SONS OF THE PROPHETS

Essays in Celebration
of the Sesquicentennial
Princeton Theological Seminary
Princeton, New Jersey
1812–1962

SONS OF THE PROPHETS

Leaders in Protestantism from Princeton Seminary

EDITED BY HUGH T. KERR

PRINCETON, NEW JERSEY
PRINCETON UNIVERSITY PRESS

1963

Copyright © 1963
by Princeton University Press
All Rights Reserved
L. C. card no.: 63-12665

❖

Printed in the United States
of America by Princeton University Press
Princeton, New Jersey

God of the prophets! Bless the prophets' sons;
  Elijah's mantle o'er Elisha cast;
Each age its solemn task may claim but once;
  Make each one nobler, stronger than the last.

—*Denis Wortman (1835-1922)*

FOREWORD

THIS volume of essays in biography, criticism, and theology celebrates the sesquicentennial anniversary of Princeton Theological Seminary. The 150th year of the Seminary was extended to allow for special convocations, lectures, concerts, and publications. During this time, dignitaries and theologians of the Christian Church throughout the world have visited the campus, colloquies have been convened, hopes for the future and reminiscences of the past have been voiced. As one of its first decisions, the Sesquicentennial Steering Committee projected a series of publications to commemorate the anniversary events. This biographical volume is the first of that series to appear.

A sesquicentennial anniversary of a theological seminary is a rare enough event in America to merit some special attention. Prior to 1800, training for the ministry of the various Churches was pursued within the regular curriculum of the colleges or by means of apprentice tutoring in pastors' homes and studies. By 1850, and until the present, most such training, numerically speaking, has been undertaken in divinity schools sponsored or supported by specific denominations. Even in colleges and universities maintaining divinity faculties, often as not these are virtually independent administrations with separate classroom facilities, dormitories, faculty, and campus life.

The establishment of The Theological Seminary at Princeton by the General Assembly of the Presbyterian Church in 1812 marked a turning point in American theological education. Within the last quarter of the eighteenth century, all learning was of a piece and could be adequately taught and studied in the schools and colleges, nearly all of which were Church-initiated. General education was also the context for professional studies in divinity, medicine, and the law. In the first quarter of the nineteenth century, professional training became disengaged from the college curriculum, medical and

FOREWORD

law schools were established, and seventeen divinity schools and seminaries came into existence.

On the threshold of the nineteenth century, powerful elements in American life, both secular and religious, were forcing some radical changes in the older, more unitive educational and intellectual climate. The emergence of scientific studies, the expansion of the college curriculum, new economic and social responsibilities associated with democratic government, industrial development in the East and geographical movement toward the West—all such factors required the Churches to reconsider their own mission and message.

To complicate the situation further, there were also intramural conflicts within the Churches. As the denominations multiplied, they became more self-conscious, polemical, and defensive. The local "parson" found he was not always the undisputed intellectual "person" in the community. The western migration created a sudden demand for ministers that could not be met under the old training programs, and the rough and ready frontiersmen were less exacting in their requirements for an educated ministry. Religious and theological tides in the meantime were running between deistical, rational influences and pietistic, revivalistic enthusiasm.

In 1812 only the faintest hints of the significance of these factors were recognized. The faculty of the College of New Jersey at the time consisted of two men, the President and one other professor, both Presbyterian ministers. Together they taught the whole curriculum, mathematics and science, moral philosophy and literature. They were also responsible for the training of young ministers for the Presbyterian Church.

The plan to establish a theological seminary at Princeton was in the interests of advancing and extending the theological curriculum. It was not, as has sometimes been intimated, a sectarian withdrawal from secular university life. The educational intention was to go beyond the liberal arts course by setting up a postgraduate, professional school in theology. The plan met with enthusiastic approval on the part of the College authorities, for they were coming to see that

FOREWORD

specialized training in theology required more attention than they could give. As early as 1768 a professor of theology had been appointed to the faculty of the College, but he was dismissed the following year because of the added expense. Ashbel Green, who became President of the College some months after the Seminary opened, had already signified his support for the new seminary by accepting the position of President of the Board of Directors. A sort of "concordat," as Harold W. Dodds was later to describe it, was agreed upon at the time whereby the College promised not to establish a chair or department of theology so long as the Seminary remained in Princeton.

In many ways, 1812 was an inauspicious time for educational innovation. The new nation that had so recently fought for its life in a war of independence was too soon plunged into another war which to many, then as now, was both senseless and inglorious. There was also war abroad. Napoleon had invaded Russia, and the event sent a shudder through the cultural as well as the political marrow of Europe. The European universities shared in the general chaos, many buildings were destroyed, libraries were scattered, ideas were few and far between, scholarship was pedantic, reactionary, timid.

Nor was it a promising time from the religious and theological perspective. A quick inventory of the first decade of the nineteenth century shows no great hymns, no persuasive preachers, no pioneering Biblical studies, no new ideas in theological methodology. The epitaph of Andrew Flynn, Moderator of the General Assembly in 1812, noted that "he was distinguished for earnestness, solemnity, and pathos." Schleiermacher, the year before, had published his *Kurze Darstellung des theologischen Studiums* (Berlin, 1811), the full effects of which were not felt until a generation later (the book waited forty years for an English translation). But the nineteenth century had begun, and with it came a new optimism and buoyancy which few could possibly predict in the year of the Seminary's birth.

With less than a dozen students, Archibald Alexander was the only Seminary professor in 1812. He was joined the following year by a second professor, Samuel Miller, who came to Princeton from the pastorate of the Wall Street Church in New York. Though the faculty of the Seminary was as big (or as small) as at the College, it was a venture of faith bordering on the foolhardy to lay elaborate plans for the future.

To read back over the wording of the original "Design of the Seminary" is to perceive the early growth of the modern development in theological education in America—though the Princeton innovators were not at all thinking of breaking new ground except in the literal sense. They were prophetic enough, however, and among other things the "Design" noted that the purpose of the Seminary was:

to unite in those who shall sustain the ministerial office, religion and literature; that piety of the heart, which is the fruit only of the renewing and sanctifying grace of God, with solid learning; believing that religion without learning, or learning without religion, in the ministers of the Gospel, must ultimately prove injurious to the Church.

The dialectic suggested in the juxtaposition of piety and learning deserves some comment. It is an apt text for expounding the peculiar genius of Princeton Seminary and its view of theological education. The piety side of the formula stems from the accent on personal salvation, the experience of repentance and forgiveness, the Christian life of faith, justification and sanctification, the reality of the new man in Jesus Christ, all of which can be traced to the roots of American religion, whether of the Puritan, Calvinist, Lutheran, Quaker, Wesleyan, or "left-wing" Reformation traditions.

There were divisive opinions about the proper and improper means of eliciting and expressing inner religious experience. Revivalistic techniques were widely hailed by some but roundly denounced by others. Princeton Seminary men more often than not were found on the side of restrained, controlled emotion, but all agreed that piety in any form was not so much taught as caught. College revivals were extra-curricular at best. Though often starting on the campuses, it was in the churches and not in the colleges that personal salvation was

FOREWORD

nurtured. The saving of souls at home and abroad, the preaching of the Gospel whether fervently or decorously, the training of ministers in the craft of homiletics and the art of pastoral oversight, the establishment of congregations and the building of churches—these arts and skills could scarcely be included in any definition of college education.

So it was that Princeton Seminary, as was true of most other divinity schools, deliberately defined itself as a school of "that piety of the heart," a training center for Church leaders of all sorts, which specialized in preaching, the cure of souls, evangelism, and missions. This is one side of the Seminary's history illustrated most obviously in the statistics of the number of pastors graduated, the large proportion of alumni in missionary service, the local and ecumenical concern for the Church. To be sure, there were many at Princeton unsympathetic with much of the methodology of the new pietism and revivalism. But regarding the religious goals interpreted as personal salvation, "the fruit only of the renewing and sanctifying grace of God," there was unanimity between thumping revivalists and proper Princetonians.

The other side of the piety-learning formula was equally important for the founders of the Seminary. The new institution was never described as a Protestant monastery or retreat, a place distinguished mainly for prayer and meditation. It was to be a school with teachers and students, library and books, ideas of the mind as well as convictions of the heart, all in the service of "solid learning." The library was one of the first major projects of the faculty, growing from the private collections of the professors to occupy, by the latter half of the nineteenth century, two fair sized but still inadequate buildings. The recently erected Speer Library building includes more than 200,000 bound volumes, 50,000 pamphlets, various special collections, and is so planned as to allow for doubling the total number of books. Even the "heretics" are present in the collection, and that, as Emil Brunner remarked when he visited Princeton for the first time, is the best test of the worth of a theological library.

The teaching of the original Biblical languages, Hebrew and

FOREWORD

Greek, has remained a prerequisite for the B.D. degree at Princeton Seminary despite the fact that the requirement has been dropped in many other seminaries. A long succession of quarterly reviews from the *Biblical Repertory*, begun in 1825, to *Theology Today*, begun in 1944, spans the history of the Seminary. Long before the Th.D. postgraduate program was inaugurated, many graduates became teachers in other institutions, college presidents, and founders of other seminaries.

Beyond all this, the Reformed tradition to which Princeton Seminary was committed has always magnified the intellectual integrity of the faith. Theology has been a highly respected word on the campus. Systems and structures of thought, reflection on the meaning and application of the faith, clarity of expression, and precision of definition—these are recognized norms for theological thinking. As a "confessional" seminary, the detailed doctrinal standard of the Westminster Confession of Faith was regarded not only "as containing the system of doctrine taught in the Holy Scriptures" but as tangible evidence of the possibility of the intellectual articulation of the faith.

What has been said about piety and learning is not meant to suggest that Princeton Seminary had a monopoly on either. And it would be sentimental and untrue to suggest that the history of the Seminary at Princeton in the intervening 150 years has admirably illustrated the piety-learning dialectic in every possible way. The chronicle makes a mixed tale. It could hardly be shown that Princeton Seminary was tempted very far in the direction of an excessive emphasis on piety, as was the case in some schools and Bible institutes. The temptation at Princeton was more in the direction of a cloistered scholasticism patterned after post-Reformation orthodoxy. This was a highly cerebral theological tradition, but it often resulted in an intellectualism unrelated to vital religion, the currents of secular and scientific thought, and the practical life of the Church. It is no secret that many contemporary professors at the Seminary feel completely out of touch theologically with their predecessors of a generation or more ago on such issues as Biblical criticism, apologetics, the sacraments, and the interpretation of the Westminster Confession of Faith.

That not everything was touched with creative imagination in the process of theological reflection is made clear in several of the chapters of this book. Those who love the Seminary and know it best would want it that way. To celebrate the contributions that have been made by the Seminary does not mean uncritical adulation of everything or everyone past or present. This would not be in the best interests of the Seminary for it would violate the Protestant principle of *self-criticism*.

Basic to the Reformed faith, to which the Seminary has always been loyal, is the categorical imperative that the church, reformed, must ever be reformed (*ecclesia reformata semper reformanda*). Even within the post-Reformation Westminster Confession of Faith, a section on "Synods and Councils" reads: "All synods or councils since the apostles' times, whether general or particular, may err, and many have erred; therefore they are not to be made the rule of faith or practice, but to be used as a help in both."

The purpose behind this volume of essays is the desire to present a dozen or so distinguished personages associated with Princeton Seminary over the years. The figures are mostly alumni, but there are also included the first professor, a lay trustee, a Japanese graduate student, a visiting lecturer. Each person, it is hoped, will in some way but not all in the same way reveal an interesting, representative, or even untypical aspect of the Seminary's long life.

The problem was not to find enough alumni to fill the pages but to choose a few from so many. Some arbitrariness no doubt crept in, and those familiar with the history of the Seminary will easily observe omissions. If it be asked why there is not a large selection of preachers and pastors, the somewhat lame but truthful answer must be that the choice was too invidious among such a large alumni body so notable in this category of ministry. One or two others who belong here have already been served by biographers or await a much

FOREWORD

fuller treatment than is possible here. In any case, this volume does not pretend to be a history of the Seminary. That, in fact, is already under way as a separate project, and, when it appears, a more comprehensive record and evaluation of the Seminary will do justice to the history that is here presupposed.

The distinguished group of authors in this volume were encouraged not only to write of the past but to speak their minds about the present. In some cases, today's theological education needs to reaffirm the substantial contributions of yesterday's leaders. But in other cases, the authors have obviously felt that the best way to celebrate the Seminary's 150th anniversary is to stand out from the Old Princeton so that all things may become new again.

The glory and the weakness of Princeton Theological Seminary are intertwined in its reputation for conservative, moderate theology. Whether this be taken as strength or limitation, the significant thing to observe is that, from the very first of its history, the Seminary produced independent, and sometimes revolutionary, minds who rejected any theological party line and instinctively accepted the apostolic injunction that "judgment must begin at the house of God." For these as for so many other alumni, the Seminary has reason to rejoice on this sesquicentennial anniversary.

There is much more to tell than is here unfolded in biographical essay and theological appraisal, but at least this needs to be told. Of special significance to alumni and friends of Princeton Seminary and Princeton University, this volume is of more than local interest. For one thing, it illustrates in an unusual and dramatic way the recreative power of the Protestant principle of self-criticism. For another thing, it discloses vast areas of American religious thought and history which are awaiting further research. It is astonishing but true that many of the men considered here in restricted space, in spite of their substantial contributions, have not generally received the scholarly attention they deserve from historians or theologians. In some instances they have not even been accorded the minimum recognition of a first class biography.

FOREWORD

Perhaps the most signal feature of these essays as a group is their tendency to look forward rather than backward. This surely augurs well for the future of theological education in America and for the future educated ministry of the Christian Church.

Hugh T. Kerr

CONTENTS

FOREWORD   Hugh T. Kerr   vii

I. ARCHIBALD ALEXANDER (1772-1851)
Founding Father   John A. Mackay   3

II. CHARLES HODGE (1797-1878)
Theology—Didactic and Polemical
    Leonard J. Trinterud   22

III. SAMUEL SIMON SCHMUCKER (1799-1873)
Lutheran Educator   E. Theodore Bachmann   39

IV. JOHN WILLIAMSON NEVIN (1803-1886)
Evangelical Catholicism   James H. Nichols   69

V. SHELDON JACKSON (1834-1909)
Christ's Fool and Seward's Folly
    Hermann N. Morse   82

VI. ASHBEL GREEN SIMONTON (1833-1867)
A Calvinist in Brazil   M. Richard Shaull   100

VII. STEPHEN COLWELL (1800-1871)
Social Prophet before the Social Gospel
    Bruce Morgan   123

VIII. HENRY VAN DYKE (1852-1933)
Many-sided Litterateur   Roland Mushat Frye   148

IX. FRANCIS JAMES GRIMKÉ (1850-1937)
Christian Moralist and Civil Rights
    Clifton E. Olmstead   161

CONTENTS

X. WALTER LOWRIE (1868-1959)
Man and Churchman Extraordinary
                        Howard A. Johnson   176

XI. TOYOHIKO KAGAWA (1888-1960)
   Blessed Are the Poor   Yasuo Carl Furuya   192

XII. JOSEF LUKL HROMADKA (1889-   )
    Theology and Ideology   Charles C. West   205

THE CONTRIBUTORS   224

LIST OF ILLUSTRATIONS

Archibald Alexander   Engraving by John Sartain after portrait by John Neagle. Courtesy Princeton Theological Seminary

Charles Hodge   Engraving by H. G. Wagner after portrait by Daniel Huntingdon. Courtesy Princeton Theological Seminary

Samuel Simon Schmucker   Portrait by unknown artist. Courtesy Gettysburg Lutheran Theological Seminary

John Williamson Nevin   Engraving by John Sartain after portrait by Jacob Eicholtz. Courtesy Lancaster Theological Seminary

Sheldon Jackson   Reproduced from Clifford M. Drury, *Presbyterian Panorama*, Philadelphia, 1952

Ashbel Green Simonton   Courtesy Presbyterian Museum, Theological Seminary, Campinas, Brazil

Stephen Colwell   Reproduced from Henry C. Carey, *A Memoir of Stephen Colwell*, Philadelphia, 1871

Henry van Dyke   Photograph courtesy Mrs. Tertius van Dyke

Francis James Grimké   Reproduced from a "Souvenir Program of the Seventy-fifth Anniversary of the Fifteenth Street Presbyterian Church, Washington, D.C.," November 1916

Walter Lowrie   Reproduced from A. W. van Buren et al., *Dr. Lowrie of Princeton & Rome*, Greenwich, Conn., 1957

Toyohiko Kagawa   Photograph courtesy Mrs. Kagawa

Josef L. Hromadka   Photograph courtesy Clearose Studio, Princeton

SONS OF THE PROPHETS

I. ARCHIBALD ALEXANDER
(1772-1851)

Founding Father*

BY JOHN A. MACKAY

Not infrequently, as history shows, the founder of an institution becomes its abiding image. When this happens, the institution manifests its genius and fulfills its destiny in the measure in which it reflects the spirit and dream of the person who brought it into being. This has been superlatively true of the theological seminary which was established in the New Jersey village of Princeton in the year 1812.

The Seminary's founder and first professor, Archibald Alexander, was described a century later by the church historian, John DeWitt, as "one of the largest and most disciplined intellects the American Church has produced." He can, without sentimentality, be regarded as the authentic soul and symbol of Princeton Theological Seminary. This Christian scholar and churchman, who throughout his long life lived on the frontiers of knowledge and the Church's total mission, is Princeton Seminary's most cherished and inspiring image.

I

Archibald Alexander was born on April 17, 1772, near Lexington, Virginia. His parents were Presbyterians of Scotch-

* The only important biography of Archibald Alexander was prepared by his son James Waddell Alexander, *The Life of Archibald Alexander* (1854). See also W. B. Sprague, *Annals of the American Pulpit*, Volume III, 1857-1869, pp. 612-626; John DeWitt, "Archibald Alexander's Preparation for His Professorship," *Princeton Theological Review*, Volume III, No. 4, Oct. 1905, pp. 573-594; the bio-bibliographical account in *The Biblical Repertory and Princeton Review*, Index Volume, 1871, pp. 42-67. Alexander's books and many unpublished manuscripts are in Speer Library, Princeton Seminary; correspondence and other materials are in Firestone Library, Princeton University.

Irish ancestry, as were so many other American colonists of the pre-Revolutionary era. Brought up in the lovely valley in which Lexington is located, young Archibald developed, in early youth, a passionate love of nature. This passion for the world around him, a veritable "emotion of the sublime," produced a life-long devotion to natural science.

Equally noteworthy was the profound religious temperament of this Virginia boy. Even before entering his teens, he developed a love for the Bible and for quiet meditation. In the years that succeeded the Revolutionary War, religion in American Presbyterian circles was of a very conventional and formalistic character. A Baptist lady of the period is quoted by the biographer of Archibald Alexander as remarking, "Presbyterians were sound in doctrine, but deficient in inward experience."[1] They reflected the spirit of the Scottish "Moderates," for whom the ethical, the dogmatic, and the aesthetic formed the core of religion, and who acclaimed cultural interests on the part of Church members as being more important than spiritual enthusiasm, which they in fact regarded with both suspicion and disdain. It is of interest to observe that a great Princetonian of an earlier period, John Witherspoon, had engaged in an historic debate with the Moderates immediately before leaving his native Scotland to become President of the College of New Jersey, now Princeton University.

In an atmosphere marked by hostility to any manifestation of ardor in Church life, where the exciting phenomenon of religious conversion was frowned upon as most un-Presbyterian and something to be discouraged, Archibald Alexander passed through a profound experience of spiritual change. While still in his seventeenth year, he entered upon a new epoch of his life. Following a period of intense dissatisfaction with himself as he was, and anxiously longing for a personal acquaintanceship with God as Saviour, he joined that succession of "new men in Christ" which includes St. Augustine, Martin Luther, John Calvin, and Jonathan Edwards. A year

[1] James W. Alexander, *The Life of Archibald Alexander*, New York: Scribner, 1854, p. 39.

before his death, when he was seventy-eight years of age, Alexander would still return in intimate conversation to the time when his natural religiosity became evangelical faith, when Jesus Christ became a transforming reality in his life and the object of his passionate devotion.

This decisive, though quite undramatic, experience shaped Alexander's thought and behavior through all the coming years. Like that famous Spaniard, Raymond Lull, he could say of Jesus Christ, "I have one passion in life and it is He." Thus Alexander came to approach all questions concerning the human and the divine from a profoundly Christo-centric perspective. "His peculiar piety," said Cortlandt van Rensselaer while delivering the memorial oration after Alexander had passed away, "was the basis of his excellence." This piety, which had its origin in spiritual rebirth, its pivotal center in Christ, its charter in Holy Scripture, its pattern in New Testament sainthood, and its objective in Christian witness in the Church and in the world, was poles apart from the purely emotional and individualistic piosity of the religious zealot. While he proclaimed the importance of zeal, Archibald Alexander never ceased to deprecate "zeal without knowledge," that is, the unenlightened fervor of the fanatic. His favorite symbol of dedicated Christian living was the green meadow refreshed by rain showers from above, rather than the fierce flame of embers kindled from beneath. But in every case the ultimate norm of true Christian devotion was, for this Virginian, a passion to do good to men because of a sincere love for people. His life as a Christian was, in theory and practice, a reverberation of the words of that dynamic Spanish saint, Teresa of Avila, who used to say to the young women of her religious order, "The Lord demands works" (*Obras quiere el Senor*). She did not mean works to merit or to secure salvation, but works that follow salvation and insure its reality.

Alexander's experience of spiritual rebirth led him to the decision to become a Christian minister. In the United States in those days, just as in Scotland about the same period, the Presbyterian ministry had become to a large extent a profession like other professions and preaching had become a mere trade. But for the young man from Lexington, to become a "minister of the Word and Sacraments" was life's highest vocation. To this vocation he felt called by God Himself. He accordingly set about preparing himself for this high office.

In days when colleges were few and theological seminaries as such did not exist, Alexander was fortunate in becoming the pupil of a very remarkable man, William Graham. Graham was a fine scholar and an inspiring teacher. Quite early in their relationship, the teacher said to the student something the latter never forgot. "If you mean ever to be a theologian, you must come at it not by reading but by thinking." In the course of the years, the pupil became a very learned man; but he consistently shunned becoming a mere unreflective dogmatist or an erudite encyclopedist. While retaining an intense thirst for knowledge of all kinds, the pursuit of which he tells us "was never a weariness to me," he cultivated the Socratic approach to truth with which his revered teacher inspired him. The student of divinity developed, among other things, an amazing interest in mathematical and physical investigation. In this, as in other respects, the future head of Princeton Seminary resembled his Scottish counterpart and contemporary, Thomas Chalmers, who was adjudged by Thomas Carlyle the most outstanding Scotsman since John Knox. Chalmers became the first principal of New College, Edinburgh. These two men, who were later to enter into correspondence with one another, incarnated each in his own way the ideals of religious living and scholarly achievement, which in the course of time were to be enshrined in the charter of a seminary in New Jersey with the designation, "piety and learning."

II

His formal preparation completed, Archibald Alexander, after a trial sermon on the text "Thy Word is Truth," was licensed and ordained a Christian minister by the Presbytery of Hanover in Virginia. It is worthy of note that this Presbytery had the distinction of being the first ecclesiastical body in the United States to recognize the new revolutionary government of George Washington.

During the closing years of the eighteenth century, the new minister did the work of a rural pastor and itinerant missionary on the colonial frontier of Virginia and Ohio. His apprenticeship as a traveling evangelist, a Presbyterian "circuit rider," helped him to become intimately acquainted with common people and their problems. It came home to him that, in the true apostolic succession, the Word must never cease to become flesh. He learned that they who would witness to the Gospel must win a right to be heard, both by what they themselves are and by what they say and the way they say it. The inspiration of this experience and the lessons derived from it remained with Archibald Alexander to the end of his life.

While he was carrying on his ministry in the American wilderness, without in any way abandoning his passion for learning, the traveling preacher was called to the presidency of a Virginia college called Hampden-Sydney. This college, which had been established in 1783 for the purpose of educating men for the ministry, found itself a decade later in a serious plight. Alexander accepted the call, and in 1796, while in his twenty-fourth year, he was installed in his new office. He took up his academic duties with characteristic enthusiasm. To the pressures of his new responsibilities as a teacher, he later attributed "whatever accuracy he possessed in classical and scientific knowledge." The life of the college received a new impulse from its scholarly young President, who added, moreover, a rich humanity and love of people to his academic labors.

Four years passed. The young President of Hampden-Sydney began to question whether the headship of a college was his true vocation. His health, moreover, had been impaired. In quest of new vigor, and because of a long cherished desire to visit New England, he resigned the presidency in 1801. The northern journey that followed his resignation was destined to exercise a profound influence on his future life.

Having already become acquainted with life on the American frontier as far west as Ohio, Alexander now moved northward into the land of the Pilgrims, the historic seat of American culture. This journey, which carried him to Boston, Harvard, and Dartmouth, had a broadening influence upon the outlook of Alexander with respect to Christians brought up in a tradition different from his own. The New England Congregationalists on their part received the Virginia educator with great kindness. While their warm hospitality won his heart, they were deeply impressed by this plain and simple man from the South whose first-rate intellectual qualities they recognized. From Dartmouth College came the announcement that he had been appointed Professor of Theology, an appointment which he, however, declined.

When Alexander returned to the South, it was with a mind cleared of many a prejudice and with a new-born appreciation of fellow Christians who engaged in ecclesiastical practices and cherished some theological ideas that he personally did not follow. While continuing through life an unashamed and ardent Presbyterian, a man committed to his Biblical and Christ-centered faith, Archibald Alexander was never a haughty dogmatist. He was nobly sensitive to the ideas and feelings of people whose viewpoints were at variance with his own.

After a year's absence from academic life, during which time his health had been restored and his spirits revived, Alexander resumed his former responsibilities at Hampden-Sydney, where he continued in the office of President until 1807. That year he accepted a call to become the pastor of the Third Presbyterian Church of Philadelphia, one of the city's largest congregations. He was at the time thirty-five years old and had just married a charming young woman, Janetta Waddell, who was to be his devoted partner for the next fifty years. Thus, in the full glow and exuberance of youth, the man from Virginia became a leading minister in the now historic city which in the first decade of the last century was achieving increasing importance in the life of the young Republic.

ARCHIBALD ALEXANDER

III

It was not long before the minister of the Third Presbyterian Church, which was known also as the Pine Street Church, was achieving renown as an impressive pulpit orator. To what has been described as a "disciplined mind, theological knowledge, rich imagination, and evangelical zeal," he added an extraordinary capacity for extemporaneous utterance which he continued to manifest throughout life. Because of this particular gift, the pastor of the Third Church made an extraordinary impact upon his people. "I have never succeeded in getting a discourse by heart," he is quoted as saying. As was the custom of the famous English preacher, F. W. Robertson of Brighton, Alexander, when he did write his sermons, wrote them after delivery.

Throughout his entire Philadelphia ministry, Alexander was an indefatigable reader of the writings of others. He devoted himself especially to mastering the theology of the sixteenth and seventeenth centuries. And it was not merely the theologians in the Reformed tradition whose works he read; his study also embraced the theological writings of Lutherans and Roman Catholics of that period. In this respect as in others, he was an everlasting frontiersman. On Sundays his words thrilled common folk; during the week the people's preacher absorbed the words of the learned whether written in English or in Latin.

The popular preacher of Pine Street was also a warm and tender pastor. In the great Pauline tradition, Archibald Alexander had a shepherd's heart. He loved people and was the friend and counselor of all who needed help. Among his writings are a series of most diverse pastoral letters, the text of which has been preserved. In this epistolary series are letters to young people and to aged folk, to persons who had suffered affliction, to widows and to widowers.

Nowhere does the soul of the preacher blend so perfectly and symbolically with the heart of the pastor as in the discourse Alexander was asked to deliver at a special service which was held on the night of December 28, 1811, following the burning of the theater in Richmond. In this conflagration, seventy-five persons lost their lives, including the Governor of the state of Virginia. Speaking from the text "Weep with them that weep" (Rom. 12:15) the preacher analyzed and applied the principle of sympathy as prescribed by the Christian religion in contrast to the cold impassivity of the Stoic ethic. "One leading difference," he said, "between the system of ethics prescribed by the Stoics and that inculcated by Christianity is that, whilst the former aims at eradicating the passions, the latter endeavors to regulate them, and direct them into their proper channels. . . . The great Author of our being has implanted the principle of sympathy deeply in human nature and has made the susceptibility of feeling the sorrows of another as extensive as the race of man. This principle of sympathy, whilst it indicates the unity of our species, seems to form a mysterious bond of connection between all its members."

After describing the horror that had befallen the city, and elaborating its significance as an example of the sorrows and uncertainties that beset man's mortal life, Alexander extolled what religion could mean for all suffering and concerned people. "But in order to enjoy the consolation of religion," he went on, "we must practice its precepts, and in order to practice its precepts, we must experience its power. True religion is not a form but a living principle within, not a name but an active energetic influence which governs the whole man and directs his views and exertions to the noblest object. . . . Therefore," he concluded, addressing himself in particular to the Virginia students of medicine who had invited him to conduct the service, "become real Christians; make religion a personal concern; attend to it without delay."

Loyal to his concept of "real Christian," Archibald Alexander did not limit his concern to the conscientious fulfillment of the duties connected with the pastoral ministry. This visionary crusader continued to be a frontiersman in the heart of the great growing city. Projects designed to meet needs in society or in the Church, whether in the city itself, throughout the new nation, or beyond its bounds, were initiated by him, or received his support. Here are some manifestations of his spirit: He introduced his congregation to the novelty of Sunday evening services, which became very popular. Concerned about the need of inculcating evangelical truth beyond ecclesiastical frontiers, he prepared the manuscript of a religious novel called "Eudocia," which, unfortunately, was never published. He launched the idea of a religious newspaper before any such journal existed. There was in Philadelphia at that time an organization called "The Humane Society." Dissatisfied with the spirit and objectives of this organization, Alexander created "The Evangelical Society." The purpose of the new society was not to employ other people to do good in the name of those who were its members. Every member was himself to be a worker by becoming directly involved in achieving the objectives of the Society.

Various other enterprises which were struggling to be born in the first decade of the nineteenth century had Alexander's active cooperation. Such were "The Philadelphia Tract Society," "The Society for Promoting Christian Knowledge among the Poor," and the nascent "Sunday School Association," which in those days was encountering opposition from traditionalists. Other projects also were in his dreams for the advancement of God's Kingdom. Among them was a scheme whereby Negroes would be able to realize their aspirations. Another was the organization of a Foreign Missions Society. A third project was the establishment of a theological seminary.

IV

The election of Archibald Alexander as Moderator of the General Assembly of the Presbyterian Church in the U.S.A. was the beginning of a new era in the history of a Church which was still the leading denomination in the country. The minister of the Pine Street Church of Philadelphia, when elected by the Assembly of 1807, was, with a single exception, the youngest Moderator ever to hold that office. (The exception was Francis Landley Patton. Patton, too, was only thirty-five when he was elected Moderator by the Assembly of 1878.

It is a striking coincidence that subsequently both these men became related to Princeton Theological Seminary. After years of service as a pastor and theological teacher, Patton was elected in 1888 President of the College of New Jersey, now Princeton University. Following fourteen years in the presidency of the College, he retired and was succeeded by Woodrow Wilson. The same year, Patton became President of Princeton Seminary. This office he held for eleven years, retiring in 1913, the year following the Seminary's celebration of its one hundredth anniversary.)

In the overruling providence of God there exists an inseparable historical link between Archibald Alexander's election as his Church's Moderator and the establishment of Princeton Theological Seminary. During his year in office, the Presbyterian Church became abundantly aware of its Moderator's dimension. At the close of his moderatorial year, Alexander preached a sermon to the General Assembly of 1808. In this sermon, he pled that adequate provision be made for the preparation of ministers of the Gospel. Taking as his text the words of St. Paul to the Christians in Corinth, "Strive to excel in building up the Church" (I Cor. 4:19), the preacher spoke with great eloquence. The time had come, he said, for the denomination to take theological education seriously. Here are his words:

"In my opinion, we shall not have a regular and sufficient supply of well-qualified ministers of the Gospel until every Presbytery, or at least every Synod, shall have under its direction a seminary established for the single purpose of educating youth for the ministry, in which the course of education from its commencement shall be directed to this object; for it is much to be doubted whether the system of education pursued in our colleges and universities is the best adapted to prepare a young man for the work of the ministry. The great extension of the physical sciences and the taste and fashion of life have given such a shift and direction to the academical course that I confess it appears to me to be little adapted to introduce a youth to the study of the Sacred Scriptures."

Archibald Alexander

ARCHIBALD ALEXANDER

The popular response to the idea of a theological seminary was such that a fellow minister of Alexander's, Ashbel Green, the minister of the Second Presbyterian Church of Philadelphia, joined him in promoting the idea in their Presbytery. The effort was successful. The Presbytery of Philadelphia overtured the General Assembly of 1809 that a theological school be duly established, as had been proposed by their fellow Presbyter in his moderatorial sermon. The Assembly approved the overture and a committee was appointed. This committee submitted three alternative schemes to the Presbyteries of the Church. Presbytery opinion favored the establishment of a single theological seminary for the whole Church. A new committee of seven was appointed, under the chairmanship of Ashbel Green, to draft a plan that would serve as a constitution of the new seminary. It included Archibald Alexander and Samuel Miller, the minister of the First Presbyterian Church of New York. A constitutional plan was submitted in 1811. After some modifications, it was adopted, and the Assembly proceeded immediately to elect the first professor.

In what appears to have been a deeply moving session, and after a period of prayer, the members balloted for the person who, in their judgment, was most fitted for the new position. The "lot fell" on the minister of the Pine Street Church.

There is evidence that Archibald Alexander did not expect or desire this appointment, his personal preference being to continue his pastorate in Philadelphia. Yielding, however, to what he felt to be the call of the Holy Spirit speaking through the representatives of the Church, he accepted the invitation. A year later, on August 12, 1812, he was formally installed into his new office in the seminary which the Assembly had decided to establish in Princeton, New Jersey, under the name of "The Theological Seminary of the Presbyterian Church in the United States of America." Alexander's colleague, Ashbel Green, who played so important a part in launching the new institution, was in the same year elected President of the College of New Jersey. He had already been elected President of the Board of Directors of the new seminary, a position he held from 1812 to 1848. In this way, two close ministerial friends became neighbors in the village of Princeton, where they shaped the courses of sister institutions, each of which was destined for world renown.

V

The Plan, or Constitution, of the "one great school in some convenient place near the center of the bounds of our Church" became the inspiration and guide for Archibald Alexander and his successors. Its basic concepts are a faithful transcript of the personal ideas of the Seminary's founder. For that reason, and because the Plan has shaped the destiny of the institution for a hundred and fifty years, it merits special attention.

A central concept in this historic document is the affirmation that a Christian minister worthy of his office and fitted for his work should combine two indispensable qualities. These qualities are defined as "piety and learning." In the original report of the committee charged with preparing the Plan, we find this paragraph: "That, as filling the Church with a learned and able ministry without a corresponding portion of real piety, would be a curse to the world and an offense to God and his people, so the General Assembly think it their duty to state that in establishing a seminary for training up ministers, it is the earnest desire to guard as far as possible against so great an evil. And they do hereby solemnly pledge themselves to the Churches under their care that in forming and carrying into execution the plan of the proposed seminary, it will be their endeavor to make it, under the blessing of God, a nursery of vital piety as well as of sound theological learning, and to train up persons for the ministry who shall be lovers as well as defenders of the truth as it is in Jesus, friends of revivals of religion, and a blessing to the Church of God."

In the final version of the Plan as it was adopted, the design of the Seminary is stated as follows: "It is to unite in those who shall sustain the ministerial office, religion and literature; that piety of heart, which is the fruit only of the renewing and sanctifying grace of God, with solid learning: believing that religion without learning, or learning without religion, in the ministers of the Gospel, must ultimately prove injurious to the Church. . . .

"It is to afford more advantages than have hitherto been usually possessed by ministers of religion in our country, to cultivate both piety and literature in their preparatory course; piety, by placing it in circumstances favorable to its growth, and by cherishing and regulating its ardor; literature, by affording favorable opportunities for its attainment, and by making its possession indispensable. . . .

"It is, finally, to endeavor to raise up a succession of men, at once *qualified for* and thoroughly *devoted to* the work of the Gospel ministry; who, with various endowments, suiting them to different stations in the Church of Christ, may all possess a portion of the spirit of the primitive propagators of the Gospel; prepared to make every sacrifice, to endure every hardship, and to render every service which the promotion of pure and undefiled religion may require."

The notes sounded here found an echo in the personality and life of the new professor. They express, moreover, his philosophy of what theological education and a theological seminary should be. Take, for example, "piety and learning," or the synonymous designation, "religion and literature." Personal devotion to God, as commitment and communion, must be accompanied in the Christian minister by a broad culture, involving an intelligent grasp of the Christian faith. When either one of these qualities is lacking, the Christian Church is in peril.

VI

Regarding people who have "learning without religion," Samuel Miller had this to say in the address he delivered at the inauguration of his friend: "O my fathers and brethren, let it never be said of us on whom this task has fallen, that we take more pains to make polite scholars, eloquent orators or men of mere learning than to form able and faithful ministers of the New Testament." For Christian truth, he went on, is to be "loved" as well as "defended." Miller, a member of the Seminary's first Board of Directors, had in mind the so-called Moderates of that day, whose sophisticated successors form a considerable group in our day. Such persons are to be found in the Church's conservative as well as its liberal tradition. They look down disdainful noses at any manifestation of religious emotion or any claim that people may make to the concrete subjective reality of communion with God in the daily round or the common task.

Equally to be avoided, however, according to the Plan, was religion without learning, zeal without knowledge, which could be also injurious to the Church. Frothy emotionalism, the reduction of religion to pure feeling, was rampant then as now. Archibald Alexander stood, as the Christian Church when true to itself has always stood, for dynamic centrality, for the commitment of the human self to the Christ who is both Life and Light, the "Power of God" as well as the "Wisdom of God." It was to be the function of the newly founded Seminary to make equal provision in its institutional life for the spiritual nurture as well as for the intellectual development of all who belonged to it.

What has been described as Alexander's "mental and spiritual universalism"[2] became strikingly evident in the Inaugural Address he delivered at the opening of the first seminary year. His thoughts ran the full gamut of intellectual interest and concern that human knowledge be regarded as relevant to a study of the Scriptures, to the interpretation of the Christian faith, and to the building of the Church.

The Plan of the Seminary had laid down that the new institution should have three chairs: Divinity, Oriental and Biblical Literature, Ecclesiastical History and Church Government. Until he was joined in 1813 by his friend Samuel Miller, who was elected professor of Ecclesiastical History and Church Government, Archibald Alexander was responsible for the entire curriculum. His competency and enthusiasm

[2] John DeWitt, "Archibald Alexander's Preparation for His Professorship," *Princeton Theological Review*, III, Oct. 1905, p. 593.

were immediately evident as he assumed responsibility for the first Seminary class of three students, which met in his home. The former President of Hampden-Sydney College became the Seminary's institutional foundation and a luminous and inspiring image for all who would succeed him down the years, whether in the classroom or on the campus, in the quiet sociability of the home or amid the agitations of public witness.

VII

In the discharge of his academic responsibilities, as well as in the writings which now began to flow from his pen, Professor Alexander manifested both his native intellectual qualities and the breadth of knowledge that made evident his mature scholarship. Alongside his fervent faith and his linguistic preparation for the exposition of Holy Scripture, his natural penchant for metaphysics was never absent. In his approach to Christian theology and to ideas in general, he never ceased to display the penetration of the philosopher. He inculcated in his students a passion for original research. He advocated, moreover, and exemplified in his own intellectual life, a spirit of fairness in dealing with controversial issues. Out of this spirit was born the Seminary's world-famous library. No books of representative significance were ever placed by a censor on a theological Index. In what is now the Robert E. Speer Library, the reader has access to all shades of opinion, however unconventional or heretical, to all sorts of supplementary literature in the realm of culture capable of shedding light upon a religious event, an historical epoch, or a doctrinal issue.

Alexander's intellect and vast knowledge had, however, one limitation. His cultural breadth and his incomparable power of penetration into a subject were not matched by a corresponding capacity for the massive organization of ideas. In this regard he was surpassed by his student, Charles Hodge, who subsequently became his colleague and successor. While Alexander was more universal than Hodge in his intellectual interests, and especially in his human concern, Hodge excelled his teacher as a systematizer.

Out of the collaboration of these two men, one an everlasting denizen of the spiritual frontier, the other a genius for bringing the farthest horizons into perspective, and of Samuel Miller, a man more "polished and literary" than either, there was born in 1825 a theological journal called *The Biblical Repertory*. This journal was one of the first theological reviews published in America and the predecessor of *Theology Today*. To *The Biblical Repertory* Alexander contributed many important articles. These were written on such varied themes as: "The Catechism of the Council of Trent," "Evidences of a New Heart," "The Present State and Prospects of the Presbyterian Church," "Mr. H. Everett's Report on Indian Affairs." These few titles indicate the author's interest in theological dogma, the inner life of the Christian, the health of the Church, and the welfare of neglected people. Among the books written during his Princeton years, the following stand out: *A Brief Outline of the Evidences of the Christian Religion* (1825), *The Canon of the Old and New Testaments* (1826), *Thoughts on Religious Experience* (1841), *Biographical Sketches of the Founder and Principal Alumni of the Log College* (1845), *History of Colonization on the West Coast of Africa* (1846), *Outlines of Moral Science*, published in 1852, the year after his death.

The inspiring teacher and writer was also a warm-hearted friend. Archibald Alexander's home was ever open to students who wanted to see him. It was said of him that he seemed "incapable of being interrupted." Between him and his colleague, Samuel Miller, there existed throughout their long lives the most intimate Christian companionship. It was customary for them not only to converse together but to pray together. With their younger colleague, Charles Hodge, they conducted each week for the students "The Sunday Afternoon Conference." This gathering, which usually lasted an hour and a half, was devoted to the discussion of all sorts of questions relating to the Christian life, to experimental religion, and to practical behavior.

Here was campus community at its best. Teachers and students shared their deepest thoughts on what it meant to be truly Christian, both in personal experience and in active obedience. The students represented, as the years went by, an increasingly diversified group both denominationally and racially. From the early decades of the Seminary's life, Episcopalians, Methodists, and Baptists shared with Presbyterians the life of classroom and campus in perfect Christian fellowship. And from its earliest years the Seminary was host to many students from abroad.

VIII

In the deepest, most classical sense, Archibald Alexander the professor was also a Churchman. He did all his thinking, and carried out his diverse forms of activity, with a sense of his calling as a member and minister of the community called the Church. Yet no American Churchman was ever less of a mere professional or cleric, less of an ecclesiastic or a hierarch, than he. Dedicated to the fellowship of Jesus Christ, he devoted his entire manhood to increasing the membership of this fellowship, calling upon people to commit themselves to Christ as Saviour. The second half of his life, forty years in all, he spent trying to equip young men for the Church's ministry under the Lordship of Christ.

The address he delivered at the beginning of the seminary year 1832 bears the title "Plea for Absolute Devotion to God in the Work of the Ministry." In the course of his remarks on this occasion he said, "You are coming forward, my young friends, at an eventful period of the world. Read then the signs of the times. Let every man be found at his post and standing in his lot. Let no one now entering the ministry dream of a quiet or easy life, or of literary leisure." He was interested in where his students went and where all Presbyterian ministers carried on their work. "There was no man living," we are told by his biographer, "whose acquaintance with the geography and topography of America was more extensive or exact."[3] Archibald Alexander used this amazing knowledge as a Churchman who was personally interested in

[3] Alexander, *Life of Alexander*, p. 540.

all his fellow ministers. "The whole territory of the Church," it was said of him, "was so mapped out in his head that it is scarcely too much to affirm that he knew who was the pastor of every Presbyterian Church in the United States."

But this Churchman, who was personally acquainted with the identity and sphere of labor of every Presbyterian minister, was no sectarian, still less a bigot, in his spirit and concerns. He was profoundly ecumenical in his commitment. "The Church of Christ is one," he exclaimed, "and all who agree in essential matters should hold communion together, notwithstanding minor differences." And again, "Let us hold together as long as the foundation can be felt under our feet."

But for Alexander, to "hold together" did not mean remaining static or becoming institutionally minded. While his judgment was invariably cool and dispassionate, and his policy conservative, "he never rejected any scheme because it was novel." To the very end of his life he was interested in new schemes. What could be more conclusive than the following testimony? "No observation was more common than that Dr. Alexander was unlike most old men, in the tolerance for the changes of his day. If a new scheme of any promise was on foot, he was really more inclined to listen and to favor than most younger men."

Nowhere was the forward looking and dynamic spirit of Alexander, the Churchman, more manifest than in his advocacy and support of the missionary movement. At the time of his death he was President of the Board of Foreign Missions of the Presbyterian Church. Two of his most famous public utterances were missionary sermons. One of those sermons he preached in Philadelphia in May 1814 at the invitation of the Standing Committee on Missions, while the General Assembly of the Church was in session. The other was delivered at Albany, New York, in October 1829 on the occasion of the Twentieth Annual Meeting of the American Board of Commissioners for Foreign Mission.

In his Philadelphia sermon, Alexander challenged the idea then common in Church circles in Scotland and the United States that "civilization should precede evangelization." He then proceeded to express the hope "that the General Assembly, which is the Missionary Society of your Church, will at their present session take the subject of foreign mission into serious consideration." Fruits of initiating mission work abroad, he declared, would be, "a missionary spirit which is the true spirit of Christianity," "the destruction of bigotry and a narrow sectarian spirit," the promotion of "peace and harmony in the Church." For Churchmen would then have no more interest in "petty contentions." Not only so, but the awakening in the Church of a missionary spirit would "increase the number of candidates for the ministry as well as the devotion to home missions."

In his Albany sermon, after discussing the prevailing objections to foreign missions, the Princeton Churchman spoke critically of the Puritan successors of the Reformers, who despite their eminent piety did not develop an interest in world evangelization and mission.

This precursor of the ecumenical spirit, true son of John Calvin, then proceeded to pay prophetic tribute to what can be expected in the realm of Church unity when Christians are gripped by a spirit of missionary enthusiasm. What statement of any Churchman in the early years of the nineteenth century is more contemporaneously significant than the following utterance from Archibald Alexander's Albany sermon? "Nowhere upon earth does the genuine spirit of Catholicism more prevail," he said, "than among missionaries and the ardent friends of missions. . . . It cannot, it must not, be that the progress of this work of God should be retarded or hindered by the petty jealousies of its professed friends. A better spirit prevails, and will, I trust, more and more prevail, until all our sectarian distinctions shall be melted into the complete 'unity of the Spirit' . . . when all the servants of God 'shall see eye to eye' and the bond of union shall be TRUTH, PEACE, and CHARITY."

This plain man, true saint and scholar, great preacher, professor and ecumenical Churchman is worthy to be, in the present sesquicentennial year and in the centuries to come, the abiding image of the institution he created.

II. CHARLES HODGE (1797-1878)

Theology—Didactic and Polemical*

BY LEONARD J. TRINTERUD

IT is widely believed that Charles Hodge lies buried in three volumes. While this may have been true, existentially, for some Princetonians through the years, the Hodge who lived was not that mythical Hodge. The Hodge who lived was so completely captivated by The Theological Seminary at Princeton, New Jersey, while yet a boy of fourteen, that henceforth his whole life was determined by what he supposed was the good of the Seminary. Throughout the century and a half of its existence no man has ever been so completely the embodiment of the school. There, in the Seminary, rather than in three volumes, lies Charles Hodge.

But whence the Hodge of the myth? Given a man of strong personality in a prominent seminary, for many years the leading mind of that school, idolized by students and alumni, in control of a privately owned journal of great influence, a writer of both popular and professional books, with a wide correspondence in various parts of the country, a man human enough to enter deeply into the lives of his friends—in short, given a man so gifted and so situated, it was inevitable that

---

* The best sources for the life of Charles Hodge are his letters and papers deposited in the Firestone Library, Princeton University. Speer Library, Princeton Seminary, has a large collection of his lecture notes, his diary, and some letters and other miscellaneous manuscripts. The correspondence of Samuel Miller now in Firestone Library and the letters of James Waddell Alexander, published and manuscript, provide much additional material. The Durrett Collection at the University of Chicago has in the Joshua L. Wilson Papers a great store of materials dealing with the Old School party in the West. Articles in *The Biblical Repertory and Princeton Review* are indispensable. The Presbyterian periodicals of the era regularly referred to Hodge and Princeton. Several unpublished doctoral dissertations on Hodge provide background material; microfilm copies of these are in Speer Library, Princeton Seminary.

he should build and guide a large and influential group of disciples. The disciples themselves became a self-conscious group amidst the controversies of the half-century of Hodge's career. Wherever these disciples went—in the pastorates, in the colleges and seminaries, and on the mission fields—they continued to look to their mentor. In any crisis, to know what Professor Hodge would say was to clarify one's thinking. To quote Professor Hodge was to bring the whole weight of the master and the discipleship to bear against an opponent.

Men such as Charles Hodge, situated as he was, can never be buried in books. But they may suffer severely at the hands of their eager disciples, or they may find themselves adopted by power groups who profess great admiration and zeal for the famous man whose public image is better than their own. The Hodge of the myth is "the authorized portrait of our leader" done by command of followers whom in the end Hodge could not control. Yet the record is quite plain that the leader squirmed a good deal while this authorized portrait was being made. It was only his unquestioning devotion to the Seminary which made the sittings for this portrait endurable.

I

Charles Hodge was born in Philadelphia, December 28, 1797, of a family rooted in the revival of 1733-1742 and in the Second Presbyterian Church, founded by George Whitefield and Gilbert Tennent. The pastor of this church in 1797 was Ashbel Green, to whose vanity and ambition Hodge was to owe much of the unhappiness of his years as a professor. In due time he attended the College of New Jersey at Princeton. While a first-year student at college, aged fourteen, he witnessed with something like religious fascination the installation of Archibald Alexander as the first professor of the newly founded Theological Seminary. Before long he came to Alexander's attention, and within months each had adopted the other. The attachment was unbroken until Alexander's death in 1851. No other influence upon Hodge ever equalled that of his "father" Alexander. After graduation from college young Hodge entered the Seminary. Upon his graduation there, Alexander told Hodge that he had chosen him to be a teacher at the Seminary. His appointment was in Biblical studies. Before long, however, he became persuaded that his training in the field was inadequate for the demands of the day. Men from New England had studied abroad, and Hodge asked permission to do the same.

In October 1826, Hodge sailed for Paris to study Oriental languages. He was not much impressed with the religious life of Paris and soon moved on to Germany. Here he found a wonderful new world. He found erudite, highly placed professors who were interested in small prayer-bands, in revivals, and in the private study of the Bible. He became a fast friend of such professors as August Tholuck, Johann Neander, Ernest Hengstenberg, and prominent nobles such as the brothers von Gerlach, Baron von Kottwitz, Chancellor le Coq, and many others. Otto von Gerlach was noted as "the Wesley of Berlin." The religious movement of which all these men were a part included men and women of rather diverse theologies, among them some liberal Catholics. Hodge was much interested in the German revivals and noted that in them there had occurred some of the "bodily exercises" or demonstrations which had accompanied the American revivals. Yet neither Hodge nor his German friends were troubled by these "excesses" nearly as much as they were by the policies of the ruling clique in the various German state churches. Hodge deplored, as did his friends, the high-handed methods of the ecclesiastical bureaucracy against the revivals and against the Bible-study and prayer groups. He little guessed that in three short years he would be thrown headlong into a similar maelstrom of conflict back home. No doubt the role he sought to play in that American conflict was in some measure influenced by his experiences while in Germany.

After nearly two years in Germany, Hodge turned homeward after a brief tour through Switzerland, France, and Great Britain. In view of the role which the terms "Scottish" and "Scotch-Irish" were to play in his later polemical writings against the New England theologians, it is interesting to note that Hodge did not visit Ireland, and that he spent less than a week in Scotland, of which his diary is silent. He met in Scotland no one who interested him, nor did he gain any interest in Scottish Church affairs from the few days' visit. In England he was most impressed by the Evangelical leader Charles Simeon. About mid-September of 1828 he reached Princeton.

II

The America to which Hodge returned in 1828 was entering a stormy and troubled era. The new West was filling up at a rate beyond the wildest imagination of men. By 1830 Ohio had a population (937,000) greater than Massachusetts and Connecticut combined. Kentucky and Tennessee each passed the half-million mark about 1820. The West was expanding so rapidly that the older East was apprehensive lest it lose control of the nation. The election of President Jackson in 1828 seemed to many easterners the beginning of the end. On the religious scene, the Congregationalists and Presbyterians, who had always regarded themselves as the religious leaders of the nation and as better-class, educated, socially responsible Churches, had been outstripped by the Baptists and Methodists before 1830. In one generation the lead had gone to the groups despised as uneducated, lower-class, and "popular."

In the first years after the founding of the new nation a variety of factors brought the Congregationalists of New England and the Presbyterians of the middle seaboard states into close cooperation in the Plan of Union of 1801 for joint home mission work. The effective power of the Presbyterian Church was in the former New Side regions and was friendly to New England. The Presbyterians were as yet very weak in the entire South and even weaker on the new western frontier. The former Old Side regions of Pennsylvania and Maryland had not opposed the Plan of Union because it was assumed—evidently by all parties—that this plan would function mostly in New York state, where the sentiment was pro-New England already. But the Plan of Union plus the changing situation in the nation and in the Church were soon to become the occasions for a series of controversies.

The theological controversies which occupied so much of Hodge's career had begun in a very small way about the time of the founding of the Seminary. In fact, theological conflict had much to do with the founding of the Seminary. In the anti-religious era immediately following the Revolutionary War, the College of New Jersey, the principal Presbyterian school, had declined in number of students and in religious influence. In New England also, the decline was being felt. In both Presbyterian and Congregational circles the cry was going up for more ministers, for better trained ministers to evangelize the new West and the changing East. The existing colleges were not doing the job. In 1808 a theological seminary was founded at Andover, Massachusetts, which sought to combine orthodox trinitarian Congregationalists with Presbyterians in a dual thrust to offset Unitarianism and to train an adequate evangelical ministry. A number of New York and New Jersey Presbyterians friendly to New England supported this move, among them Gardiner Spring of New York and Edward D. Griffin of Newark. Other Presbyterians such as Ashbel Green, Samuel Miller, and Archibald Alexander held back from making common cause with the Andover group. These men were averse to certain newer trends in New England Calvinism, and, though they were anxious to continue cooperation with New Enlgand on many fronts, they wished to have a seminary which would teach their views in theology. This they achieved with the founding of the seminary at Princeton in 1812. They set forth the ideal of one great central seminary which was to unify the Church by having all its ministers trained by one faculty at one place. But this ideal of one seminary through which to "type" the Church had been opposed by many. Only ten out of thirty-six presbyteries had approved it. Nonetheless its promoters had managed to get it through the General Assembly.

Andover Seminary had been founded in 1808 as a Maginot

Line against Unitarianism. Its defensive work was a doctrinal subscription of unprecedented detail and rigor. When Princeton was founded four years later it was given an ironclad subscription formula written by Ashbel Green and ardently supported by Samuel Miller. Whereas the New York-New Jersey Presbyterians of New England orientation supported the Andover subscription formula because it was aimed at Unitarianism, by 1818-1819 Spring, Griffin, James Richards, and others were aroused by the Princeton subscription formula. Griffin wrote an attack upon it calling it "The New Test." These men charged that the Princeton-Philadelphia group were in fact seeking to make their personal interpretation of the Church's standards the test by which all others were to be judged orthodox or unorthodox. This, they charged, was an attack upon the rights of all other Presbyterians. The Princeton-Philadelphia group took the attitude that they were merely being good Presbyterians. And so the wars within nineteenth-century Presbyterianism began as the Princeton-Philadelphia group assumed the honorific claim to be Presbyterians of the "Old School" over and against the innovators who drew non-Presbyterian ideas from New England and were thus merely "New School" men.

It now became clear that the real purpose behind the determination of Green, Miller, Alexander, and the Philadelphia group to have only one seminary for the entire Church was that in this way—as the plan of the school indeed said—controversies might be avoided by having all the future ministers of the Church taught by one faculty rigidly bound to one interpretation of Presbyterianism. By 1830 the inevitable answer was apparent: five other Presbyterian seminaries had been founded in various parts of the nation.

Even before Hodge went abroad, the rumblings of the controveries which were to involve him throughout his career had begun. In 1826 Ashbel Green had noted bitterly that whereas Pennsylvania (for him the center of his power and prestige) had a total of 196 Presbyterian licentiates and ministers, New York had a total of 426. In 1829 New York had more students in colleges than did the combined colleges of

Pennsylvania and New Jersey (which regarded themselves as the bastions of the Presbyterian Church). One half of these students, moreover, were in New York state colleges. What was to become now of Princeton? While Hodge was in Germany (1827), Alexander had written to him of his apprehension for the future of the Seminary. Alexander feared that a New England-New West axis would leave Princeton to shrivel and die. In 1828 he wrote to Hodge (in Germany) that the new Presbyterian seminary founded that year in Pittsburgh was being "viewed by many as the last stronghold of orthodoxy, and the most secure deposit for funds intended to support the truth; and at this time, I have little doubt but that Dr. [Ashbel] Green and others of our staunch friends feel a deeper interest in that institution than in this. . . . After all we shall be forced to look to New England for our students."

In 1830 there were a total of seventeen Protestant seminaries in the nation. From the New England seminaries a goodly number of men were coming into the Presbyterian ministry each year. In western Pennsylvania, western New York, Ohio, Indiana, Tennessee, and Virginia, Presbyterian seminaries were competing with Princeton for students and money. If, as Alexander gloomily wrote to Hodge, Princeton were confined to eastern Pennsylvania and New Jersey it would be helpless, for the population in the area was not expanding much. In Hodge's lifetime his native city of Philadelphia went from the largest in the nation to a rather stagnant city less than half the size of New York City.

III

Worse by far than this form of competition for Princeton was the growing threat of popular religion. Both Alexander and Hodge regarded themselves as favorably disposed toward revivals, free religious associations, lay piety, and the like. Miller stood aloof from most of such movements, though no tensions had emerged before Hodge left for Europe. But beginning in 1827 Princeton began to be increasingly aware of

Charles Hodge

the violent controversy raging in New York state and in New England over the revivals conducted by Charles G. Finney and his followers. To the anxious Princeton professors it seemed by 1830 that the whole of New York state Presbyterianism, with its 426 ministers and licentiates, and all its college students would go over to a kind of popular religion which was anathema to them. From both the West and the South Princeton was already under heavy fire for, it was charged, making its students first gentlemen, and then ministers. In so doing, the charge went, Princeton unfitted men for the work of the Church in the new states on the frontier.

Despite what Hodge and the other Princeton professors thought of themselves, throughout the nineteenth century they found themselves unable to understand the popular religious movements of the day. The popular movements in turn rejected Princeton as "high-toned," "book-learned," and interested only in the upper classes. Hodge and J. W. Alexander (the son of Archibald Alexander) recognized the tension but did not know how to deal with the problem. As J. W. Alexander wrote, with italics, "To the poor the Gospel is *not* preached in our crack Presbyterian Churches." He told a friend, the famous elite preacher John Hall, that bad as Finney's "new measures" in truth were, they were better than no measures at all—i.e. the Philadelphia indifference to people. For several years Hodge, Archibald Alexander, J. W. Alexander, and Albert Dod of the College, tried to steer a middle course on the popular religious movements of the day, critical of their theological vagaries but seeking to win and to change them rather than attempting to blot them out. The attempt proved futile.

Among the many aspects of the popular religious movements of the day none was more characteristic, and none was destined to cause Presbyterianism, Princeton, and Hodge more trouble, than the so-called voluntary benevolent societies. By the time Hodge returned from Germany these benevolent societies included a number of anti-slavery societies, plus the missionary, education, and reform societies. As though this were not ferment enough, long smoldering anti-Yankee feelings and theological differences burst all the seams just about the time Hodge returned. The ensuing struggle caught him up, gave him grievous trouble, and occupied him until the end of his life. He was always very distrustful of ecclesiastical power, and he questioned the characters and motives of "the Philadelphia junto" (as he called them), which was driving for a powerful ecclesiastical machine. Yet theologically and socially he was utterly opposed to the total ideology of those who were resisting the Philadelphia group led by Ashbel Green. In the bitter end the good of the Seminary, as he understood it, made him the foremost apologist of the Philadelphia policies and the great opponent of all popular movements and ideas in Presbyterianism.

Charles Hodge returned from abroad to a troubled Church, an insecure school, and a nation which was undergoing rapid and radical change. The leadership of the Seminary was solidly in the hands of Alexander and Miller. Their answer to the problems of the day was simple: allow no changes. This position Hodge loyally accepted and supported. In 1825 a group of men in and about Princeton had founded a small quarterly journal called the *Biblical Repertory*. It had carried at first mostly reviews, reprints, and general surveys. It was now re-organized with the added backing of several New York area New School Presbyterians. Princeton, led by Miller and Alexander, had embarked upon a policy of steering a middle course between Old School and New School lest she be left to wither and die as the other seminaries became party organs. The *Repertory* was to be a major instrument in this endeavor. It was to carry articles of opinion and comment, thoroughly orthodox but uncommitted to any of the warring parties. A local editorial committee from the Seminary and the College was to control its contents. All articles were to be unsigned, and for decades most of the material was written by this local group. All controversial topics were subjected to the decision of this group, usually numbering from six to ten men. Hodge became the "beast of burden," as he called it, of the venture but by no means the master or driver.

IV

It is often assumed that Hodge was a leader in the violent controversies of 1831 to 1837 which broke the Presbyterian Church into two denominations. Though he later became the great defender of the Old School party and denomination, he was actually an opponent of the rupture at the time. Both the opposition to the rupture before 1837 and the defense of it afterward were motivated in large measure by the good of the Seminary as he understood it. Even so, Hodge's role must not be over-stressed. Throughout this period it was Alexander and Miller who controlled policy, not Hodge and the other younger members of the faculty. Moreover from 1833 to 1838 Hodge was confined by illness to his house and unable even to leave it for classes. A great part of this time he was forced to read and write while lying on his back. His malady was an infection in one leg. Of the more extreme remedies, he wrote his wife from Philadelphia, where he had been taken once for treatment, "I had sixty leeches applied to the groin last evening. . . ." A newly invented treatment was "a piece of lighted punk, or rather thin tree bark, is put on the flesh and allowed to burn out. It of course burns to a crisp the skin under it. . . ." This was done to him daily for a time. By the winter of 1838 he was able to go about on crutches, though he did not resume preaching until 1842.

By 1830-1831 controversy was rife in the Presbyterian Church yet without any very clear pattern of parties or of issues. Dominant Old School demagogues like R. J. Breckinridge condemned the doctrine of a limited atonement as vigorously as did New School heretics like Albert Barnes. Yet to Princeton this was one of the three essentials of the "Triangle." Joshua L. Wilson, the heresy hunter of Cincinnati and the unsuccessful prosecutor of Lyman Beecher, was almost fanatically anti-Yankee, if not anti-easterner. Yet Wilson was a bitter personal enemy of the entire Pittsburgh Old School group who with Breckinridge and Ashbel Green were most responsible for the rupture of 1837. Breckinridge, Wilson, and their friends, were more outright and outspoken against slavery than was Beecher. Yet the Pennsylvania Old School men fought *all discussion* of slavery lest the South secede from the Church leaving the northern Old School party a minority.

Until 1834 Thomas Baird of Pittsburgh, who later was to claim credit for having first seen the need for dividing the Church, was asserting in his paper that the whole controversy in the Church was due to the personal ambitions of the Philadelphia clique. At the height of the heresy trial of Albert Barnes, Ashbel Green raised the cry that bad as Barnes' heresies were, the greater crisis was the danger of the voluntary societies to the boards of the Church, all of which, Green boasted, he was a member of and the head of several. On the western frontier, mission board secretaries like Joshua T. Russell, Green's man, subsidized local journals and pastors who could be useful to the cause of the Old School. In New York state, New School Presbyterians were divided between a pro-Finney group and an older New School group based on New York City and Auburn Seminary. The latter was as opposed to Finney's new measures as were many Old School men. Yet Joshua L. Wilson had himself been a campmeeting evangelist employing all the Finney techniques, even the anxious bench and early admission to the church, as late as 1832. R. J. Breckinridge as late as 1834 defended camp meetings and the new measures when Wilson had turned against them. In the East, Hopkinsianism, the advanced New England "heresy" of the early 1800's, had all but been forgotten by 1832. The leading men of the party, such as Gardiner Spring, were now Old School men, and the former opponents of Hopkinsianism, such as Ezra S. Ely, were now New School men. Both parties had changed sides. Wilson saw the dangers of Hopkinsianism everywhere. Baird of Pittsburgh, who later claimed to have been consistently anti-Hopkinsian and anti-New England since 1814, seldom noticed the Finney revivals at all in his paper.

In this crazy-quilt pattern of affairs, with the Church burdened by several dozen half-pint demagogues backed by a newspaper of some kind, or a synodical or assembly board, or a voluntary society, or an emergency committee, the reaction of the Princeton faculty was typically academic. They set out to *educate* the Church. Miller wrote several small books on various controverted issues, Hodge and the two younger Alexanders, Joseph Addison and James Waddell, projected a complete popular commentary on the Bible, of which Hodge's volume on Romans became the best known. No doubt this set was intended, in part at least, to compete with Barnes' phenomenally successful *Notes* on the various books of the New Testament. Most important, however, was the role of the *Biblical Repertory*. In this journal the Princeton group sought desperately to moderate the controversies and to guide the Church to a wise solution of the problems. In article after article they sought to show that the basic problems were doctrinal and could only be settled over a period of time. They sought to conciliate the South by opposing abolitionism and by emphasizing piety and sound revivalism. They opposed the Taylor-New Haven theology and the revivalism of Taylor and Beecher as well as the revivalism of Finney. They also tried earnestly to secure the aid of the famous New England conservative evangelist Asahel Nettleton. At their solicitation he visited Princeton several times and made one extended trip in the South. The Princeton group treated the Philadelphia, Pittsburgh, Cincinnati, and Kentucky Old School groups as doctrinally sound but wrong in their ecclesiastical policies.

V

The Old School groups reacted violently to the Princeton program. Beginning in 1831 the various Old School papers, especially the *Presbyterian* of Philadelphia, so frequently attacked Hodge that a member of his family kept a running account of the articles. The Old School party regarded the Princeton program as a betrayal of the cause. On numerous occasions, in various papers, in various synods and presbyteries, and in the General Assembly, threats were made to discipline or to re-organize the faculty. From 1833 to 1838 the faculty was frequently left without salary for as long as eight or nine months. Hodge borrowed money from his well-to-do brother, but the senior Alexander was several times in a pitiful situation. Yet until 1834 the personal ambitions, petty vanity and demagoguery of the various Old School parties kept them from making any common cause. The Old School clique which met after the General Assembly of 1834 to unite upon a common platform which it called *The Act and Testimony* was, therefore, a thunderclap to the Princeton group. It meant that Princeton, which was in fact solidly Old School in theology would now have little hope of resisting the Old School politics in the Church. Samuel Miller wrote anxiously and secretly to Gardiner Spring asking if he thought the Princeton group should make peace with the Old School politicians and how they could best do it without admitting too much error.

Though Miller and others of the Princeton group who are not now identifiable began to ease over to the politicians, the group as a whole (about ten from the Seminary and from the College) moved more slowly. Hodge began in 1835 an annual feature review of the actions of each General Assembly. This he was to keep up until 1867 (with the possible exception of 1841). In these reviews he sought to analyze critically and theologically the work of each assembly. In view of the extreme pressure upon the Seminary faculty, unpaid salaries and more besides, this was a courageous venture indeed. Though Hodge wrote these reviews, they were frequently censored drastically by the group. On several occasions Hodge was forced under great protest to write that which he did not think.

In spite of these cautious censorings the Old School reactions became even more menacing. The "Ultras," as Hodge called them, demanded that the Princeton faculty be disciplined for presuming to sit in judgment upon the highest judicatory in the Church. They demanded also that the Assembly forbid any Seminary faculty from publishing a journal or periodical. Secret and public conclaves were held on whether or not to change the faculty. Miller's son-in-law, a committed member of the political group, was placed on the faculty. In late 1836 a delegation of Old School men came to Princeton to "persuade" the faculty to change its course. They informed the faculty that unless it did so, the Old School financiers, Robert and James Lenox, had the money, the plans, and the land ready to found a new, thoroughly Old School, seminary in New York City, where the New School had just founded Union Seminary.

That same year, 1836, Hodge wrote and published in the *Biblical Repertory* what became his most notorious article, a long book review on the issue of slavery. He argued that slavery as such was accepted in the Bible and that only its abuse was to be condemned outright. The article was bitterly anti-abolitionist and full of signs of the extreme pressure under which the Princeton group was living. Alexander, Miller, Hodge, and others of the Princeton group had at one time or another held slaves themselves or had purchased indentured white or black servants. Alexander had a very sentimental, romantic, patriarchal interpretation of slavery, which regarded it almost wholly from the standpoint of domestic household servants, and he ignored as much as possible the problems of plantation slavery, slave-trading, slave-breeding, etc.

Hodge followed Alexander's views. He had no personal knowledge of the South, and seems to have made no effort to learn anything about the situation. The article was several times reprinted, once as late as 1860, and was widely circulated. Of him, the Old School theologian E. D. McMaster wrote, "Dr. Hodge has done more to pervert the public mind on the subject of slavery than any hundred men in the Church." Hodge wrote the article as part of the Princeton group's desperate attempt to keep the South from seceding from the Church and leaving the New School with a working majority in the Assembly. He little realized what use interested parties would make of his article, and of the names Princeton and Presbyterian.

VI

His illness prevented Hodge from attending the fateful meeting of the Assembly of 1837, which resulted in the rupture of the

Church. Miller was there working solidly with the Old School party. Alexander was active also but seems to have had some reservations about the methods of the Old School clique. When Hodge came to write his annual review of the actions of the Assembly there was great dissension in the Princeton group. Hodge wished to condemn the New School, to approve some aspects of the Old School policy, and to question the constitutional grounds of the Old School's exscinding acts against the New School. In the end he was forced to come almost all the way to Miller's approval of the acts. Yet even the slight critique which he was allowed aroused a barrage of protests from Pennsylvania to Kentucky and further threats against the faculty. Miller and John McLean of the College, both on the *Biblical Repertory* committee, wrote in vigorous defense of the Old School actions in various weekly papers. Only two younger Princeton men stood with Hodge, J. W. Alexander and Albert Dod.

Once it was clear that henceforth there would be two Presbyterian Churches in the nation, the New School and the Old School denominations, Princeton's course became clear. Peace had to be made with the politicians if the Seminary faculty was to continue. The problem for the faculty was eased somewhat, however, by the public reaction to the rupture. No one had supposed that fourth-ninths of the Church would follow the New School denomination. The politicians themselves were in need of peace and public support. The more moderate Old School men approached Hodge in 1839 to write a history of the Church which would vindicate the Old School point of view. So difficult still were relations between Hodge and Ashbel Green, who had possession of most of the official records, that a third party had to make the arrangements for Hodge to use the documents. Yet when Hodge was through with his *Constitutional History*, he had so wholeheartedly defended an ultra Old School interpretation of things that Alexander was deeply pained.

In 1840 Hodge was made Professor of Theology, taking over most of Alexander's work. From this time also his health improved rapidly. The two older men became less active, and

Hodge for the first time moved toward actual leadership in the Seminary. Alexander and Miller retained a hold on affairs, however, until their deaths in 1851 and 1850. With the passing of some of the more ultra Old School men, and of the pressing needs of the Church, peace came for Hodge in other ways. He became accepted on several Church boards and was Moderator of the Old School General Assembly of 1846. His influence as a teacher was broadened by further writing and by travel. By the time of the Civil War he was regarded by many as the leading theologian of the denomination. The war put him again to a severe test. Until the last he sought to play down controversy and to conciliate the South in every possible way. Once the war had gone on for a year, he changed enough to charge that it was being fought largely at the behest of the slave-interests of the South. Yet before he was through, he had returned to his old insistence that slavery as such could not be condemned because the Bible approved of it.

The war came to an end, and the Old School found itself unable to reunite with the former southern Old School Churches which had formed a new denomination during the war. Moreover the younger generations in both the New School and the Old School in the North were agitating for a reunited northern Church. Hodge fought the proposal vigorously but failed to prevent the reunion. The terms of the reunion were hard for the Princeton group because they allowed constitutional status for the Princeton theology only as one possible interpretation of the Church's standards. Since 1812 Princeton had assumed that its theology was *the* faith of the Church. This Hodge had always maintained against the New School. After 1870 Hodge was again merely the theologian of a party. Yet he set out vigorously now to make for that theology its grandest monument. Hitherto the Board of the Seminary had prevailed upon him not to publish his theology lest it thus become available for use in any Old School seminary. Princeton might lose students if Hodge's theology could be studied anywhere. Between 1871 and 1873 he issued his now famous "three volumes." Very quickly they became the standard conservative Federal theology among the English-speaking Reformed Churches. The work was the capstone of his long career. Fittingly, upon the fiftieth anniversary of his entrance upon teaching at the Seminary, a celebration of considerable importance was held. He had indeed been the greatest of the Seminary's students and the greatest of its professors. When he passed from the scene on December 19, 1878, he had been the acknowledged leader of the Seminary for more than a generation. No other individual has ever served the Seminary so long, or so greatly furthered its cause.

III. SAMUEL SIMON SCHMUCKER
(1799-1873)

Lutheran Educator*

BY E. THEODORE BACHMANN

IF Professor Archibald Alexander had continued his lectures in pastoral theology at Princeton Seminary for the remainder of the academic year, Samuel Schmucker would have finished with the class of 1820. Instead, Schmucker acceded to his father's urging and resumed his studies in German. Before doing that, however, he visited friends in New York in order to acquaint himself with the church situation there. Then, after a final session of lectures and a round of farewells to faculty and students at the end of March, young Schmucker hit the highway from Princeton westward toward Philadelphia —and an inscrutable future.[1]

---

* In addition to the indicated sources, further material resides in the archives of the Lutheran Theological Seminary at Gettysburg, Pennsylvania, as well as in the possession of Dr. Abdel Ross Wentz (see Note 8). This includes letters of Schmucker to his wife and numerous other items hitherto unpublished. Dr. Wentz's forthcoming biography of this Lutheran educator promises to fill an obvious need. Upon finishing with Schmucker's sojourn at Princeton, 1818-1820, Dr. Wentz declared in a letter to the author of this essay, "I am amazed to find how much Princeton influenced him, both positively and negatively" (December 11, 1962).

[1] Born February 28, 1799, Schmucker was the son of the Rev. John George Schmucker and his wife Elizabeth (Gross). He attended Princeton Theological Seminary from August 17, 1818, to March 30, 1820. He died July 25, 1873, at Gettysburg, Pennsylvania. The only full-length biography that has appeared to date is the old and inadequate one by P. Anstadt, *Life and Times of Rev. S. S. Schmucker, D.D.*, York, Pa.: Anstadt & Sons, 1896. Excerpts from primary sources are its main merit. For the Princeton period, see pp. 60-79.

A still untold story, of ecumenical significance, is that of Schmucker's ensuing relations with the friends he made at Princeton, especially with fellow students like Charles Hodge, '19; William B. Sprague, '19 (Congregational, later editor of *Annals of the American Pulpit*); John Johns, '19 (later Episcopal Bishop of Virginia); Charles P. McIlvaine, '20 (later Episcopal Bishop of Ohio); Robert Baird, '22, Schmucker's

SONS OF THE PROPHETS

I

A native of Hagerstown, Maryland, and son of the then president of the Lutheran Ministerium of Pennsylvania, young Schmucker was Princeton Seminary's first student of German Lutheran descent. Gifted, earnest, and methodical, his bilinguality made him at home in both German and Anglo-Saxon cultures. A profound religious experience during his mid-teens opened to him the legacy of the Halle-type of pietism, which had been personified by Henry Melchior Muhlenberg,[2] the so-called patriarch of Lutherans in colonial America. In Schmucker this brand of pietism was blended with that of American revivalism as personified by Jonathan Edwards. Animated by this unity of spirit Schmucker moved easily in two linguistic worlds. His own experience in studying theology both as a student under Justus Helmuth,[3] the last of Muhlenberg's associates at Philadelphia, and as a student in the new Presbyterian Seminary under Archibald Alexander[4] and Samuel Miller,[5] showed him what requirements would have to be met for a soundly prepared ministry. No doubt his earlier experience as a Latin teacher at York[6] had given him ideas too. For, as he later told friends, he left Princeton with three burn-

---

roommate during his last year (an outstanding Presbyterian ecumenical leader, influential also in Europe), and others. See *Biographical Catalog of the Princeton Theological Seminary 1815-1932*, Princeton, 1933.

[2] Anstadt, pp. 31-35, 40-59. For the cultivation of piety in the life of the people in the formative colonial era, see *The Journals of Henry Melchior Muhlenberg*, trans. T. G. Tappert and J. W. Doberstein, 3 vols. Phila.: Muhlenberg Press, 1942-1958. E.g., I, 10ff.

[3] Anstadt, pp. 30, 35. Abdel Ross Wentz, *History of the Gettysburg Theological Seminary, 1826-1926*, Phila.: United Lutheran Publication House, 1926, pp. 50ff., 60f. (hereafter cited simply as Wentz). E. Theodore Bachmann, "The Rise of Missouri Lutheranism," Chicago: University of Chicago Library (microfilm), 1946, pp. 1-18.

[4] James W. Alexander, *The Life of Archibald Alexander, D.D.*, N.Y.: Scribner, 1954, pp. 373f., 393f. Anstadt, pp. 61-62.

[5] Samuel Miller, Jr., *The Life of Samuel Miller, D.D., LL.D.*, 2 vols. Phila., 1869, *passim*. See also, Samuel Miller, *A Brief Retrospect of the Eighteenth Century*, 2 vols. N.Y., 1803, an amazing compilation that grew out of a New Year's sermon at the turn of the century and drew Miller into fruitful international as well as national contacts.

[6] Anstadt, pp. 30-31, 36-39.

ing desires: to translate some solid Lutheran theological work from the German; to found a theological seminary; and to found a college.[7]

A fuller recounting of Schmucker's career must be left to his biographers.[8] What concerns us here is how he attained these three ambitions. Our attention, therefore, centers on the years between 1820 and 1832. For it was within this short span of time that Schmucker's latent genius unfolded with remarkable effect. To be sure, he got off to a seemingly slow start. Although he left Princeton early in the spring, almost the entire year passed before he was situated in his first parish. Not that the time was wasted. On the contrary, through his father's involvement in the formation of the Lutheran General Synod,[9] and then through his own interest in the founding of the Synod of Maryland and Virginia,[10] he gained a keen appreciation of the problems facing Lutherans in America. Meanwhile, at Lancaster in early June he had been examined and then licensed by the Ministerium of Pennsylvania.[11]

Thanks to parental ties in Virginia, the problem of finding a vacant parish for him was solved. Uncle John Peter Schmucker's parish in the Shenandoah Valley comprised ten congregations. A couple of these, including New Market, were detached—perhaps with some misgivings on the part of the farmers and villagers—for the studious Princetonian Lutheran.

[7] *Ibid.*, p. 112. See also "Schmucker, Samuel Simon," *Dictionary of American Biography*, 16:443.

[8] A full-length biography is being prepared by Abdel Ross Wentz, Church historian and President-emeritus of Gettysburg Seminary. See also his article, "The Work of Samuel Simon Schmucker," *Lutheran Quarterly*, 57:61-89 (1927). Frederick K. Wentz, Church History Professor at Gettysburg Seminary, is editing a selection of Schmucker's writings.

[9] *Documentary History of the Evangelical Lutheran Ministerium of Pennsylvania and Adjacent States . . . 1748-1821*, Philadelphia: General Council, 1898, pp. 524ff., 545ff. Robert Fortenbaugh, *Development of the Synodical Polity of the Lutheran Church in America* (unpublished Ph.D. thesis, University of Pennsylvania), 1926, pp. 146-171.

[10] Abdel Ross Wentz, *History of the Evangelical Lutheran Synod of Maryland*, Phila.: United Lutheran, 1920, *passim*.

[11] *Documentary History*, pp. 546ff. Anstadt, p. 80.

An early visit to the countryside in September, when the first autumn colors touched the Blue Ridge, was shortly followed by his permanent arrival. In his journal, a few days before Christmas, he made this terse entry: "December 21. Arrived at New Market, Shenandoah County, Va., and by the grace of God, in reliance on the aid of God, took charge of my churches."[12]

Samuel Schmucker entered New Market with no illusions. He knew of the intellectual gulf between himself and most of his parishioners; and he determined to bridge it with faithful pastoral care and catechetical education. He also knew that he was in "Henkel territory," where the followers of an aggressively conservative Lutheranism—led by the enterprising frontier preacher Paul Henkel—had in that very year banded themselves together as the Tennessee Synod; in some respects it was a rival of the Synod of Maryland and Virginia, also created in 1820.[13] Ironically, Paul Henkel, years earlier, had been the one to urge Samuel Schmucker's father and two uncles to consider the ministry and had been their first theological tutor.[14] But now, alas, New Market's new pastor confided in his journal: "Henkel and sons persecute instinctively everything that bears the name of Schmucker."[15] Small wonder that on New Year's Day, 1821, Samuel Schmucker preached to his New Market congregation on the text from Job 16:22: "When a few years are come, then I shall go the way whence I shall not return."[16] During the ensuing years he went to work with ardor, saw his membership increase from year to year, married and soon lost his first wife, and then steeped himself in productive study and more than parochial teaching. It is to his study that we turn first.

[12] *Ibid.*, p. 98.
[13] "Henkel, Paul," *D.A.B.*, 8:538. Socrates Henkel, *History of the Evangelical Lutheran Tennessee Synod*, New Market: Henkel & Co., 1890, pp. 13-25. See also C. W. Cassell, W. J. Fink, and Elon O. Henkel, *History of the Lutheran Church in Virginia and East Tennessee*, Strasburg, Va.: Shenandoah Publishing House, 1930, pp. 96ff.
[14] "Schmucker, John George," *D.A.B.*, 16:442.
[15] Anstadt, p. 85.
[16] *Ibid.*, p. 98.

SAMUEL SIMON SCHMUCKER

II

"A translation of some one eminent system of Lutheran Dogmatics" stood first among the three *pia desideria* with which Schmucker left Princeton. New Market might not be a good place to found a seminary or a college, but it would be a useful place to translate a book. But what book? While still at Princeton, his father as well as his former theological tutor, Helmuth, recommended that he translate something by Mosheim.[17] Johann Laurentz von Mosheim had been Chancellor of the rising new University of Göttingen and internationally known as a church historian and highly competent scholar; he was a Lutheran theologian who set his course midway between deism and pietism. Although he had died in 1755, sixty years later there were still Mosheim clubs in Europe and America which gathered to read his works. One such club for young men had Helmuth's encouragement in Philadelphia.[18] For these reasons Sam Schmucker gave serious thought to translating Mosheim's *Elementa Theologiae Dogmaticae*—an impressive opus of nearly 900 pages.[19] Whether his mentors at Princeton, Professors Alexander and Miller, encouraged him cannot now be determined. Miller's own expansive two volumes on the eighteenth century included Germany and, at least in a projected additional volume, would necessarily have mentioned Mosheim.[20] However, Archibald Alexander was probably a good deal more wary of German

[17] *Ibid.*, p. 112.

[18] Henry A. Pochmann, *German Culture in America*, Madison: U. of Wis., 1957, pp. 522f. See other citations under "Mosheim," *New Schaff-Herzog Encyclopedia of Religious Knowledge*, 8:28-29. Also the fuller article on Mosheim by Bonwetsch in *Realencyklopädie für protestantische Theologie und Kirche*, 3d ed., 13:502-506.

[19] Edited by Prof. Christian E. von Windsheim, Erlangen, Nürnberg, 1758.

[20] Cf. n. 5, above. The two volumes were but the first half of a projected sequence of four, the last being intended to cover developments in religion and theology. *The Princeton University Library Chronicle*, XIV (Winter, 1953), No. 2, pp. 55-58. Had Miller been able to follow through, especially in the areas of philosophy as well as theology on the Continent, the highly Anglo-Saxon climate of American thought, along with its French ingredients, might have been measurably affected.

theology than was Samuel Miller. To Alexander it appeared mainly as "neology" and verged on infidelity.[21] How Schmucker finally settled for something other than Mosheim's *Elements* opens up a new range of contacts.

Just how Schmucker began to correspond with Professor Moses Stuart[22] at Andover Theological Seminary, the new Congregationalist stronghold near Boston, or with Friedrich August Koethe,[23] the scholarly Lutheran Church superintendent at Allstaedt, in the Duchy of Weimar, the extant records do not precisely say. Both of these men were well informed on theological developments in Germany since Mosheim's death. Stuart's emergence as America's pioneer Hebraist and Old Testament scholar of modern cast rested heavily upon just such German sources as—in Schmucker's day—tended to be avoided at Princeton. Ironically, it was largely by way of books first imported by Boston Unitarians that

[21] A. A. Hodge, *The Life of Charles Hodge, D.D., LL.D.*, N.Y.: Scribner, 1880, p. 161.

[22] "Stuart, Moses," *D.A.B.*, 18:174-5. This sketch, by William F. Albright, the noted Biblical archaeologist, shows how German scholarship made an impact on Stuart's development as an Old Testament scholar. Especially illuminating is Stuart's "Letter to the Editor, on the Study of the German Language," *The Christian Review* (Boston), vi (Sept. 1841), No. 23, pp. 446-471. There Stuart describes how he began his study of German about 1810. In the Hebrew grammar, edited by the English scholar, Parkhurst, he came upon occasional references to Luther's German Bible. These referred him to Georg Fr. Seiler's *Hermeneutik*, a work "that opened my eyes . . . and made me see that I had everything to do, and yet had done nothing," p. 449.

For more on Seiler's work, see W. Gass, *Geschichte der Protestantischen Dogmatik*, IV (Berlin: Reimer, 1867), p. 105. When Moses Stuart purchased some books for Andover Seminary from the library of the late Unitarian leader, J. S. Buckminster, in Boston, he came upon the *Magazin für Dogmatik und Moral* put out in Tübingen by Christian Flatt, the younger colleague of Christian Friedrich Storr. This magazine, he said, is "excellent and staunch orthodox . . . still remains a standard and noble work"; *Christian Rev.*, p. 449. As Gass points out, an affinity existed between Seiler, at Erlangen, and Storr, at Tübingen. But cf. Mathias Simon, *Evangelische Kirchengeschichte Bayerns*, Nürnberg, 1952, who sees in Seiler the father of rationalism in northern Bavaria. He taught at Erlangen, 1770-1807; p. 519.

[23] *Allgemeine Deutsche Biographie*, xvi.

SAMUEL SIMON SCHMUCKER

Stuart came on to the trail of intensive Biblical study in the German manner.[24]

On the other side of the Atlantic, Koethe, despite his quiet scholarliness, was a lively champion of evangelical faith as an essential element in any study of Christian theology. During the Napoleonic era, a spiritual awakening was stirring in many, often obscure, quarters on the Continent. In Germany, as well as in Britain and America, the Christian faith was experiencing a resurgence, and Koethe was one of its spokesmen.[25] As early as February 1820, while visiting his friend Frederick Schaeffer, a young Lutheran pastor in New York, Schmucker had learned about Koethe's work and made a contribution.[26] One thing led to another, and presently both Stuart and Koethe were advising Schmucker to forget about Mosheim and to consider Storr. Mosheim, after all, was a pre-Kantian theologian; and to be that was to be at a decided disadvantage in the rising world of theological thought. Mosheim was also pre-French Revolution, and that, too, could make a difference in outlook upon modern society. Not that Storr was the ultimate answer, for he himself was pre-Schleiermacher. But he was the best author available.

Gottlob Christian Storr, professor of theology at the University of Tübingen, in South Germany, had died in 1805. A dozen years earlier he had published his *Doctrinae Christianae pars theoretica e sacris leteris repetita*. Storr's younger colleague, Carl Christian Flatt, in 1803, brought out a German translation, with notes, entitled, *Lehrbuch der christlichen Dogmatik*.[27] Storr, it was said, had begun to make use

[24] Cf. n. 22, above, re Joseph Stevens Buckminster (1784-1812). *New Schaff-Herzog Encyc.*, 2:290.

[25] For an account of this simultaneous phenomenon see e.g. Heinrich Hermelink, *Das Christentum in der Menschheitsgeschichte* (1789-1835), Stuttgart: Metzler, 1951, I, 219-265. See also K. S. Latourette, *A History of Christianity*, N.Y.: Harker, 1953, pp. 1013ff. Also C. W. Ranson, *That the World May Know*, N.Y.: Friendship, 1953, pp. 62-78.

[26] Anstadt, p. 75.

[27] Stuttgart: Metzler, 1803. Cf. n. 22 above re Flatt. Anonymously a small opus of Storr's was translated from the Latin and published in Boston in 1817, entitled *An Essay on the Historical Sense of the New*

of Kant, but he was not an outright Kantian. Nor had he assimilated French revolutionary thinking into his system. However, he was recommended as a theological author reasonably up to date and worthy also of an audience in the English-speaking world. Schmucker acquired a copy of Storr and energetically set about the task of translating its 800-odd pages. By the spring of 1824—despite domestic grief and a wide array of church responsibilities that had taken him repeatedly away from his parish and had demanded much effort as well as time—he was on his way from New Market with the translation finished.

En route to New England, Schmucker stopped briefly at Princeton and received Professor Alexander's approbation for the additions he had made, especially for his defense of the doctrine of the Trinity.[28] The latter was a timely rebuttal to Unitarian dogma which had been popularized by William Ellery Channing's noteworthy "Baltimore Sermon" (1819). At Andover, Schmucker delivered his manuscript to Moses Stuart, who saw it through publication. Two years later, in 1826, Messrs. Flagg and Gould at Andover brought out the two-volume opus, whose title page read: *An Elementary Course of Biblical Theology*, translated from the work of Professors Storr and Flatt, with additions, by S. S. Schmucker. Its five parts included: the authority of Scripture; the work and providence of the Triune God; the Christian understanding of man; the redemptive work of Christ; justification by faith and the Christian life.[29]

Young Schmucker had thus publicly identified himself with

Testament. Storr's *Doctrinae Christianae*, meanwhile, had virtually become the official theological textbook for the Evangelical State Church of Württemberg. H. Hermelink, *Geschichte der Evang. Kirche in Württemberg von der Reformation bis zur Gegenwart*, Stuttgart: Wunderlich, 1952, pp. 301-9. Note Hermelink's reference to the influence on Storr of the great pietist New Testament scholar, Johann Albrecht Bengel, and also that of Kant.

[28] Anstadt, p. 108.

[29] Two volumes bound in one. The dedication was "To the Reverend Clergy of the Evangelical Lutheran Church in the United States, this attempt to promote the cause of evangelical truth and theological science."

the leading protagonists of what later came to be called the "older Tübingen school."[30] For his own subsequent development, as well as for the future course of theological thought among the advocates of a deliberately styled "American" Lutheranism,[31] this association was significant. Being denominationally loyal, Schmucker early showed signs of being not so much original as eclectic in his thinking. He was devoted to orderliness and was drawn—at least within the scope of traditional Protestant thought—toward synthesis rather than sharp differentiation.[32] Such sharpness was reserved by him for Roman Catholicism on the one hand and for Deism or Unitarianism on the other. Meanwhile, his own knowledge of Lutheranism, or, more specifically, of the writings and teaching of Luther, at least at this stage in his life, appears to have been rather limited.

Perhaps it is not too much to say that, for better or for worse, Schmucker associated himself with the Biblical supernaturalism of Storr and the older Tübingen school of thought. This was an irenic Biblical trend, characteristic particularly of the Lutheran Church in Württemberg. While it opposed the rationalism of the Enlightenment it also dissociated itself from the traditional formulations of seventeenth-century Lutheran orthodoxy. Storr's efforts lay in seeking to establish Christian truth and doctrine on the sole authority of a self-authenticating divine revelation in Scripture. It has been said that Storr's position was distinguished from orthodoxy by his substitution of the authority of Jesus and his apostles for the inspiration of the Scriptures, by making the Scripture the sole source, even the textbook, of Christian teaching. In that case, not only "human faith" but, indirectly, also "divine faith" was derived from empirical historical deduction, and left in doubt the attribution of proof to the "testimony of the Holy Spirit." After establishing the authority of Christ and the

---

[30] Of which, in one sense, Bengel was the forerunner.

[31] For an account of the term and the movement see, Vergilius Ferm, *The Crisis in American Lutheran Theology*, N.Y.: Century, 1827, pp. 71-116.

[32] Wentz, *History of the Gettysburg Seminary*, pp. 106-115.

Bible, as one scholar has observed, Storr "needed no further internal proof of Christian truth from reason or experience." Besides, there could be no occasion for the influence of philosophy on the content of Christian doctrine. In consequence, while professing the deity of Christ, he avoided the doctrine of the *communicatio idiomatum* and thus lost hold of the true incarnation of the Word.[33]

III

How much of Storr's thinking was assimilated by Schmucker is not easy to say, because there was also an imponderable persistence of the influence of Archibald Alexander. In the fields of Biblical and doctrinal study Alexander had contagious interests in hermeneutics and archaeology as well as in orthodox Calvinist teaching as adapted to a methodical scheme of "mental philosophy."[34] To Thomas Reid (d. 1796), and other members of the Philosophical Society of Aberdeen, Alexander joined the apologist William Paley (d. 1805). Like the rest of the students at Princeton, Schmucker also became acquainted with the Genevan orthodox dogmatician Francis Turretin (d. 1687), whose *Institutio theologiae elencticae* served as the text upon which Alexander based his lectures in systematics.[35]

Unfortunately, it is not possible here to say how much Schmucker had been influenced by his aged tutor, Justus Helmuth, or what theological works the latter relied upon for the doctrinal orientation of his students. At this period in his life, however, Schmucker seems to have favored certain formulations of the Lutheran Confessions as set forth in the Book of Concord. Indeed, following his visit to New York in 1820, he had written to his father: "The Augsburg Confession should again be brought up out of the dust." He would insist that everyone must "subscribe to the twenty-one articles, and de-

[33] Otto Kirn's analysis in *New Shaff-Herzog Encyc.*, 12:34-36. See Kirn's fuller analysis in *Realencyklopädie für protestantische Theologie und Kirche* (3d ed.), 20:153f.

[34] Alexander, *Life of Alexander*, pp. 366-67. *New Shaff-Herzog Encyc.*, 2:372.

[35] *Ibid.*, pp. 368-9, 372-3.

clare before God by his subscription, that it corresponds with the Bible, not *quantum* [*sic*] but *quia*." What concerned Schmucker most, and what constituted the point of synthesis for many divergent elements, was the spiritual life of the individual minister. "Personal Christianity" was exhibited and cultivated best for him especially in the *Meditations on the Sufferings of Christ*, by the great Francke's successor at Halle, Johann Jakob Rambach (d. 1735).[36]

In the light of these influences in Schmucker's life it is easier to see why he was probably drawn with deep conviction to the theological position of Storr, and how, in the process of translating, his own diversified experiences were brought into focus. As Storr had sought to adapt Christian theology to the demands of a new day, so Schmucker could find encouragement in that work for seeking to adapt Lutheranism to the demands of the American scene. It is probably safe to say that in New Market, in close contact with and reaction to a Henkel-type of conservative Lutheranism, Schmucker developed the ingredients of what he was later to disseminate as "American" Lutheranism.[37]

What better way, moreover, could there be for launching Lutheranism into the currents of American theological discussion than by making available in English a major work of one of its more recent noteworthy scholars? In New England, where the Congregationalist-Unitarian controversy was bitter, two journals gave extensive reviews of Schmucker's translation. In New Haven, *The Christian Spectator*,[38] after acknowledging the long-standing weaknesses and dangers of German Lutheranism, saw in Storr's presentation the force of logical Biblical argument that would have to be recognized even by Unitarians. The reviewer claimed: "The argument of Storr on this subject [Biblical authority] is conducted in a masterly manner and with irresistible evidence, and if our young theologians shall ever need to look around for the weapons of such a warfare [to defend the Biblical doctrines] they will find here

[36] Anstadt, p. 63.
[37] Cf. n. 31 above.
[38] New Series, I (Jan. 1827), pp. 35-42.

a well stocked armory." Besides, "it is chiefly because the work is thus *Biblical*, that it deserves, as far as it is a system of theology, the attention of the student."

The *Christian Spectator* reviewer was not uncritical of the translator. He regretted that Schmucker had retained not only the full sixteen pages on the Real Presence in the Lord's Supper but had added ten more of his own to defend a doctrine marked by "Lutheran peculiarities." Conversely, his supplement on the doctrine of the Trinity was welcomed. Most of all the reviewer deplored the pedantry of the translator. To be sure he had improved upon Storr by embodying Flatt's notes directly into the context. Other than that, however, Schmucker had included no English theological works in the references; he had simply plugged along with the German, so that even where there is reference to a German translation of an English book he "most scrupulously retained the reference to the translation instead of to the original."[39] Far from being considered a popular work, this English version of Storr was nevertheless hailed as a solid support of traditional evangelical Christianity.

A cutting rebuttal, however, came from Boston's Unitarian journal, the *Christian Examiner and Theological Review*.[40] There the reviewer criticized Storr's work as having far less to do with the Bible than was claimed. In addition, it chided a scholar such as Storr for perpetuating the misleading notion that the doctrine of the Trinity is of Biblical rather than of patristic origin. To go further into this controversy would lead us too far afield. It is sufficient to note that as a young pastor of twenty-seven Samuel Schmucker had broken into the company and controversy of American theologians. Perhaps it was on grounds of discreet silence that Princeton Seminary's *Biblical Repertory* made no mention of Schmucker's translation, although certain of Storr's works had already been mentioned.[41]

[39] *Ibid.*, p. 41.

[40] IV, pp. 334–47. The reviewer rebuffed Schmucker's attack on the Unitarians in the second volume, pp. 279-81.

[41] Cf. note 28 above. Alexander and Miller had seen Schmucker's translation in manuscript. So had Hodge; Anstadt, p. 108. Hodge reported

In any case, by the time his first ambition had thus been realized, Schmucker was already accomplishing his second.

IV

On September 5, 1826, at Gettysburg, Samuel Simon Schmucker, Professor of Christian Theology, delivered his inaugural address before the directors of the Theological Seminary of the General Synod of the Evangelical Lutheran Church.[42] This event fulfilled a long-felt need of American Lutherans in general and the imaginative aggressiveness of one young pastor in particular to do something about the theological education of future pastors. In most denominations there persisted until it was satisfied the same concern that had moved the Puritans to found Harvard College lest they leave behind them an unlettered ministry.[43] For Lutherans, remembering their Reformation legacy and its origin in the theological faculty of a university, this concern could not easily be erased; nor, however, could it be easily satisfied.

The seminary which Schmucker had learned to know at Princeton in 1818 was then a half-dozen years old. Andover had been founded only in 1808; and the Dutch Reformed Seminary, now located at New Brunswick, New Jersey, antedated all other American theological seminaries by virtue of its founding in 1784. Indeed, seminary education for ministers-to-be, in contrast to theological education within the college context—as at Harvard or Yale—was a relatively new development. As early as 1749, Henry Melchior Muhlenberg had proposed the opening of a theological seminary at Philadelphia. Yet this as well as later proposals brought no action.

---

that Friedrich August Tholuck, whom he had met in Germany, also considered Storr "often very unnatural." Hodge, *Life of Charles Hodge*, p. 121. Perhaps it was for reasons of mutual friendship that Hodge, as editor of the *Biblical Repertory*, preferred to keep silent on Schmucker's translation rather than offend by offering criticism.

[42] Published at Carlisle, Pa.: Tizzard & Crever, 1826.
[43] "New England First Fruits. 2. In Respect of the College and the Proceeding of Learning Therein." (1643). *The Puritans*, ed. Perry Miller and Thomas H. Johnson, N.Y.: American Book Co., 1938, p. 701.

Muhlenberg's son-in-law, John Christopher Kunze, conducted a kind of theological prep school at Philadelphia from 1773 to 1782. Its functions were subsequently embodied in the rising University of Pennsylvania.[44] In 1797, at New York, Kunze began to tutor young men in theology. By the time of his death ten years later he had turned out a small but remarkably select number of theologues, who were among the first American Lutheran pastors thoroughly at home in the English language. Many other ministers, meanwhile, had also been tutoring young men. But it was Kunze's efforts that in 1815 had led to the opening of Hartwick Seminary, the first Lutheran theological school in America. Its location was near the present town of Oneonta, New York, at the headwaters of the Susquehanna River—where lay the large but remote lands which the eccentric clergyman, John Christopher Hartwick, had bequeathed to the Lutherans for an educational institution.[45]

In the almost equally remote New Market, Virginia, Samuel Schmucker had added the task of theological tutor to his other duties. Other pastors in the Shenandoah Valley had done it before him, notably Paul Henkel. But with Schmucker, the born scholar *and* organizer, things were different. His teaching experience as a youth at York Academy now proved useful. The death, after childbirth, of his wife, Elizabeth, in early 1823, actually seemed to plunge him, in self-forgetfulness, into a teaching ministry of high determination. Into his parsonage, at the southwest corner of what is now Congress Street and Seminary Lane at New Market, there came a number of young lads. Actually, the first had already come in 1822.[46] The adjoining little house became a theological preparatory school, a pilot project. Among the six students was John Gottlob Morris, who had already known Schmucker as a teacher at York. He and the other five seldom got to see

[44] Wentz, *History of the Gettysburg Seminary*, pp. 28-48.
[45] *Ibid.*, pp. 64-73.
[46] B. M. Schmucker, *Pennsylvania College Book*, Phila.: Lutheran Publ. Soc., 1882, p. 155.

SAMUEL SIMON SCHMUCKER

their teacher outside of class and pictured him as a "grind," holed up in his study writing and reading.[47]

What his students could not know was that young Schmucker was really living in the future. Schmucker knew that unless the Lutherans had both a well organized and united church and a viable enterprise in higher education, notably in theology, things would get even worse than they looked in 1823. To be sure, already, in 1821, Schmucker had given attention to the need of sound church organization and, as secretary of a special polity committee of the infant synod that had just ordained him, he adapted from Presbyterian sources a "Formula for the Government and Discipline of the Evangelical Lutheran Church in Maryland and Virginia." Adopted and published by that synod in 1823, this formula subsequently became widely influential as an instrument of Lutheran Church polity.[48] With these early insights into the significance of polity in the life of the Church he could thus argue all the more effectively when, quite unexpectedly late in 1823, the Ministerium of Pennsylvania suddenly withdrew from the General Synod. Undismayed by the loss of this largest unit, young Schmucker and his friends worked for the preservation of the General Synod, while Schmucker Senior, a former president of the Ministerium, lent a strong hand in forming the Synod of Western Pennsylvania out of the congregations west of the Susquehanna.[49]

For Samuel Schmucker, however, the preservation of the General Synod was essential to the successful completion of plans for a theological seminary. The church needed the sem-

[47] John G. Morris, *Fifty Years in the Lutheran Ministry*, Baltimore: James Young, 1878, p. 128.

[48] *Pennsylvania College Book*, p. 155. Cf. "The Form of Government," drawn up in 1788, adopted the following year by the Presbyterian General Assembly. Text in *The Constitution of the Presbyterian Church in the United States of America*, Phila.: Presb. Bd. of Publication, 1842. Cf. Charles Hodge, *The Constitutional History of the Presbyterian Church in the United States of America, Part II. 1741-1748*, Phila.: Marten, 1840, for background.

[49] H. E. Jacobs, *A History of the Evang. Lutheran Church in the United States*, N.Y.: Scribners, 1893, p. 363.

inary; the seminary needed the church. Under Schmucker's leadership, theological education was shifted away from the New York and Philadelphia areas to western Maryland and Virginia. With younger pastors in the synod Schmucker pursued frequent discussions. Eventually a consensus developed. In 1824 Schmucker was ready with a plan for a theological seminary. In a sermon to the Synod of Maryland and Virginia he set it forth.[50] Meanwhile, with its constitution already making provision for action in the field of theological education, the General Synod at its third biennial convention, meeting in Frederick, Maryland (1825), voted to proceed with the founding of a seminary.[51] As to location, Philadelphia had become synodically "off limits." Big cities were held in fear for their presumed corrupting influence on students; therefore Baltimore as well as New York was also ruled out. The presence of Hartwick Seminary, some 65 miles southwest of Albany, New York, and the ready accessibility of the Lutheran settlements in Maryland and Virginia, focused the choice on central Pennsylvania. Gettysburg, located on the Lancaster Pike, the main route between Philadelphia and Pittsburgh, was the location finally selected. For a constituency as it then existed, and for the means of transportation then available, this was a central location. The town also made the "greatest pecuniary offer."[52] As the first professor at this new institution, in March 1826 the directors selected the one man who really mattered. Samuel Schmucker accepted their call.

The text of his sermon on New Year's Day, 1821, was presently fulfilled for his New Market parishioners: "When a few more years are come, then I shall go the way whence I shall not return." Schmucker was soon on his way to Gettysburg. Among his first duties was the drafting of a constitution, which he patterned after the constitution of Princeton Seminary.[53] When September 5th came, and directors, pastors,

[50] Wentz, *History of the Gettysburg Seminary*, pp. 90-92.
[51] *Ibid.*, pp. 92-100.
[52] "Inaugural Address," p. 3.
[53] Wentz, *op.cit.*, p. 100.

students, and friends gathered in the Gettysburg church, deep feeling and significance could be discerned in Schmucker's inaugural address. This was the attainment of his second ambition. What he said then, and what others said, deserves special scrutiny.

V

In delivering the charge, the Rev. David F. Schaeffer, of Frederick, recalled the legacy of learning in the Lutheran ministry and the high repute in which colonial America held Lutheran pastors who had received their education at the University of Halle. Recognizing the honest effort which many pastors had put into the task of tutoring, he admitted how inadequate such efforts inevitably were, especially in view of the rapidly expanding missionary responsibilities of the Church. Taking his cue from a sister denomination, he declared: "The Presbyterian church was among the first to do so, and the number of her learned and pious clergy is sufficient to establish the fact, that theological seminaries are among the most valuable institutions, which christians can and should support."[54] Schaeffer then pledged Schmucker to teach in conformity with the Biblical tenets of "the immortal reformer." Any students who disagreed basically with such tenets should be given freedom to join such denominations as "may suit them better." Hence, he said, "I charge you, to exert yourself, in convincing our students that the Augsburg Confession is a safe directory, to determine upon matters of faith, declared in the Lamb's book." Above all, he charged Schmucker "to ground our students well in the doctrine of the atonement by Christ" and never to recommend to the Church a student who is heterodox on this point, that "Jesus of Nazareth is very God."[55]

Addressing the fifteen students who comprised the first class Dr. Schaeffer exhorted: "Upon you will in a great measure depend, the prosperity of our seminary. If you leave it erudite and pious, and become active, zealous, prudent and faithful

[54] "Inaugural Address," p. 6.   [55] *Ibid.*, pp. 8, 9.

ambassadors of Jesus, then will our seminary rise and flourish; but if on the contrary, you should be unmindful of your duties as students—if your hearts and heads are not improved—if piety and knowledge be wanting, then may our seminary sink —which may God avert!"[56]

In taking the oath of office, Schmucker approved the design of the Seminary as an institution of the General Synod and pledged himself to the Constitution and Statutes of the Seminary. Moreover, he solemnly declared that "I do *ex animo*, believe the Scriptures of the Old and New Testament to be the inspired Word of God, and the only perfect rule of faith and practice." He made his confessional position clear, saying "I believe the Augsburg Confession and the Catechism of Luther to be a summary and just exhibition of the fundamental doctrines of the Word of God." He declared his approval of the polity by which the Lutheran Church in America was governed and solemnly promised to teach nothing contrary to the pledges he had made in his oath of office.[57]

In his inaugural address, entitled "The Theological Education of Ministers," Schmucker held up two prerequisites: fervent piety and good natural talents. With piety as the cornerstone, the intellectual structure of the seminarian would include an impressive array of disciplines: the Biblical languages, Greek and Hebrew, Biblical interpretation and archaeology, dogmatics, homiletics, polemics, church polity, practical divinity, pastoral theology, and natural theology.[58] As might be expected, he underscored the advantages of "associated study" in a theological seminary over against private study under a tutor. Specifically, what are these advantages? "They are," he said, "the pious example and exhortations of the instructor, access to a multitude of practical works, frequent opportunity to engage in the exercise of practical religion, and the influence of surrounding circumstances." The latter referred also to the subject of location: "That theological seminaries, like the Saviour whom they teach, should court retire-

[56] *Ibid.*, p. 10.
[57] Wentz, p. 101.
[58] *Ibid.*, p. 102.

ment, that smaller towns rather than cities ought to be their favorite seats, appears to us an obvious principle, and is sanctioned by the mass of churches in this country."[59]

As to the position of theological education in the field of higher education as a whole, Schmucker expressed the confidence that "a religion that is from God, will not shrink from investigation, not tremble before the intellectual altitude of friends or foes." He had no time for those who claimed that there is a boundary to knowledge "beyond which no believer can adventure without danger to his faith." With pardonable exultation—because today's Lutheran scholars would not make the boast—Schmucker contended for a kind of Biblical fundamentalism which could prove with pride that the proponents of Biblical criticism are wrong.[60] In words suggesting something of what Professor Samuel Miller had said upon his inauguration at Princeton Seminary,[61] Schmucker concluded that education in a seminary "will promote *unanimity of views*, and *harmony of feelings* among future ministers of the church." Indeed, for the promotion of unity in the Church such education was recognized as indispensable. "Similarity of doctrinal views," Schmucker went on, "is promoted by uniformity of instruction. Long continued habits of personal intercourse, intwine together the cords of social feeling, and make the ecclesiastical sympathies of the students flow in the same channel. Love one another, is among the Saviour's prominent commands. And he, who can believe that a number of truly pious men, can for years drink together out of the same fountain of revealed truth, can worship together around the same altar, and mingle on it their sacrifices of prayer and praise, and not find their hearts insensibly knit together in love, betrays an entire want of acquaintance with the principles of true piety."[62]

After the festivities and oratory, the real work of the Seminary began. The story has been told in detail elsewhere,[63]

[59] "Inaugural Address," pp. 31, 32.   [60] *Ibid.*, pp. 24, 25-26.
[61] Alexander, *Life of Alexander*, pp. 338-39.
[62] "Inaugural Address," p. 40.
[63] Wentz, *op.cit.*, pp. 100-3.

but here several matters deserve to be drawn together to round out this brief account. First, the directors had wisely appointed agents in the several Lutheran synods to collect funds for the Seminary; and contributions were already coming in. Next, the directors had desired keenly a first-rate theological library. For this purpose books were being collected in the United States, and an ardent supporter of the enterprise, Benjamin Kurtz of Hagerstown, Maryland, was gathering funds and books in Europe. From London to St. Petersburg (Leningrad), from Stockholm to Berlin, and many other German cities,[64] Kurtz's twenty-two month search eventually netted Gettysburg contributions of $10,000 in cash plus 5,000 volumes for the library. The latter is said to have made the library of the young seminary the largest in the theological field in America.[65]

As to physical facilities, the Adams County Academy building in Gettysburg was made available to the Seminary. As sole professor, Schmucker began teaching a full schedule at once. With fifteen students, including again the ever-present "former student" John G. Morris, he had his hands more than full; the entire curriculum depended upon him. Finally, after four years of carrying on alone, Schmucker was joined by Professor Ernest Lewis Hazelius. Called from the faculty at Hartwick Seminary, Hazelius' arrival in Gettysburg added an experienced teacher and accomplished scholar. A Prussian by birth, he had emigrated from his native Silesia in 1800. Associated with the Moravians for a time, he later returned to the Lutheran Church. Union and Columbia Colleges in New York both honored him in 1824 with the degree of Doctor of Divinity. Professorships had been offered him by Lafayette College and by Princeton.[66] In the same year that Hazelius was welcomed at Gettysburg, Schmucker himself was honored by the New Brunswick Seminary with a D.D. degree.

Within four eventful years a gratifying number of students had been graduated, and the Seminary seemed to be living up

[64] *Ibid.*, pp. 128-32.
[65] *Ibid.*, p. 132.
[66] *Ibid.*, pp. 302-3.

to expectations. For Schmucker, however, this was no time to relax. While some of the seminarians were college graduates, or were otherwise suitably prepared, others were not. Urgently needed was an institution fulfilling the functions of the pre-theological program that Schmucker had set up in his parsonage at New Market. This, after all, was the third ambition with which he had left Princeton.

VI

If Lutherans were slow in founding theological seminaries, they were even slower in entering the field of secondary and higher education. To be sure, their parochial schools had, since colonial times, been an adjunct to many a local congregation. On the whole, however, there was little popular favor among the Lutheran laity for anything beyond an elementary education.[67] The earliest effort to provide something approximating a liberal arts—or a general studies—preparation for pre-theological students had been, as we have seen above, the effort by Kunze in Philadelphia. However, after 1783 this kind of education was given over entirely to the new University of Pennsylvania.[68] From the beginning, able Lutheran professors were on the University's faculty, and an ever increasing number of Lutheran students matriculated there. Elsewhere, however, overtures for Lutheran participation, first at Dickinson College, and then at Franklin College, failed to produce any lasting partnership or fruitful enterprise.[69] Indeed, when the Lutheran Theological Seminary opened at Gettysburg in 1826, there was as yet no Lutheran college either in Pennsylvania or in any of the other states.[70] Lutherans were in the peculiar position of having elementary schools and a couple of theological seminaries but no adequate educational facilities in be-

[67] Walter H. Beck, *Lutheran Elementary Schools in the United States*. St. Louis: Concordia, 1939. *Passim.*
[68] *Pennsylvania College Book*, p. 95.
[69] *Ibid.* Also Wentz, *op.cit.*, pp. 81f.
[70] See D. G. Tewksbury, *The Founding of American Colleges and Universities before the Civil War*, N.Y.: Columbia, 1932.

tween. The logic of this need was enough to prod Schmucker into action.

As early as 1827 the directors of the Seminary at Gettysburg resolved to establish a preparatory school. This action was taken on May 16, and in short order a teacher had been selected and the "school" was opened on June 25. As one of a committee of two, Schmucker proposed a seminary student as teacher. David Jacobs, at the age of twenty-one, was the second student to have enrolled at the Seminary. With an excellent preparation in Latin and Greek, previous teaching experience, and a congenial concern for students, Jacobs was a good choice. Prior to his entering the Seminary he had already received tutorial training in theology, so that he was able to give time to the classics department entrusted to him. He began with two students.[71] Two years later, in 1829, David's brother, Michael Jacobs, was engaged to head a scientific department, which meant the teaching of mathematics and natural science.[72] A five-year program of secondary and collegiate education was projected, the first two years being roughly equivalent to today's junior and senior year of high school, and the third year being nearly parallel to the freshman year at college. Latin and Greek were the mainstays of the first two years, with the arts and sciences filling in the other three. For lack of an official name, this was called the "Gettysburg Academy."[73]

New developments presently gave this educational enterprise a promising turn. In September 1829 the Adams County Academy building, in whose four large rooms both the Seminary and the collegiate classes were being held, was sold by the sheriff. Built in 1810 by means of a $2,000 appropriation that Thaddeus Stevens, a citizen of Gettysburg and strong advocate of popular education, had obtained from the Pennsylvania Legislature, the structure was located at the southeast corner of Washington and High Streets.[74] What precisely

---

[71] *Pennsylvania College Book*, p. 145.
[72] *Ibid.*, p. 158.
[73] *Ibid.*, p. 96.
[74] Wentz, *op.cit.*, pp. 102-3.

Samuel Simon Schmucker

led to the sale is not clear. Professor Schmucker, however, was ready. He purchased the building for $1,150, the amount of its encumbrances. He agreed that it should be used for educational purposes and not sold for other uses without giving the citizens of Gettysburg an opportunity to redeem it at cost.

Now began an educative process designed to broaden the base of support as well as to diffuse interest in the institution, especially among a larger number of Lutheran clergymen. To that end Schmucker proposed the formation of "An Association for the establishment of a Classical and Scientific Department in subservience to the objects of the Theological Seminary at Gettysburg, and for the purchase of the Adams County Academy." Articles to this effect were drawn up, and a stock issue of $1,000 floated. The twenty-two shares, valued at $50 each, were then to be sold to interested parties who, in turn, would become the stockholders and patrons of the institution. Five elected trustees were to manage its affairs, while the professors and directors of the Seminary were to be a School Committee. This committee was to appoint all teachers, prescribe the course of study, and direct discipline. In case of need, the professors of the Seminary could act alone, which at that time meant Schmucker could act alone. Children of the original stockholders were to be taught without charge.[75]

As it turned out, the stockholders were all Lutheran ministers. These included both Schmucker and his father, as well as twenty others, many of whom later became prominent in the educational and missionary outreaches of the Lutheran Church. The first meeting of the stockholders took place in May 1830, at which time the enterprising promoter of the Seminary, Benjamin Kurtz, was elected president. Perhaps Kurtz's travel in Europe and his acquaintance with the German educational scheme—as devised originally by Philip Melanchthon, the so-called *Praeceptor Germaniae*—had something to do with the name selected for the re-organized school: "The Gettysburg Gymnasium."[76]

[75] *Pennsylvania College Book*, p. 96.
[76] *Ibid.*, p. 96. One of these was Christian Frederick Heyer, a close

SONS OF THE PROPHETS

The entire academic community was saddened by the sudden death of the "Gymnasium's" first teacher, the Rev. David Jacobs. Not the kind of young man to spare himself, he had thrown himself fully into his teaching ministry. Death came to him in November, 1830, while traveling in the South, presumably to rest and regain his health, although actually preaching and arousing interest in higher education wherever he went. It was David and his brother, Michael Jacobs, who together helped to set a high standard of excellence both in their teaching and in their concern for their students generally.[77] Called to succeed David Jacobs was Henry Louis Baugher, a graduate of Dickinson College, at Carlisle. Originally intending to study law, he had made arrangements to do so under the tutelage of Francis Scott Key at Georgetown, D.C. However, the death of Baugher's mother changed his plans, and he decided to prepare for the ministry. For two years, 1825-1827, he studied theology at Princeton Seminary, and then took his final year at Gettysburg, graduating there in 1828. In April, 1831, he began his teaching career at the Gettysburg Gymnasium.[78]

The chief mover in the successive stages of what was now the Gymnasium was Samuel Schmucker. From 1826 to 1830 he was the sole professor in the Seminary. He had urged the establishment of the Academy, had been charged with the selection of the first two teachers as well as with all the arrangements for opening the school. He had purchased the Academy building so as to secure housing for this enterprise. He had formed the Association which took possession of it, and secured—by his persuasiveness in letters and conversation—subscriptions of stock. And he had constantly overseen the operations of the school. "He now hoped," as his son later

---

friend of Schmucker in promoting the educational and missionary task of the Lutherans in America and, later, in India. E. T. Bachmann, *They Called Him Father, The Life Story of Christian Frederick Heyer*, Phila.: Muhlenberg, 1942, pp. 65f. On Melanchthon, a favorite of Schmucker and Kurtz, see James W. Richard, *Philip Melanchthon, The Protestant Preceptor of Germany, 1497-1560*, N.Y.: Putnam, 1907, pp. 125-41.

[77] *Pennsylvania College Book*, pp. 145, 158f., 97.

[78] *Ibid.*, pp. 149-51. Wentz, *op.cit.*, p. 366.

reflected, "that it was both needful and possible to enlarge the Institution."[79]

VII

In the autumn of 1831 Schmucker believed the time had come for enlarging the Gymnasium to a college. For that purpose he invited several prominent Gettysburg citizens to talk things over. They were by no means all Lutherans but were representatives of the interests of various denominations as well as of the community at large. The plan which Schmucker proposed was given warm approval. The essential next step was the securing of a charter. General Thomas Craig Miller was appointed to accompany Professor Schmucker to Harrisburg and to aid him in securing a charter from the Pennsylvania Legislature. During the weeks which he was thus required to spend at the state capital, Schmucker discovered that much more was required than a simple request. There had to be information and interpretation, in addition to the cultivation of the right contacts. Receiving the desired permission, he addressed the Legislature on "The Eminent Character and Services of the Germans in Pennsylvania, and their claims for recognition by the Legislature." The charter was granted. Governor Wolf signed it on April 7, 1832.[80] The charter was compiled by Schmucker himself from similar charters and was written by him in a sideroom of the State Senate. The official name: Pennsylvania College.[81]

Particularly in light of ecclesiastical involvements in higher education, the emergence of the Gettysburg Gymnasium into a college is instructive. In the charter, as drafted by Schmucker, the stockholders of the Gymnasium, with the addition of certain interested citizens of Gettysburg, were made the Patrons of the College. The Patrons, in turn, elected the Trustees. In short, initiative came from interested churchmen,

---

[79] *Pennsylvania College Book*, p. 97.
[80] *Laws of Pennsylvania, 1831-32*, p. 365. Text in Samuel G. Hefelbower, *The History of Gettysburg College, 1832-1932*, Gettysburg: Gettysburg College, 1932, pp. 447-56.
[81] *Pennsylvania College Book*, pp. 97-98, 2. Name changed to Gettysburg College, 1921. Hefelbower, *History of Gettysburg College*, p. 325.

response and support came from the community; and the enabling act of the Legislature cleared the way for a self-governing academic enterprise. The whole venture was open to Lutheran influence, but ownership resided in the self-perpetuating Board of Trustees. While the majority of the Trustees were Lutherans, no religious conditions were attached either to the position of trustee or of patron. The charter declared: ". . . at elections either for patrons, or trustees, or teachers, or other officers, and in the reception of pupils, no person shall be rejected on account of his conscientious persuasion in matter of religion, provided he shall demean himself in a sober, orderly manner, and conform to the rules and regulations of the college."[82]

As President Milton Valentine stated in 1882 on the College's fiftieth anniversary: "The institution is, therefore, nonsectarian, as are most American colleges established under church auspices, the denominational relation expressing only the fact that the College has been organized and is carried on under the special patronage and efforts of the Lutheran Church, and for the purpose of bearing part in the work of the higher Christian education."[83]

The formal organization of Pennsylvania College took place on July 4, 1832. For this festive occasion a large crowd had gathered. The long procession, including the Gettysburg Guards, Strangers and Citizens, Students of the Gymnasium, Students of the Seminary, Teachers and Professors, Clergy, Patrons, the Orator of the Day, and the Officiating Clergymen, moved from the Academy to the Presbyterian Church. Following the invocation by the Church's minister, Dr. William Paxton,[84] Judge Calvin Blythe of Harrisburg gave the oration. Extolling the cause of higher education and the maintenance of free civil institutions, he saw in the nascent Col-

[82] *Ibid.*, p. 448.
[83] *Pennsylvania College Book*, pp. 4-5.
[84] Paxton was minister of Marsh Creek Presbyterian Church, Carlisle Presbytery, Millertown P.O., Pa., and an honored clergyman. Local Presbyterian minister at the time was the Rev. J. F. Irwin.

SAMUEL SIMON SCHMUCKER

lege "every reason to believe [that it] will prove a valuable auxiliary in the great cause of education." Following a hymn by the choir, Professor Schmucker pronounced the benediction. Later, at the first meeting of the Board of Trustees, Judge Blythe was elected its first president, and the Rev. John G. Morris—who had been a student of Schmucker's at three different places—was elected secretary; a Gettysburg banker, J. B. McPherson, was made treasurer.[85] Of the twenty-one man board, fourteen were Lutheran ministers, including Professors Schmucker and Hazelius of the Seminary.

Pennsylvania College at Gettysburg went into operation on November 7, 1832. Despite certain local opposition, the College made gratifying gains. Its five-man faculty included both Seminary professors, who served part-time, and three other teachers. Samuel Schmucker, D.D., was listed as Professor of Intellectual and Moral Science, and he was limited to the junior and senior classes, teaching philosophy, logic, ethics, and Bible. Ernest Hazelius, D.D., Professor of Latin Language and German literature, gave courses to all four college classes. The full-time College faculty included Henry L. Baugher, A.M., Professor of Greek Language and Belles-Lettres; Michael Jacobs, A.M., Professor of Natural Philosophy, Chemistry, and Mathematics; J. H. Marsden, A.M., Professor of Mineralogy and Botany. The first matriculation of students took place on December 15, 1832. The student body of the College included three juniors, eight sophomores, and twelve freshmen. In addition to these twenty-three there were also forty "Preparatorians" in the three high school grades of the Academy.[86]

When Professor Hazelius left Gettysburg in 1833 in order to take up teaching at the newly set up Lutheran Theological Southern Seminary at Lexington, South Carolina, his place was filled by the Rev. Charles Philip Krauth, a highly promising young scholar whom the Seminary Board called from

[85] *Pennsylvania College Book*, pp. 5-6.
[86] *Ibid.*, pp. 7-8.

St. Matthew's Church in Philadelphia. A native of Pennsylvania, but tutored in theology in Frederick, Maryland, and Winchester, Virginia, he was linguistically gifted and well informed on theological developments in both Continental Europe and the United States. Beginning his teaching at the Seminary as Professor of Biblical and Oriental Literature, he also taught part time at the College as Professor of Intellectual and Moral Science. When, in 1834, the College was fully organized, Krauth was unanimously elected its first president.[87]

Until 1834, Samuel Schmucker had been serving as the *de facto* president of the College. With Krauth's election these responsibilities ceased. Their ending, moreover, coincided with the successful conclusion of Schmucker's extended negotiations at Harrisburg for an appropriation from the State Legislature. A number of other colleges were receiving such help, including Dickinson, Washington, Jefferson, Allegheny, and Lafayette. Some, indeed, had apparently not been making very good use of their grants in land or cash which had made Schmucker's task difficult. Besides, there was the clamor of diversified regional lobbies for aid in the construction of canals, roads, and railroads. Understandably, there were some at Gettysburg who would rather have seen a railway spur come into their town than a college. But in June 1834 the Legislature voted an appropriation of $3,000 annually, for five years, for Pennsylvania College at Gettysburg. It was actually this grant that enabled the College to complete its organization and to install a full-time president.[88]

VIII

Samuel Simon Schmucker, Princeton Theological Seminary, class of 1820, Educator. This should be *finis*. Yet this fragmentary story deserves an epilogue. Samuel Schmucker had left Princeton with three objectives. These objectives were to shape much of his life's activity. His translation of Storr's *Biblical Theology* proved to be valuable but dull. Yet he had

[87] *Ibid.*, pp. 146, 8.
[88] *Ibid.*, pp. 98-99.

learned his lesson. In 1834, in response to many requests, he brought out his *Elements of Popular Theology*, which eventually went through eight editions. Second, his founding of Gettysburg Seminary was obviously not as much of an individual undertaking as an over-simplified historical record might suggest. Rather, it was a fruitful enterprise that drew many into partnership. Other Lutheran seminaries, as they emerged, were directly or indirectly indebted to Gettysburg; among them were such seminaries of General Synod orientation as Southern (1830); Wittenberg/Hamma (1846), at Springfield, Ohio; and, unhappily, by schism, Philadelphia (1864). The list could be extended beyond Schmucker's lifetime to show how well he pioneered. Third, his leadership in establishing Pennsylvania College (re-named Gettysburg in 1921), gave rise to daughter schools which are flourishing today: Wittenberg University, Roanoke College (1842), at Salem, Virginia; Newberry College (1860), Newberry, South Carolina; Muhlenberg College (1867), Allentown, Pennsylvania; Thiel College (1866), Greenville, Pennsylvania; and in the West, the establishment of Illinois State University (1852), at Springfield, Illinois, out of whose demise there emerged four Lutheran colleges in the Midwest, including Augustana (1860), at Rock Island, Illinois (supported mainly by those of Swedish origin); and Carthage (1869), where the tradition of the General Synod was perpetuated.[89]

Churches in later generations are coming more and more to recognize in Samuel Schmucker, dubbed "Steam Boat" by his students, an ecumenical pioneer.[90] Full of mistakes as pioneering inevitably is, his efforts in the promotion of comity and unity among kindred confessions deserve more attention than they have thus far received. Schmucker's "American Lutheranism" may, in many respects, be justly censured; but what would Lutheranism in America be today without knowl-

[89] *Ibid.*, pp. 174-86. E.g., W. E. Eisenberg, *The First Hundred Years of Roanoke College, 1842-1942*, Salem, Va., 1942, pp. 15ff.

[90] See various references to Schmucker in *History of the Ecumenical Movement, 1517-1948*, Phila.: Westminster, 1954, pp. 243ff. Also to Schmucker's roommate at Princeton, 1819-1820, Robert Baird, pp. 244, 635.

edge of the errors and successes of his bold experimentation? Finally, what kind of story might some historian write about the ecumenical movement in the 1960's, or, more specifically, about the current conversations between Lutherans and Presbyterians in America, if—five generations earlier—Sam Schmucker had never gone to Princeton?

IV. JOHN WILLIAMSON NEVIN
(1803-1886)

Evangelical Catholicism*

BY JAMES H. NICHOLS

In the *History of the Yale Divinity School* Roland Bainton devotes a chapter to Horace Bushnell, the patron saint of romantic liberalism in theology and of the religious education movement. Bushnell launched his new venture by rebellion against Yale and the "New Haven Divinity" of his professor Nathaniel Taylor. By similar ties of antagonism John Williamson Nevin, Bushnell's contemporary, belongs to the history of Princeton Theological Seminary. He broke from the scholastic orthodoxy which characterized nineteenth-century Princeton and carried on all his life a running theological feud with the Princeton coryphaeus, Charles Hodge. Nevin and Bushnell alike opened up theological perspectives which were to be more fruitful for the future than the doctrinal systems established in their respective alma maters.

I

Nevin's definitive break with Turretin, the Moses of Princeton, did not take place while he was there. His years there as student and instructor (1823-1828) were harmonious and, as he later wrote, "in some respects the most pleasant part of my life." His upbringing in the Cumberland Valley, predisposed him to find at Princeton "a second home." He arrived, to be sure, as a convalescent from a nervous breakdown, and with a painful chronic illness, and throughout his course he felt

---

* Factual and biographical documentation as well as extensive bibliographical information are provided in *Romanticism in American Theology: Nevin and Schaff at Mercersburg*, by James Hastings Nichols (Chicago: University of Chicago Press, 1961). See especially the Bibliographical Note, pp. 313-316.

himself spiritually inadequate to the calling of the ministry. President Alexander's probing "conferences" moved him deeply but left him even less assured. Yet he was in his proper element. At first rebellious against the requirement in Hebrew, which was sufficient to be onerous but inadequate for any useful command of the language, he determined to make educational sense of it. He set himself extra assignments and eventually read through the whole Old Testament by himself, while his class labored through the few required chapters. As the best Hebrew scholar in the school he was the obvious choice for an interim instructorship to replace Charles Hodge when the latter went to study in Germany in 1826. When Nevin found he could not make ends meet with the $200 stipend the Seminary paid him, his father was proud to make up the difference, and equipped him with a good horse and fodder so that he could maintain a suitable style on the classic ground of the Presbyterian Athens.

Nevin left Princeton at Hodge's return but only to engage in a continuation of the Princeton enterprise. A new seminary beyond the Alleghenies was organized near Pittsburgh, modeled on that at Princeton. The two full-time faculty members, Luther Halsey and John W. Nevin, had both taught at Princeton, the one in the College, the other in the Seminary. They did their best to transplant the Princeton conception, curriculum, and textbooks. For a full decade (1830-1840) Nevin thus continued to serve the Presbyterian Church as a theological teacher in the Princeton tradition. At Western Seminary he taught some 160 men, and probably more than that number in his two years at Princeton.

Nevin was perhaps a more militant moral crusader than was typical of Princeton. His father had been a temperance man and an opponent of slavery even before the end of the eighteenth century, and the son improved this heritage. He lashed distillers and purveyors of strong drink from the pulpit and in the press, esteeming the temperance movement a "new Reformation." A sermon at the time of the cholera epidemic of 1832, "The Scourge of God," related the pestilence to the sin of vending and consuming ardent spirits, and unfortunately he commended to his hearers the fatal advice—drink water. He was threatened with a whipping for his opposition to the frontier theatre in Pittsburgh and antagonized most of the daughters of the Presbyterian Zion by comparing their ladies' fair to a bullfight. From being a colonizationist he was converted to abolitionism, probably by Theodore Weld. Abolitionism was most unpopular in Pittsburgh, and Nevin was forced to relinquish his editing of a weekly newspaper.

He was described by a prominent physician as "the most dangerous man in Pittsburgh." Only the most urgent representations as to the injury he would thereby bring to Western Seminary dissuaded him from speaking for abolition at the Pittsburgh General Assembly of 1835. He was never tempted, however, to be a mere reformer, but remained a devout and active churchman, a doctrinal and Biblical preacher.

On the controversies of the 1830's of Old School and New, Nevin was less militant than some of the fire-eaters would have liked. He took up and developed President Alexander's scheme of an amicable decentralization of the Church into a loose federation of synods. He deplored the bitter factionalism of the Philadelphia Synod and opposed the new creedal test of the "Act and Testimony" clique. Here again he maintained consistently the original position of the Princeton faculty, and he was later glad that he had not permitted himself to be bullied, as they were, against their better judgment. When the "excision" came he elected for the Old School Assembly without hesitation, but was never convinced that the action had been constitutional or that the Old School Assembly was the exclusive continuation of the Presbyterian Church.

Even when Nevin accepted a call in 1840 to the theological seminary of the German Reformed Church at Mercersburg, he went as an Old School Presbyterian of the Princeton stamp. President Alexander encouraged the move as a transfer to another branch of the one Reformed Church. Nevin was merely moving from the Scotch Reformed to the German Presbyterians. His first three years of teaching at Mercersburg were still, on the whole, in the spirit of scholastic predestinarianism.

II

It was in 1843, at the age of forty, that Nevin passed through a radical theological reorientation to a new high-church and sacramental tendency of which he was to be the most significant American spokesman. He now broke sharply with the static unhistorical orthodoxy of Princeton, its individualistic view of the Church, its philosophical predestinarianism, its less than Zwinglian view of the sacraments. Or rather, the sharp break came from the other direction. Nevin and his colleague Schaff at Mercersburg had hoped for at least benevolent neutrality from Princeton. But in 1847 and 1848, at first without mentioning names and then by excommunication in terms, Hodge "lowered the visor" and smote them.

Nevin was not a man to be attacked with impunity. Despite his chronic illness he presented a formidable presence and personality. He was not yet forty when he arrived in Mercersburg, yet he gave the impression of much greater age. "His face was marked with the deep lines of thought, and his gait was that of a person who had been accustomed to carry heavy burdens."[1] Tall, erect, used to command, with a deep remarkable voice, he was a more dominating figure than Hodge. The story is variously told of Orestes Brownson and Isaak Dorner, each of whom had engaged in literary debate with Nevin, that they were at length presented to him in the flesh with the question, "Do you know who this is?" "No," they are supposed to have replied, "but I know that this is a *man*." With the pen also, Nevin was a dangerous polemic theologian. He lacked the adroit thrust and parry of a Newman, but had greater philosophical power. On his chosen territory he was more learned than Hodge. And in fact for the next quarter-century the two men carried on a recurrent debate in which Hodge usually came out a poor second.

Hodge's last testimony to Nevin was the more impressive after these exchanges. When Nevin's seventieth birthday was celebrated in 1873 he recalled with "fond recollection" friend-

[1] T. Appel, *Recollections of College Life* (Reading, Pa., 1886), p. 297.

JOHN WILLIAMSON NEVIN

ships and experiences from the Presbyterian half of his career but observed that this was now for him "like the memory of a dream," while for those now around him it was as if it had never existed. But at his funeral in 1886 Princeton and the Presbyterian Church were represented in the person of Archibald Alexander Hodge. Hodge remembered sitting in Nevin's lap sixty years before in Princeton. He declared that Charles Hodge had always regarded Nevin "as the greatest of his pupils" and had never relinquished his friendship for him. Nevin belonged first to the German Reformed Church, but also to the Reformed community generally and to the whole church.

Did Charles Hodge really regard Nevin as "the greatest" of the three thousand men who had sat under him? There were among these several men of considerable parts who were far more congenial to Hodge's theology. But if Hodge himself would include in the Princeton heritage this maverick who had so mauled him in debate, who else should deny him his place there? And in fact decades later Princeton Seminary would come to prefer Nevin to Hodge on many of their points of difference.

The occasion for Nevin's reorientation of 1843 was his reaction from "new measures" revivalism. Here again, he was able to quote from Professors Alexander and Miller numerous warnings against the religious dangers of popular revivalism; and his tract *The Anxious Bench* was favorably reviewed in the *Princeton Review*. Finney's excesses supplied data for a major portion of the Old School polemic of the 1830's, and Nevin had been disgusted personally by the six weeks' sensation of James Gallagher, the "notable Kentucky operator," in Pittsburgh in 1835. Winebrenner's camp meetings in the German Reformed constituency later brought him to resume in print his objections to the "system of the bench." This tract, and Bushnell's parallel pamphlet, constituted perhaps the two most notable nineteenth-century critiques of manipulative revivalism. Insofar as such revivalism still plays a role in American religion much of the argument is still pertinent and telling. Nevin and Bushnell both insisted, with differing nuances, that painstaking undramatic nurture and education are the proper and indispensable means of extending the Church and cannot be replaced by cheap excitement without disastrous effects.

Nevin's dislike of more or less illiterate itinerant evangelists on the frontier had early led him toward high views of ministerial authority. Early in his Pittsburgh days he had edited a new printing of Joseph Lathrop's volume, *Christ's Warning to the Churches, to beware of False Prophets who come as Wolves in Sheep's Clothing, and the marks by which they are known.* Herein it was claimed that the state churches of Massachusetts and Connecticut possessed a ministry derived in unbroken succession from the Apostles according to Christ's authority, and that admission to that succession should be only by the approval of existing ministers. While still in his twenties Nevin was moving in a direction in which he was later to stand on Anglican, if not even Roman Catholic, ground.

III

Nevin's churchly conversion of 1843 had been long preparing. From early in his Pittsburgh days he had adopted a philosophical position radically different from the Lockean and Scottish "common sense" camp to which Princeton adhered. Like Bushnell, Nevin was deeply influenced by Coleridge and his Platonist idealism. Coleridge led him back to British Platonists such as Leighton, Scougall, Howe, Shaw but also made him aware of the explosion of philosophical and theological genius in Germany at the turn of the century. When Nevin went to Mercersburg it was in part to help the Germans in America exploit their natural connections with the most powerful theological movements then in existence. It was such theologians as Sartorius, Dorner, Olshausen who helped him most to his new understanding of Christ and the union of the believer with Him, and of the Church.

Nevin himself laid greatest emphasis on the dawning of historical consciousness as the bridge by which he left Princeton scholasticism. At Princeton in his time there had been an utter lack of historical sense. He would have been shocked at the suggestion that the doctrine of the Trinity, for example, had "developed." There was one timeless body of doctrinal truth, most conveniently arranged in Turretin's *Institutes*.

It was Neander, the greatest Church historian of the day, who broke up Nevin's dogmatic slumbers in "an actual awakening of the soul." Now for the first time the early fathers, and even the medieval schoolmen, made sense to him. Lutherans and Roman Catholics were intelligible and in part respectable expressions of Christian faith when seen in an historical context rather than being ticked off in an index of heresies from the point of view of a static unhistorical confessionalism. Princeton had never really taken seriously (apart from the Bible) anything prior to the seventeenth century or outside the Reformed tradition; it lived in intellectual insularity and provincialism. In all this Nevin was well ahead of his alma mater. Hodge explicitly repudiated conceptions of historical development. Not until half a century later and then only grudgingly did Princeton begin to admit the implications of the historical method in the study of the Bible, the Church, and doctrine, and to enter the ecumenical theological conversation which follows such an admission. From the 1840's, however, Nevin had burst the walls of provincialism and was reading and debating with Lutherans, Roman Catholics, and Anglicans, and trying to relate his theologizing responsibility to the early fathers as well as the Reformers.

There is a further range of concerns in which Nevin speaks with startling actuality to the American Church of the mid-twentieth century. The topics which engaged him most passionately, the doctrine of Christ in relation to that of the Church, Church unity, the Lord's Supper, baptism, the ministry, worship and liturgy, Scripture and tradition, these are precisely the topics which, after decades of relatively little attention, have become since the 1930's the agenda of the ecumenical debates on "faith and order." To some of these issues Nevin speaks with more point than any other nineteenth-century American or, in fact, than many twentieth-century theologians. He may be called the chief American prophet of the ecumenical movement in matters of faith and order.

In his day Nevin and his supporters were able to dominate the college and the seminary of the Eastern Synod of the German Reformed Church and to maintain a personal and intellectual ascendancy in the courts of the Church. The *Mercersburg Review* was the chief organ of the movement and the medium through which Nevin set forth his case against such opponents as Hodge of Princeton, the Roman Catholic Orestes Brownson, the Anglo-Catholic R. I. Wilberforce, the Congregationalist Horace Bushnell, and the German theologian Isaak Dorner, to say nothing of members of his own denomination. The little German Reformed Church was fiercely attacked on his account, especially by its sister Church, the Dutch Reformed, and by the Lutherans, and it sometimes felt itself to be a beleaguered city. After the Civil War the Church was bitterly torn between the Nevinist camp and their opponents concerning a proposed prayer book, and it narrowly avoided actual schism. The liturgy is still the badge of the Mercersburg wing of the Church, which is, or at least this section is, the most churchly and sacramental of all the Reformed bodies in America. In recent years the Mercersburg tradition has not produced aggressive theological advocates, but the writings of Nevin himself have drawn increasing attention.

IV

A century ago most American Protestants conceived of the Christian religion as a relation with Christ established one by one in individuals who thereafter normally joined the Church. Nevin, on the contrary, held that individuals do not, by association, constitute the Church, rather the Church is the context within which alone men have access to Christ's saving presence. The Church is not an optional apparatus attached to the Gospel, but an essential part of the Gospel itself; that is why Christians confess belief in the Church as an article of the creed. The Church is the sum of all the means by which the living Christ gives himself to his people, and thus consti-

John Williamson Nevin

tutes a kind of continuing Incarnation in human history, the "new creation" begun in Jesus Christ.

For Nevin, thus, the Church is constituted by communion with Christ. Hodge disagreed. The true Church as understood at Princeton was not a communion at all, but simply the sum total of all the predestined, past, present, and future, a speculative inference. Nevin's contrasting conception of a communion is best understood in terms of the sacraments, especially the Lord's Supper. In the mystical participation of the faithful in the life of Christ the Church is most itself, for to Nevin's mind the Church is itself best comprehended as a sacrament. The Mercersburg movement can be defined, on the side of practical religion, as a eucharistic movement. Its distinctive emphases in relation both to the Church and to Christ can be most easily understood from this perspective.

Nevin's first major work dealt with this theme, *The Mystical Presence, a Vindication of the Reformed or Calvinistic Doctrine of the Holy Eucharist*. In this work Nevin convicted the American Reformed Churches generally, and for that matter the Episcopalians and Lutherans also, of substantial unfaithfulness to their several classical teachings with regard to the Lord's Supper. He restated Calvin's conception of eucharistic participation in the glorified humanity of Jesus Christ, not just his spirit, or divine essence, but the real whole Person, divine and human.

It was this publication which led to Hodge's first head-on attack, which came in a long article in the *Princeton Review*. Hodge's sacramental theology was at most Zwinglian, better suited by far to Baptists than to Calvinists. He sought to contest with Nevin the teaching of the Reformed confessions on the subject. Nevin demolished him in a magisterial article on "The Reformed Doctrine of the Lord's Supper," which has scarcely been replaced as an historical exposition. A radical challenge was thus posted as to the adequacy of current Princeton representations of the Reformed tradition, to say nothing of those of New Brunswick, Union, Yale, or Andover. As Nevin observed, the Calvinistic view of the sacraments was far more definitely and centrally anchored in the confessional structure of the Reformed tradition than was the doctrine of predestination which Hodge took to be the foundation of Reformed theology. American Reformed theology since has generally come to prefer Nevin's Christocentric orientation, if not his sacramental views, to a theology built on the Divine Decrees. And Calvin's doctrine of the spiritual real presence is surely much stronger even in the Presbyterian Church today than it was before the Civil War. Nevin was a pioneer in this reorientation and is perhaps still its most competent theological interpreter.

V

Nevin also distinguished himself as the most conspicuous American heir of the ecumenical passion of Bucer and Calvin for the unity of the visible Church. This Nevin held to be the greatest issue of his day. To many of his contemporaries, the supporters of the Evangelical Alliance, for example, or the exponents of reunion on the "restorationist" program of the New Testament alone, or on the least common denominator basis, he seemed a crabbed critic of ecumenical endeavors. Indeed Nevin's critiques of three or four superficial types of ecumenical strategy are still highly applicable to much current American discussion of the problem. But he was in no way captious; he was wholly serious and constructive. His sermons "Catholic Unity" and "The Church," and the little book *Antichrist, or the Spirit of Sect and Schism* are virtually as pertinent in 1962 as they were in the late 1840's. He knew and demonstrated that there are no administrative short-cuts to Church unity, that the prerequisites are repentance, religious renewal, and faith in the Church as the locus of Christ's continuing presence. Schism, like other forms of sin, will not be perfectly conquered in history; against all of them the Church must wage unending war, seizing occasions as they are presented. The American Reformed Churches have had few sounder counsellors in such matters.

Nevin's whole habit of thought, sacramental, metaphysical, Platonic, reverent of tradition, was especially sympathetic to the fathers. Through his work Irenaeus, Athanasius, Basil, and the Gregories as well as Augustine and Cyprian came alive theologically among the Puritans and evangelicals of America, or at least new possibilities of understanding them emerged. Nevin insisted on the necessity of a positive Protestant doctrine of tradition. He championed especially the Apostles' Creed as the prime instance of dogmatic tradition. The creed seemed to him less the product of theological reflection than the spontaneous acknowledgment of the Church to the presence of God. The order of doctrines in particular supported his view of the relation of Christ to the Church and its means of grace. It was the explication of what was already implicit in Peter's first confession, "Thou art the Christ, the Son of the Living God." As such the creed was eminently suited to bind the generations together in one testimony of faith. Nevin wished the creed used regularly in worship as in the Reformation liturgies. He lamented that in five years at Princeton he had never once heard the creed in Church.

Tradition was also necessary as an authority in the Church in addition to the Bible. Nearly all Nevin's Protestant contemporaries contended for the Bible alone, interpreted by private judgment. Nevin argued that this was not the view of the Reformers, nor the actual practice of the nineteenth-century Protestants. They all read the Bible in the light of a confession or other tradition. The Bible alone was scarcely an adequate guide, for example, as to infant baptism or the doctrine of the trinity. It was to be read, not by individuals abstracted from the Church, but from within the Church and its tradition. The Bible was the last authority, but tradition was also indispensable and the two had a reciprocal relation. There were difficulties here which Nevin did not solve, but he pushed American Protestants to face the inadequacies of the popular solutions.

Nevin also championed the importance of tradition in worship. At first he led in a movement to restore the use of the Palatinate Liturgy along with the Heidelberg Catechism. But he became increasingly dissatisfied with the heavily didactic tone of the Palatinate Liturgy and preferred ancient models. The whole enterprise was uphill work. Most Presbyterians of the time did not even know that the Reformation Churches all had and used liturgies. By the nineteenth century they had been completely captured by Puritan and evangelical ideas of spontaneity and individuality in worship. Nevin's emphasis was all at the other pole of the corporate sense in worship, calling for set and familiar forms for devotion and praise. When a service book was finally prepared embodying Mercersburg views on the ministry, ordination, the Lord's Supper, baptism, the Church year, and related topics, controversy was heated. But by the early twentieth century nearly every major American Reformed Church had equipped itself with a service book. Almost none of them, to be sure, were for congregational use, like the German Reformed book, and few if any were edited with comparable competence.

From about 1851 Nevin's writings displayed strong sympathies for Roman Catholicism and an emotional alienation from Protestantism. He resigned all his offices in the German Reformed Church and retired to private life to wrestle with the question. Many expected him to follow R. I. Wilberforce, with whom he was in correspondence, and Newman and Manning. His struggle coincided with a psychic collapse in which he felt the need of authoritative support. As in his earlier breakdown, which occurred between college and seminary, he fell into great depression and paralysis of will for months and years. But gradually he recovered health and vigor and resumed his labors still in the German Reformed Church.

The aspect of his teaching which was most problematical from the Reformed viewpoint was his conception of the ministry. He treated ordination as a "third sacrament" and considered that the sacraments of clergy, lacking regular and canonical ordination into the succession from the Apostles, were of dubious "validity." He insisted, for example, on the reordination of ministers who entered the German Reformed Church from such sects as the Evangelical Association or the Church of God. By the same logic, the sacraments of clergy not in communion with the whole ministry were also in doubt, even in "branches" with separated successions. The Anglo-Catholic view was self-contradictory. This was the line of thought which inclined him to turn to Rome as the most plausible claimant to the succession of ministry from the ancient church. And if this claim were not allowed, what alternative was there to a view which found *all* in schism and consequently *all* sacraments of dubious validity? Nevin would be definitely on the "Catholic" side in the twentieth-century faith and order debates on the ministry, although he would have difficulty with every concrete embodiment of Catholic sympathies. As was said of him, "he is always instructive, even when he is in error."

Nevin's most significant contributions seem to have been those of his middle or Mercersburg period, before his Romanizing phase. On the program of "evangelical catholicism" he contributed significantly to the deepening and broadening of the Reformed tradition in America for which Princeton stands, bringing again into force high Calvinistic convictions about the Church catholic and the sacraments, and opening channels of communication with the fathers, with Lutheranism, with Anglicans, and with Roman Catholics.

V. SHELDON JACKSON (1834-1909)

Christ's Fool and Seward's Folly*

BY HERMANN N. MORSE

As much as one man can ever be said to typify a great movement, Sheldon Jackson was the personification of Home Missions in its greatest period of continental expansion. Dedicated to the ministry by his parents at the baptismal font, he grew up never doubting that he was born to be a preacher of the Gospel and a missionary. Rejected for reasons of health when he offered himself for missionary service abroad, he entered upon a career in this country that made incredible demands upon his not too robust physique through fifty years of strenuous activity.

This was no ordinary man. No one whose path he crossed could be indifferent to him. He made warm friends and bitter enemies. He received extravagant praise and equally extravagant abuse. At times he perplexed and dismayed his supporters by his seeming recklessness. When he saw a need it was not in his nature to count the cost before committing himself. He felt this way when he began his career and still

* The following lives of Sheldon Jackson are typical: *Sheldon Jackson*, by Robert Laird Stewart (New York: Revell, 1908); *The Alaskan Pathfinder*, by John Thomson Faris (New York: Revell, 1926); *The Bishop of All Beyond*, by Winifred Hulbert (New York: Friendship Press, 1948); "Sheldon Jackson, Planter of Churches," by Alvin K. Bailey, *Journal of the Presbyterian Historical Society*, Volume xxvi, No. 3, Sept. 1948, pp. 129-148; Volume xxvi, No. 4, Dec. 1948, pp. 193-214; Volume xxvii, No. 1, March 1949, pp. 21-40; *Presbyterian Panorama*, by Clifford M. Drury (Philadelphia: Board of Christian Education, 1952); *Alaskan Apostle*, by Arthur J. Lazell (New York: Harper and Brothers, 1960); "Sheldon Jackson, Presbyterian Lobbyist," by Theodore C. Hinckley, *Journal of Presbyterian History*, Volume 40, No. 1, March 1962, pp. 3-23. The Presbyterian Historical Society, Witherspoon Bldg., Philadelphia, has files of Jackson's articles and correspondence and copies of the *Rocky Mountain Presbyterian* periodical he founded and edited (1872-1886). Speer Library, Princeton Seminary, has copies of his letters and many of his copybooks relating to Alaska.

felt this way when he ended it a half-century later. But what he accomplished is a story without parallel in home mission annals. Restless, dynamic, always on the move; indefatigable and undaunted in the face of any difficulty or danger; always reaching for more than he could grasp but ending up grasping it; sensitive to the needs of others but careless of his own; completely trusting what he believed to be God's promises while obeying what he believed to be his commands—it is easy to understand the many epithets that were applied to him. He was called "The St. Paul of America," "The Wild Horseman of the Rockies," "The Continental Circuit-Rider," "The Missionary with the Flying Coattails," "The Bishop of all Beyond," and, of course, "pioneer," "pathfinder," "prospector," and the like.

Theodore L. Cuyler, writing of the biography of Sheldon Jackson, said: "Amid the crowd of new books I bespeak a clear track for one that reads like an added chapter to the 'Acts of the Apostles.' . . . A herald of Jesus Christ who has traversed nearly a million miles by stages and buckboards, by ox-carts and reindeer sledges—who has faced hostile Indians and arctic ice-floes—who has founded one-hundred Presbyterian Churches and a large number of Sunday Schools—who has delivered nearly four thousand public addresses as hot as an anthracite coal fire—who has done the same kind of pioneer work for the vast region of Alaska that Livingstone did for Africa, and has made his name as visible in the spiritual history of the 'New West' as Pike's Peak or Mount McKinley. Such a man, who has wrought such achievements, is not surpassed by any living Christian minister on this continent."

Just one thing makes Sheldon Jackson's story explicable: he was through and through a missionary. The knowledge of any place that lacked the preaching of the Gospel and the ministration of the Christian Church was to him an irresistible appeal. The text by which he lived and would have the Church live—and from which he often preached—was Moses' command to the people of Israel: "Begin to possess, that thou mayest inherit the land" (Deut. 2:31).

As this is the story of a native of New York State who

wrote his name over the face of the West, from the Missouri River to the Pacific and from the Mexican border to the shores of the Arctic Ocean, it is an interesting coincidence that the year of his birth, 1834, was the year in which another great pioneer missionary, Marcus Whitman, also a New Yorker, committed himself to his trail-blazing mission to the Indians of the Northwest. The two never met since Whitman's death by massacre occurred while Jackson was still a school boy. But one can think of Jackson as Whitman's spiritual heir. On Whitman's statue in the National Capitol are carved these words, taken from his journal, which apply as well to one man as to the other: "My plans require time and distance." How much time, how great a distance no one could have foreseen.

I

In an autobiographical sketch prepared for the Women's Board of Home Missions, Jackson covered the first twenty-four years of his life in just three sentences: "I was born in Minaville, New York, in 1834—Valley of the Mohawk. My father was a well-to-do farmer. I was sent through the usual routine of schools, Union College, Princeton Theological Seminary, where I graduated in 1858, when I was ordained; graduated, ordained, and married within one week." He often commented on how many important things had happened to him in the month of May. In this month he was born, graduated from college, graduated from seminary, ordained, married, received his first missionary appointment, began his career as Superintendent of Home Missions in the West, was elected Moderator of the General Assembly. And it was in this month that he died.

During his seminary years he felt a strong call to the foreign mission field. He wrote that "a band of us held a Sabbath evening prayer-meeting in our rooms where we cultivated a spirit of missions." He offered himself to the Board of Foreign Missions for service in Asia, Africa, or South America, but the unfavorable report of a physician closed those doors to him. However, the board offered him a commission to work among the Choctaw Indians (who were then regarded as a responsibility of Foreign Missions) "as they could get me home easy ... they thought I was not strong, but I had an iron constitution with the exception of dyspepsia." He accepted the appointment and with his wife, during the summer of 1858, traveled across the country by train, boat, stage coach, and private conveyance to Spencer Academy in the Indian Territory.

This, as it turned out, was a brief and not too satisfactory experience since his susceptibility to malaria compelled him to withdraw from the field in the following spring. However, several circumstances combined to give it significance for his later career. His experience convinced him of the importance of the mission school in the opening of work in new areas and particularly in ministry to exceptional populations. Later he was the most persistent advocate of such schools in Utah and on Indian- and Spanish-speaking fields. To him belongs most of the credit for the organization, nearly twenty years later, of the Women's Board of Home Missions, which had this as its special responsibility. Further, his missionary instinct did not permit him to confine his work to the school room. Between his bouts with malaria, he made the rounds of the settlements within his reach, living with the Indians and preaching to them; for a time he averaged a service a day.

In the spring, when Jackson and his wife could be released without embarrassment to the work of the mission, they started north to get away from the malaria. After a brief visit with his family, who sometime before this had moved from New York to Illinois, he accepted a commission from the Board of Domestic Missions for work in Minnesota. This began an association that, in one form or another, was to continue for the rest of his life. The commission stated that it was issued "on the application of the Churches of La Crescent, Hokah and vicinity, Minnesota; and by the recommendation of the Presbytery of Winnebago" and that the members of the board "have appropriated the sum of Three Hundred ($300) Dollars, to aid in the support of the Reverend Sheldon Jackson as Pastor or stated supply of such Churches." As Jackson's biographer, Robert Laird Stewart, points out, one of the notable things about this commission was that "the Churches named in it were non-existent at the date of its issue, or, in other words, they were not yet organized." As for the salary of $300, Dr. Jackson many years later remarked, "in Minnesota we sometimes suffered on this salary." Nevertheless, he accepted and at once began his work.

La Crescent, a village of fifty or sixty homes on the Mississippi River opposite La Crosse, Wisconsin, was on the route that many westward bound migrants followed. The whole territory around it was practically destitute of religious privileges. Characteristically, Jackson interpreted his commission as applying not only to La Crescent and nearby Hokah but to every settled place in any direction that he could possibly reach on horseback, by buggy or sleigh, or as often as not on foot. His circuit quickly came to include thirteen counties in Minnesota and five in Wisconsin.

His ministry in Minnesota continued for ten years, 1859-1869, the last five of which he made his home in Rochester, where he had earlier assisted in organizing a promising church. During this ten years he organized or assisted in organizing twenty-three churches. He was instrumental in securing ministers for most of them and made himself personally responsible to see that they did not lack support. He established what he called his "Raven Fund" and solicited gifts of money and missionary boxes of clothing that saved the day for many a hard-pressed minister and his family. What the Mission Board's chronically depleted treasury did not permit it to do, Jackson, as a one-man, volunteer missionary agency, somehow managed to do. Not all of his work endured but much of it did. Through this difficult decade of the Civil War, with one brief intermission for service as a chaplain with the Union forces in Tennessee, he kept the Gospel light burning in many a frontier community.

The experience of these years was preparing Jackson, just as the circumstances of the times were preparing the nation, for what was ahead in the vast westward expansion with which the next period of his life was to be associated.

II

On Prospect Hill in Sioux City, Iowa, overlooking the Missouri River, stands a monument bearing the following inscription:

> To commemorate the Prospect Hill Prayer
> Meeting held by Sheldon Jackson, Thomas H.
> Cleland, John C. Elliott, Ministers of the
> Gospel, on this hilltop, April 29, 1869,
> which inaugurated the movement for the
> evangelization of the great North West
> and the regions beyond.
> Erected by the Presbyterian Church,
> A.D. 1913. Prayer availeth much.

Many years later Dr. Jackson wrote of the emotion that overwhelmed them as these three Presbyterian ministers, contemplating the extent of the spiritual desolation of the great area of the West, prayed "for divine help and strength and self-denial and consecration" and "for faith that the all-conquering Cross would yet triumph over these desolations."

They could see then, as in retrospect we can see even more clearly, how fraught with destiny that day was for the Church and for the nation. Seven years earlier, before the war ended, Congress had passed the Homestead Act opening the West to settlement. By the end of the decade, throngs of settlers were on their way west. This movement was to continue at an accelerating pace until, twenty years later, the Census Bureau would announce that the day of the frontier had ended. Shortly after the close of the war the task of completing the construction of the first transcontinental railroad was undertaken, with the Central Pacific working eastward from San Francisco and the Union Pacific working westward from Omaha. On May 10, 1869, less than two weeks after Jackson and his friends prayed on Prospect Hill, the two branches met at Promontory Point, Utah, the golden spike was driven, and the transcontinental railroad was a reality.

It took very little imagination to see what would happen

along that line and throughout the territory that it served. Indeed, it was already happening. Up to this time, the westward progress of the Presbyterian Church had practically ended at the Missouri River, except for a half-dozen churches in Nebraska, a few scattered Indian missions, and some twenty churches on the Pacific slope. The significance and urgency of this were not lost on the Presbyterians of the Synod of Iowa. The Presbyterian Church as a whole was preparing itself for a new day with the impending reunion of the Old and New School branches, but it did not yet see clearly what its task of Church extension in the West was to be. The Old School Board of Domestic Missions lacked money and probably also lacked vision. The Board of Home Missions, which was to be the agency of the reunited Church, was not to be organized until July 1870.

In the fall of 1868 the Synod of Iowa petitioned the board for a district missionary to have charge of the evangelization of their frontier, but the request was denied due to lack of funds. The following spring three presbyteries of the synod took action and invited Sheldon Jackson to serve them as district missionary. The most significant of these actions was that taken by the Presbytery of Missouri River. As the western-most presbytery of the synod, it assumed that all the territory to the west as far as the eastern border of the Presbytery of Stockton in California was under its jurisdiction. Therefore its invitation to Sheldon Jackson was to serve as "superintendent of missions for Western Iowa, Nebraska, Dakota, Idaho, Montana, Wyoming and Utah or as far as our jurisdiction extends."

This action was taken on May 1, 1869, the second day after the Prospect Hill prayer meeting. The terms of the invitation were not calculated unduly to restrict Jackson in his movements or plans. As a job description it was generously broad and vague. There was only one drawback. Unfortunately none of the three presbyteries had any money for the salary and expenses either of Jackson or of any missionaries whom he might secure. In fact, nothing was said about money. Nevertheless, Jackson accepted the appointment and went immediately to work. As the monument proclaims—"prayer availeth much." Within a week he had appointed three men to work along the line of the Union Pacific, one in Nebraska, one in Wyoming from Cheyenne to Rawlins, and one in western Wyoming and Utah. During the summer ten churches were organized in Nebraska, Wyoming, and Colorado. By the end of the year ten new missionaries had been put to work in Iowa, Nebraska, Wyoming, Colorado, and Utah.

During the first eight months Jackson raised from private sources approximately $10,000 to support this work. Rather unexpectedly, in the fall he and the missionaries whom he had appointed were commissioned by the Board of Domestic Missions. His own salary was set by the board at $1,500 but without provision for travel expense.

III

In the extraordinary experiences to which this was the prelude, the characteristics and abilities which had been evident during the ten years of Jackson's service in Minnesota were given ample scope. First of all was his inborn missionary zeal, the constant, irresistible drive to extend the Church and to preach the Gospel to all who might otherwise be without it. "Go ye" meant to him just that, a highly personal command which kept forcing him to break through any barriers that impeded the advance of the Church. Second was his indefatigable energy. He was a small man of no unusual strength, built, as he used to say, to fit into small places. But nothing daunted him. He would tackle any difficulty, whether placed in his way by nature or by man. A fifty-mile tramp through drifting snow, a hundred miles on horseback or by sleigh or buckboard or canoe, five hundred miles by stage coach—this was routine.

A third trait was his willingness to assume responsibility. There is no evidence that he was personally ambitious for place or power, though this was occasionally alleged; but he was not reluctant to take the initiative beyond any authority duly assigned to him when this seemed necessary. Sooner or later he would be officially justified for what he did, but he often did it first and received his authorization later. Fourth, he was possessed by an apparently naïve faith that what ought to be done could be done. His aptly named "Raven Fund" is indicative of his belief that resources would always be forthcoming. Certainly it is true that neither he nor any of the missionaries whom he sent out on the basis of that faith ever starved, though all of them frequently had anxious moments. Fifth, with all his faith, he was not one simply to wait until the Lord sent his ravens. He was a persuasive speaker and letter writer. We would say he had promotional gifts. Increasingly he won the confidence of the Church. The number of people who believed in him and were willing to back their belief with substantial gifts grew steadily. Sixth, he had a rare quality of imagination and ingenuity. He needed both in the tasks he undertook. He could keep a large stretch of territory and span of years more clearly in his mind than could most men. As far as his purposes went he was quite uncomplicated, but to get things done—so much with so little —he had constantly to improvise.

Of course, Jackson had also the defects of his virtues. There was the constant temptation to overreach, to undertake more than anyone could do, which left him open to the charge of recklessness and a lack of thoroughness. His relative failure in Montana, to which he could never give sufficient attention, is a case in point. It is also true that at times he ignored properly constituted authorities and used powers he did not really possess. One can sympathize with the often sorely harassed secretaries of the board. But, if they did not always appreciate his impetuousness and his gift for not listening to what he did not wish to hear, over the years they were grateful for what he accomplished and gave him their hearty support. In general his motives were not properly open to question—though often questioned—and in most instances his judgment in debatable situations was ultimately vindicated.

This period of Jackson's career covered approximately ten years, decisive years in the opening of the West and in the extension of the Church. During this one decade the total population of the area for which he assumed missionary responsibility practically trebled. In Colorado it increased fivefold, in Nebraska and Arizona fourfold, in Idaho, Montana, and Wyoming twofold. New towns were constantly appearing. Churches would be established while the towns were new and the country was developing. Some mistakes would be made. Some promising-looking places would fail to grow; that was a risk that had to be run. Jackson's policy here was dictated by theology rather than by sociology. Preach the Gospel to people where they are today and deal with the future when it comes.

Without question, a considerable measure of denominational rivalry was involved. That was part of the spirit of the time. But a prodigious job was done against great odds. Jackson himself participated in the organization of some eighty churches. He moved constantly back and forth across this great territory, with frequent trips east in search of funds. After the first year he had the energetic backing of Henry Kendall and Cyrus Dickson, the able secretaries of the newly constituted Board of Home Missions. In addition to the task of Church extension, he gave time and attention to mission work among the Indian tribes, particularly in Arizona, which officially came under his charge in 1875, and in the Mormon-dominated area of Utah.

In 1872, as a private venture, Sheldon Jackson began the publication of the *Rocky Mountain Presbyterian*, which he sent free to every active Presbyterian pastor. He published this paper for ten years and then gave it to the board. At about the same time he began vigorously to agitate for some means of establishing mission schools, particularly in Utah and in Indian- and Spanish-speaking fields. The Board of Home Missions withstood him in this, deeming the support of schools not properly within their responsibility. Therefore he turned his attention to the development of a Home Mission agency among the women of the Church. In this too he met opposition, some feeling that this would weaken the women's support of Foreign Missions. He persisted, with the somewhat reluctant support of Dr. Kendall, until in 1878 the Women's

Executive Committee of Home Missions was duly organized, to work in cooperation with the Board of Home Missions, with a special concern for the support of missionary teachers. In this Jackson was moved by a profound conviction that in many missionary situations education was the real cutting edge of the missionary effort. Some years later, in an extension of this belief, he was instrumental in the organization of Westminster College in Utah, to which he personally gave $50,000 that had come to him as a legacy.

It was Jackson's destiny, as it was his disposition, always to go before to prepare the way. This he did in a dozen western states. It was left to others to build as best they could on the foundations he laid. Writing in 1904 he pointed out that by then from the original actions of the Iowa presbyteries in 1869 had grown five synods with twenty presbyteries, 520 churches with 430 ministers and 41,252 members. But the credit for this was shared by many. By the end of the first decade his attention was being increasingly diverted to another field which was to be the crowning work of his missionary career although he continued to have an official relation to the work in the West until 1884.

IV

After the purchase of Alaska from Russia in 1867, an act for which Secretary Seward was widely ridiculed and berated, for some years neither the United States Congress nor the Christian Churches of America took seriously their responsibility for the welfare of the native population of that vast territory. It was not until 1884 that Congress passed a bill providing for a civil government in Alaska and making a modest initial provision for the education of its children. The Churches were almost as dilatory. Some beginnings of Christian work were made in the middle seventies by Christian Indians from British Columbia. These efforts and the very great need toward which they were directed deeply impressed several Christian men connected with the military forces stationed in Alaska as well as a British missionary who made a brief visit in

Sheldon Jackson

1876. Appeals to different mission agencies were declined for lack of funds.

A. L. Lindsley, then pastor of the First Presbyterian Church of Portland, Oregon, was one who was deeply impressed with Alaska's need. Through his efforts the urgent appeal was brought to Sheldon Jackson during the meeting of the General Assembly in 1877. Alaska was quite outside Jackson's field of responsibility, but it could not long remain outside his concern. He had been instructed during that summer to make a missionary journey into the northwest. When he reached Walla Walla he found that a revolt among the Indians would make it impossible to carry out the original plan for his trip. He therefore decided to go to Portland for conference with Dr. Lindsley and, if the way opened, to visit Alaska. He was encouraged in this by the fact that the Home Board had approved the opening of work in Alaska.

In Portland he found an old friend and former co-worker, Mrs. Amanda McFarland, the widow of the Reverend D. F. McFarland who, ten years before, had opened the first Presbyterian mission in New Mexico. It was at once decided that she should accompany Jackson to Alaska with the intention of establishing a Christian school. Of this trip he later wrote: "My trip, as far as Walla Walla, was in obedience to the direct instructions of the missionary secretary, concerning which I had no discretion. From Walla Walla to Portland, the trip was discretionary, and the secretary expected me to take it. From Portland to Alaska the trip was finally taken upon my own judgment, and at the earnest request of Dr. Lindsley and others interested in Alaska." One guesses that the "missionary secretary," though he had not directed the trip, could not have been overly surprised.

Jackson was now forty-three years of age and had had nearly twenty years of pioneering experience. There was nothing devious about him. He had learned to follow a straight course toward his objective and his objective now was to minister to Alaska. This was in 1877. It was not until 1884 that his commission from the board made any reference to Alaska and even then he was simply appointed as the missionary at

Sitka. For several years he continued in charge of work in the West. Then in 1882 he was moved to New York as editor of the *Presbyterian Home Missionary* (successor of the *Rocky Mountain Presbyterian*). Yet he managed to make repeated trips to Alaska, several times conducting parties of Church and public leaders to see for themselves the needs of the territory. On such a trip in 1879, with Drs. Kendall and Lindsley and their wives, the first Presbyterian Church in Alaska was organized at Fort Wrangell. Within a year after his first visit he raised over $12,000 for the construction of a mission school. He brought continuous pressure to bear on Congress to provide a civil government and schools for the native population. The United States Commissioner of Education in his report for 1883 paid special tribute to this aspect of Jackson's work, noting that between 1878 and 1884 Jackson had delivered about 900 addresses on Alaska, including several before important educational groups whose help he enlisted in his effort. In 1884 he conducted a large party of educators to Alaska.

Having taken Mrs. McFarland to Alaska in the summer of 1877 and left her there alone with the most meager equipment and support, a circumstance that shocked many in the Church, Jackson saw to it that reenforcements arrived the next year and still others later. These all looked to him as the one on whom they could chiefly rely for help. In 1883 all the missionaries in Alaska joined in requesting the board to appoint him Superintendent of Missions in Alaska. This the board declined to do. However, the next year he was offered an appointment as missionary at Sitka. He promptly accepted and moved his family there in the summer. In September the Sitka Church was organized with forty-nine members. The boarding school was transferred from Fort Wrangell to Sitka and combined with Mrs. McFarland's school. In the same month the Presbytery of Alaska was organized.

Earlier in the year two other important events had happened. The first was the granting of his request for a government appropriation of $15,000 for the enlargement of the industrial school at Sitka. The other, of far greater significance, was the passage in May 1884 of the act providing a civil government for Alaska and directing the Secretary of the Interior to make provision for the education of children of school age in the territory, with an appropriation of $25,000 for this purpose. Early in 1885 this educational task was assigned to the Bureau of Education, whose Commissioner, General John Eaton, had known Jackson since 1878. General Eaton promptly offered Jackson the appointment as General Agent of Education in Alaska at a salary of $1,200 a year. It was assumed that he could continue his missionary responsibilities, receiving an equal amount of salary from the Board of Home Missions. This type of arrangement was not unusual at this time in connection with educational work for Indians. Jackson accepted the appointment and plunged at once into a prodigiously difficult task.

It would, in fact, be almost impossible to exaggerate Jackson's difficulties. Concerning a really minor illustration, encountered in the erection of a building at Wrangell, Jackson wrote: "No one that has not tried building a thousand miles from a hardware store and a hundred miles from a sawmill, in a community where there was not a horse, wagon, or cart, and but one wheelbarrow, can realize the vexatious delays incipient to such a work." The native population was scattered over a vast territory. In southeastern Alaska, where the majority lived, the island communities could be reached only by water, which usually meant by canoe. The Eskimo settlements in western Alaska and along the Arctic Ocean constituted the most isolated and relatively inaccessible mission stations in the world.

V

It was Jackson's strategy—the only one that was feasible with the limited resources at his command—to relate the government schools as far as possible to the work of the various Church missions already established or soon to be established. To secure a wide distribution of missionary and educational efforts without any harmful competition, he worked out a comity plan with representatives of the Presbyterian, Episcopalian, Methodist, Baptist, Congregational, and Moravian

Churches. Other bodies, including the Roman Catholic Church, later cooperated with the government's school program. Among the more remote places where schools were established during the first few years were Cape Prince of Wales, Point Hope, and Point Barrow, the latter being the northernmost point on the continent. For these and other points Jackson recruited teachers from the states and found no lack of suitable applicants. From his limited government appropriation he provided materials for the erection of school buildings and homes, delivering workers and building materials to their destinations by the revenue cutter *Bear* or, when necessary, by chartered ship. He personally made five trips on the *Bear* to Point Barrow.

It was not only the obstacles interposed by distance, terrain, and weather that Jackson had to overcome. For sometime the human obstacles were equally formidable for there were men, some white and some Indian, who did not welcome the influence on the natives of mission or school. The first appointed civil officers resisted the missionary strenuously and had him arrested on a series of trumped-up charges. When the facts came to light, President Cleveland summarily removed these officers and appointed others. The charges against Jackson were dismissed. Later efforts of the same nature, including widespread attacks made on him in the metropolitan press, were exasperating but not more successful in discrediting him or diverting him from his objectives. He had powerful friends as well as bitter enemies.

Without question Jackson's most widely publicized achievement was the introduction of reindeer into Alaska. Nothing else that he accomplished so directly affected the economy of the territory and the material welfare of the population. On one of his trips to the Arctic coast he found the Eskimos in danger of starvation as a result of the unrestricted destruction of whales, walruses, and seals by American whalers. This deprived them of practically their only native source of food and clothing. At the same time he learned that the natives of Russian Siberia had in their herds of reindeer an unfailing supply of food and furs. His first proposals for the purchase and importation of reindeer were ridiculed as impracticable and his effort to secure government funds for this purpose was unsuccessful. He therefore raised from private sources enough money to purchase sixteen reindeer, which were successfully landed in Alaska in 1891. More were secured the same way the following year. By 1893 his judgment had been sufficiently vindicated so that Congress made a small appropriation for this purpose. In all, over twelve hundred reindeer were imported from Siberia before Russia prohibited further exportations in 1902. This number was augmented by others brought from Lapland and Norway. Within forty years the reindeer herds in Alaska numbered half a million, about seventy percent native-owned. Between 1891 and 1900 Jackson made thirty-three trips to Siberia in connection with this project.

In 1897 Sheldon Jackson was elected Moderator of the 109th General Assembly of the Presbyterian Church. His moderatorial year was typically Jacksonian. Upon adjournment, after a hurried trip to his home and office in Washington, D.C., he crossed the continent and took a ship to St. Michaels, Alaska, at the mouth of the Yukon River. He was here when a Yukon River steamer arrived with the cargo of gold dust that marked the real start of the Yukon gold rush. He then went by steamer on a missionary exploration the entire length of the Yukon to Dawson, Canada, a distance of over sixteen hundred miles. Returning, he was stranded for nineteen days on a sand bar. From St. Michaels he then sailed on the *Bear* to make the rounds of the mission stations and schools on the Bering Sea coast. This completed, he returned to Washington, where, shortly after, he was requested to go to Lapland as a special agent of the War Department to purchase reindeer to be sent to Alaska for the relief of miners stranded in the upper Yukon valley, who were reported to be in danger of starvation. This midwinter journey, in a year of exceptional storms, the return trip with over 500 reindeer and 68 Lapp herdsmen and their families, and their journey across the country and to Alaska, occupied Jackson fully until the end of April. Shortly thereafter he convened the General Assembly and preached its opening sermon on his familiar text—"Begin to possess, that thou mayest inherit the land."

In 1902 he made his twenty-sixth and final voyage to Alaska. While he retained his official connection and continued to give active attention to Alaskan needs, seriously impaired health compelled him to confine himself to office work in Washington. He retired in 1908 and died the following year, May 2, 1909.

VI

This is the story of a missionary. He received many honors and won distinction in other fields. But this, one feels, is how he would have wished to be remembered—as a missionary. Of a truth his plans "required time and distance." From his first commission to his final retirement had passed a full fifty years, years of unbroken, unremitting missionary service. His missionary travels covered almost a million miles. This was in a day when the fastest one could travel was fifty miles an hour by train; but much of his travel was on foot, by stage coach, canoe, dog sled, or by a steamer bucking its way through ice fields. He knew danger. Three times he read his own obituary in the newspapers. As he spent his own time and strength, he inspired many others to spend theirs that the Church might be extended and the Gospel preached in far places. That was how he understood the Lord's command.

Such a story may seem unreal today. This was true pioneering. A trip to which Sheldon Jackson devoted weeks of the most severe physical strain could now be made in comparative ease in a matter of hours. Where he once spent days and weeks in stark isolation, his modern successor can be in constant communication with the far ends of the earth. Much of what to him was the commonplace of a day's work would now seem merely quaint. His circumstances are not ours, nor his problems, nor his methods; so we might say this is just something out of a storied past.

But this may be too hasty a conclusion. If we have plans to extend the Kingdom they may still "require time and distance." Every age has its own frontiers, its own edge of the unknown and of the unconquered, and it needs those who will go before to prepare the way. In our day as in his, the Church must be a moving Church, an exploring Church, a pioneering Church, a missionary Church.

Here was a man whose one thought of his ministry was as mission. He cheerfully performed all the chores that his ministry required of him—whether to write his thousands of letters, make his thousands of speeches, buttonhole congressmen, solicit money, drive nails into a new building, argue with boards and committees, put the fear of God into the hearts of his enemies. Whatever the chores, they could not obscure his sense of mission, which was strong enough to tie all these things together and give them a spiritual unity. This was not less real to him as the Church grew and prospered than it had been when it was weak and feeble. There was always some place further on that he must "begin to possess." A simple lesson but not easy to learn—it may be the lesson the Church chiefly needs to learn in our time.

VI. ASHBEL GREEN SIMONTON
(1833-1867)

*A Calvinist in Brazil**

BY M. RICHARD SHAULL

WHEN Ashbel Green Simonton arrived in Rio de Janeiro on August 12, 1859, after having graduated from Princeton Theological Seminary, he entered upon a work which was to make him a central figure in the establishment of Protestantism and the Reformed Faith in Brazil. He succeeded where a group of French Calvinists had failed three hundred years earlier. His life, seen in the perspective of the century that has passed since his arrival in Brazil, provides us with an outstanding example of the stature and achievements of an unusual group of Princetonians who were pioneers in the missionary enterprise on three continents. As we examine his work in this same perspective, we will also be obliged to consider the limitations of his training and some of the implications of this for theological education in our time.

Simonton's work was set in an unusual context, for Rio de Janeiro had been the site of one of the few missions outside of Europe in which the Reformers of the sixteenth century

---

* The most important sources for our knowledge of Simonton's life and work are: *Journal of the Reverend Ashbel Green Simonton, Missionary to Brazil* (unpublished manuscript); personal and official letters to the Board of Foreign Missions of the Presbyterian Church, New York; the *Historic Record of Mission Work in Brazil from July 25, 1860,* by the Rev. A. L. Blackford. These, together with other source materials from the period, are available in the library of the Commission on Ecumenical Mission and Relations of the United Presbyterian Church, New York, and in the Presbyterian museum in Campinas, Brazil. The major facts about Simonton's life are presented briefly in Robert L. McIntire's *Portrait of Half a Century: Fifty Years of Presbyterianism in Brazil (1859-1910),* unpublished doctoral dissertation, Princeton Theological Seminary, 1959. See also Julio Andrade Ferreira, *História da Igreja Presbiteriana do Brasil,* Editôra Presbiteriana, São Paulo, 1959.

were directly involved. In 1555 Admiral Villegagnon had enlisted the support of Admiral Coligny and of John Calvin for an expedition to Brazil, the purpose of which was to drive out the Portuguese, establish Calvinism, and provide a place of refuge for persecuted Protestants from Europe. The group arrived and settled on a small island in what is now known as Guanabara Bay. Three years later a second expedition was sent, which included fourteen Huguenots, two of them ministers, selected by Calvin and the Church of Geneva.

The colony soon ran into troubled times. It did not have a solid economic base and was torn by internal dissension. The climax came when Villegagnon decided to return to the Roman Catholicism he had earlier renounced. The Calvinists were expelled and were to be returned to Europe. When their boat was in danger of sinking in the harbor, however, five of them decided to return to the colony, where they soon became the first Protestant martyrs in Latin America.[1] In 1560 the Portuguese defeated the French colonists, and this Calvinistic mission completely disappeared.[2]

Early in the seventeenth century, the Dutch invaded North Brazil and established themselves in Bahia, which they controlled from 1635 until they were driven out in 1654. From the very first, they took pastors and missionaries with them. Eventually two presbyteries and a synod were formed with forty pastors and eight missionaries working among the Indians. There was, however, no significant penetration among the Brazilian people, and when the Dutch colonists were expelled Calvinism disappeared with them.

These two missionary ventures occurred at a time when Portugal maintained its colony in complete isolation from the rest of the world. Moreover, the religious situation was dominated by the Jesuits, who had begun work in Brazil in 1549. By the early decades of the nineteenth century, however, sig-

[1] Three were killed by Villegagnon; one was allowed to live because he was the only tailor in the colony; the fifth escaped only to be executed by the Inquisition a few years later.

[2] One of the Calvinists who took part in this venture and returned to France, Jean de Lery, later wrote a history of it: *Histoire d'un Voyage fait en la terre du Brasil*, Paris, 1880.

nificant changes had taken place. A royal edict of 1808 that opened the ports of Brazil to all friendly nations was followed in 1822 by the Emperor's declaration of Brazil's independence. With these events a new world suddenly opened up before the Brazilian people. As the élite began to read French books, liberal ideas spread, and a new mentality developed, while the French and American revolutions aroused new political hopes. The ideals which began to inspire the younger generation seemed closely akin to thoughts and events in Protestant countries; this created a certain predisposition in favor of Protestantism and what it stood for.

Brazilian Catholicism was unprepared to deal with this new mentality. As Professor Leonard has shown, the religious situation in Brazil at that time was very similar to that of western Europe before the Reformation.[3] The decline of the work of the Jesuits, culminating in their expulsion from Brazil in 1759, left the field wide open to a type of primitive Catholicism that had become a social religion so adapted to the culture that it had lost its spiritual vitality. The number of priests was very small; their training, poor; their level of spirituality, low. Superstition abounded. What deep Christian concern existed was often Jansenistic in character, reflecting, as Leonard has noted, warm interest in the Bible, austere piety, and a strong tendency toward independence from Rome. Those who were most influenced by the new intellectual climate would have nothing to do with this religion; at the same time, many felt a deep religious longing which sought satisfaction in Masonry, esoteric cults, and in Protestantism as it appeared through the instrumentality of the North American missionary.

In this new wave of Protestant penetration, Simonton was not the first to arrive. The Anglicans had begun work early in the century. The Methodists started a mission in 1836

[3] See Émile-G. Leonard, "O Protestantismo Brasileiro. Estudo de eclesiologia e de história social," Cap. I, *Revista de História*, São Paulo, January-March, 1951, No. 5, pp. 117ff. This work, which appeared in successive numbers of this review, is the only serious historical study of the development of Brazilian Protestantism which has been published to date.

which was closed down soon afterward. Representatives of the Bible Societies traveled widely, distributing the Scriptures. In 1855 Robert Kalley, a Scotch physician who had begun missionary work on the Island of Madeira, fled to Brazil with some of his people to escape persecution. Three years later he organized a Church and carried on a very discreet type of evangelistic work which early won support in certain circles at the Court. It was left for Simonton, however, to begin the first organized effort of missionary penetration which was to sink roots in Brazilian soil and spread throughout the country.

II

Some of the early missionaries to Brazil were sons of the American frontier, prepared by this experience for pioneer work under difficult circumstances. Ashbel Green Simonton was not of this company. Son of a physician in Dauphin County, Pennsylvania, and named after a Presbyterian minister who had served as President of the College of New Jersey and also of the Board of Trustees of Princeton Theological Seminary, Simonton was reared in the solid middle-class culture of that time, in a home in which Presbyterian faith and tradition were strong. He was sent early to the College of New Jersey, from which he graduated in 1852. After eighteen months traveling through the South and teaching in Starkville Academy in Mississippi, he returned home and began the study of law. Soon thereafter his spiritual pilgrimage began that led him to abandon law, study for the ministry, and commit himself to the foreign missionary enterprise.

Simonton had been consecrated to the ministry by his parents when still a small child. He had attended church and had taken part in various revival meetings across the years but felt no deep religious convictions or experience. At the same time, his *Journal* reveals a growing spiritual dissatisfaction and a feeling that, as he writes on his twenty-second birthday, his life has "so little purpose." About that time there was a new wave of revivalism in Harrisburg. After attending several meetings, Simonton came to a decision. For a long time, as he states in his *Journal*, he had been aware not only "that the affairs of eternity are of much greater moment than the affairs of time . . . but that even in this life, to be a Christian is the highest wisdom."[4] As up to that time he had had no experience "in the heart," he had not acted on this conviction. Now, although such an emotional experience was still lacking, he decided to accept as valid the promises of the Gospel and live them out. On the day that he reported having joined the Church, he wrote thus in his *Journal*: "The more I analyzed and looked into my feelings and exercises of mind the more I have been perplexed and involved in doubt, and it is only when I turn from myself to the plain, clear and full promises of the Gospel that I find any stable footing. I have therefore after earnest prayer to God for direction decided to give over these efforts to obtain comfort or clearer evidence of my acceptance by Christ by looking into my own frames and feelings, and putting my trust in the plain word of the Scriptures, to endeavour in the promised assistance of the Holy Spirit to do my duty."[5] It was on this foundation that he based his whole future course, and it was both the motivation of his work and the source of deep spiritual unrest, as his *Journal* clearly shows.

This decision was followed almost immediately by his resolution to study for the ministry and to thus give expression to a desire that had been growing in him for several years. For him the ministry offered the opportunity to be decisively involved in the events taking place in his time. As he wrote while meditating on the question during his time in Starkville, "There is . . . a great day coming—an era in the world's history—when vast results are to be brought about and great changes wrought, and they will be honored who are the instruments in this work."[6] More central for him was the conviction that, as a minister, he would be required to trust only

[4] *Journal of the Rev. Ashbel Green Simonton, Missionary to Brazil* (1855). Original manuscript in the library of the Commission on Ecumenical Mission and Relations of the United Presbyterian Church in the U.S.A.; copy in Historical Museum of the Presbyterian Seminary in Campinas, Brazil.
[5] *Journal*, May 3, 1855.
[6] *Ibid.*, June 3, 1854.

in God, serve him alone, and live only by his succor. This was the path by which he could be fully a servant of Jesus Christ, in total self-giving, "with joy and zeal." From the moment when, upon entering Princeton Seminary, he worked out a program for discipline and growth in Christian faith and life until the end of his short career as a missionary in Brazil, this purpose and passion shaped his life.

We know very little about Simonton's years at Princeton Seminary. His *Journal* has few entries during this period and practically no references to his studies. He does inform us, however, of the factors that led him to become a foreign missionary. His thoughts were first directed toward the mission field by a sermon of Charles Hodge. What this decision meant for him is stated clearly and concisely in a paragraph in which he comments on this sermon:

"I have listened today to a very interesting sermon from Dr. Hodge on the duty of the church as a teacher. He spoke of the absolute necessity of instructing the heathen before success in the spread of the Gospel could be expected, and showed that any hopes of their conversion based upon the extraordinary agency of the Holy Spirit directly communicating truth were unscriptural. This sermon has had the effect of leading me to think seriously of the foreign mission field. The little success apparently attending missionary operations has tended to dissuade me from thinking of going. But I see I have been wrong. That the heathen are to be converted to God is clearly revealed in the Scriptures and I am convinced that day is coming rapidly. Those who are now laboring are preparing the way and God will not suffer their labor to be in vain. He who lays the foundation will receive an equal reward with those who perfect the building. I have never before seriously considered the question as to my duty to go abroad, always taking for granted that my sphere of labor would be somewhere in our great and rapidly growing country. It is, however, I feel convinced, a matter to be taken into deep consideration whether since most prefer to remain it is not my duty to go."[7]

[7] *Ibid.*, Oct. 14, 1855.

After this it was only a question of time until he applied to the Board of Foreign Missions in New York. His application was accepted, and he was appointed to Brazil. After his graduation from Princeton Seminary in 1859, he was ordained by Carlyle Presbytery and on June 18 sailed for his new field of labor.

III

Simonton arrived in Brazil with a message which was to speak to the Brazilian soul at a time when many were dominated by superstition, fear, and uncertainty of salvation; at a time when others were searching for a new and vital spiritual reality relevant to the hopes and concerns of their time. Protestant preaching brought the message of justification by faith, a new type of religious experience, and a new form of Christian life.[8] José Manoel da Conceição, the priest who was converted by the missionaries in the first years of their work, gave expression to what this meant for him. Speaking of the ecstatic experience which was his at the moment of his reception into the Protestant community, he wrote: "Do you find this mysterious? Mysterious it shall remain while you have not emptied even unto the dregs the cup of purification, a drink which shall set your teeth on edge. All this bitterness, however, will be followed by an inexplicable sweetness. You shall slumber. You shall faint of love for God; but you shall awaken in triumph most glorious, even that one which is most difficult to reach: triumph over yourselves. You shall feel yourselves converted to God, identified with Christ. Only then shall you know what it is to live and breathe the pure atmosphere of the Christian life."[9]

As the bearer of this message, Simonton had a very clear

[8] For evidence of the centrality of these themes in Simonton's preaching, see *Sermões Escolhidos*, by G. L. Shearer, New York, 1869.

[9] *Profissão de fée evangélica*, cited by Robert L. McIntire, "Portrait of Half a Century," unpublished doctoral dissertation, Princeton Theological Seminary, 1959, p. 106. I am also indebted to Dr. McIntire for much of the information about Simonton's life and work used in this chapter, and for his kindness in reading the chapter and offering valuable suggestions.

understanding of the task before him, which is expressed in the title of a paper he read to the presbytery a short time before his death: "The Proper Means for Planting the Kingdom of Jesus Christ in Brazil." He was not content merely to proclaim the Gospel as widely as possible, nor to set up a "mission" which would do the job of evangelism. His supreme purpose was to lay the foundations for a *Church* that would be the instrument of evangelistic penetration throughout Brazil.

Simonton gave himself to this task with a rare intensity of devotion. He would have only eight years before being stricken down by yellow fever at the age of thirty-four. Of that time, one year was spent learning the language, another on furlough in the United States. As a pioneer on a new frontier, he could look for help neither to the study nor the experience of others. Living in a tropical climate to which he was not accustomed and laboring in an alien culture, he began his work entirely alone and during the last years of his life bore the sorrow caused by the death of his wife one year after their marriage. Yet in this short time and in these circumstances, Ashbel Green Simonton accomplished what he set out to do, for he laid the foundation and set the pattern for the growth of one of the strongest and most creative among what is today called the "Younger Churches."

From the very start he was confronted by a problem that has been one of the most crucial in the whole Protestant missionary enterprise and to which missionaries by and large have given little attention: that of the *base* of the Christian community within the society in which it is taking form. We have no reason to believe that Simonton was originally disturbed about this. When he arrived in Rio, Robert Kalley was already attempting to establish just such a base at the Imperial Court. Simonton rightly concluded that the time was ripe for the widest possible diffusion of the Gospel by the distribution of the Scriptures and other literature, itineration, preaching, and personal evangelism. It was his hope that as this was done some would respond and be gathered into the

Christian community which would then provide the base for evangelism.

Things did not work out that easily. After a year and a half Simonton reported his discouragement. A very small nucleus had been formed in Rio, but it showed few signs of growth. It was composed of a few North Americans and other foreigners and a number of other isolated individuals; it had not sunk its roots into a natural community in which it could be firmly established and grow. Simonton gradually became aware of the seriousness of this problem. He began a weekly service in the home of one of the first families to be converted, the Eshers, and urged other members in the congregation to offer their homes for such meetings. In his own words, each such family nucleus could become a "new center of Christian influence, from which grace flows." There is no indication that he was very successful in this attempt.

In the face of this problem, A. L. Blackford, Simonton's brother-in-law and first missionary colleague, soon concluded that they should transfer the headquarters of the mission to São Paulo. Eventually Blackford went there, but the small nucleus that took form was very similar to that in Rio. As early as 1860 Simonton made a long trip through the interior of the province of São Paulo, where he discovered a large number of German Protestant colonists. He saw here the possibility of a new base and convinced the board to send an American of German descent to begin work with them. This attempt also failed.

The answer appeared quite unexpectedly at a very different point. José Manoel da Conceição had spent nearly twenty years as a priest in small villages in the interior of the State of São Paulo. As the bishop did not trust this man, who was even then known as the "Padre Protestante," he did not allow him to stay more than a year or two in any one village. His last field of service before becoming a Protestant had been a new agricultural community called Brotas. To this he returned as an itinerant evangelist and soon several of the leading families in the area had been won to the Protestant cause. When the missionaries arrived, they found that a dynamic

Ashbel Green Simonton

government of our church; which being satisfactory the examination on science, languages, etc. were dispensed with."[11]

This uncritical importation of ecclesiastical structures would raise, in later decades, serious problems that were not evident at the time. In one sense, however, the presbytery represented a significant new development, for it included from the beginning an outstanding Brazilian pastor, who was to be followed soon by other strong national leaders.

Simonton gave special attention to the formation, in the Calvinistic tradition, of a strong national ministry for the leadership of the new Church. With discernment not common among missionaries of his time, he sensed that the work of the foreign missionary would have to be temporary and of secondary importance in the development of a missionary Church. He wrote: "If these workers come from foreign countries, they are obliged to learn a new language and become accustomed to the ways of a new land. This fact in itself makes one believe that the greatest part of the workers have to be of this country."

Several young candidates soon appeared. They began to accompany Conceição on his missionary travels, but were soon taken to Rio, where Simonton founded the first Presbyterian seminary in May 1867. From what we know of the program of study, it was quite academic and followed closely that of seminaries in the United States. After a few years the seminary had to be closed because of a shortage of teachers, but an emphasis had been placed on theological education that the Presbyterian Church of Brazil soon took up and has continued to this day.

One other initiative of Simonton's deserves mention: the publication of the *Imprensa Evangélica*, the newspaper that he began in November 1864, and which continued as the official organ of the Church for twenty-eight years. This paper, with the tremendous burden it placed upon its director, was

[11] *Journal Record of Mission Work in the City of São Paulo, Brazil,* from October 9th, 1863 to December 25th, 1865. Quoted by McIntire, "Portrait of Half a Century," p. 114.

an expression of his double concern: to provide the strongest possible nourishment for the new evangelical community and at the same time to diffuse the faith as widely as possible. In it we find articles on a wide variety of subjects, witnessing incidentally to Simonton's extraordinary skill in the use of the Portuguese language.

In the midst of all these activities what most stands out is Simonton the man, the incarnation of a new form of Christian life and commitment for Brazil. In him Christian faith expressed itself in a totally dedicated person who was at the same time warmly human, who rejoiced in meaningful friendships and relations, and who was interested in all aspects of the human situation. He gave expression to a type of personal piety that reflected constant communion with Jesus Christ, deep humility, and the recognition of personal limitations and failures. The last entry in his *Journal* expresses this well: "In the retrospect of my own life during the year now closed, I feel self-condemned. I can point to some labor performed as best I could but have I progressed heavenward? Here it is that I feel myself lacking. I cannot get beyond the prayer of the publican: God be merciful to me a sinner! Shall it be always thus with me? The very press and activity of my outer life has hindered my communion with Him to whom this service is paid. How often have my devotions been formal and hurried, or disturbed by thoughts of plans for the day! And sins often confessed and bewailed have asserted their power over me. Oh! for a baptism of fire to consume my dross; oh! for a heart wholly Christ's."[12]

It was this man who was the bulwark of a new mission, the center of strength in the midst of tensions and crises, and a person whom a leader of the Presbyterian Church a century later could consider "one of the saints of modern Christianity."[13]

[12] *Journal,* December 31, 1866.
[13] Boanerges Ribeiro, *O Padre Protestante,* Casa Editòra Presbiteriana, São Paulo, 1950, p. 115.

ASHBEL GREEN SIMONTON

V

To relate Simonton's life and work to the situation of the Reformed faith in Brazil today is a difficult and treacherous task for anyone deeply involved in that situation. Looking back from this vantage point, the first thing which impresses us is that Simonton succeeded in so short a time to do what he set out to do. Even more impressive is that this man conceived of his task in terms which only recently have come to the fore in Protestant missiology: the development of the Church as a missionary community with a solid foundation and adequate forms for its life and growth and in which the missionary would occupy a secondary place from the start. And, as we have seen above, he and his colleagues—missionary and national—succeeded where missions failed in many parts of the world, in finding a solid base in the community structures of the society to which they went. In these respects we can say that Simonton stood out among his contemporaries and was far ahead of many of those who came after him in both Church and mission in Brazil.

We have now arrived at the end of an era in both the Church and the mission for which Simonton laid the foundation. Once again Calvin's mission to Brazil is threatened, not this time with extinction, but with the possibility of becoming irrelevant if it fails to respond to the challenges of the new world in which it suddenly finds itself. We are being forced to the conclusion that our faithfulness to Simonton and to the cause for which he gave his life now demands that we go about our mission in a very different way and change, perhaps radically, the patterns and structures of the Christian community which came into being as a result of his efforts.

What makes this a crucial problem for missiology and for theological education is the discovery that the issues we face have their present form and intensity because they have been serious issues for Church and mission for many decades. But we have either not been aware of them or have been unprepared to meet them. In fact, they may have existed as far back as the first decade of Presbyterian work in Brazil. Simonton and his colleagues had to face these problems, and the decisions he and his successors made helped to determine the way the problems are raised today. It may be useful to look at several which are particularly evident and which must be seen in this historical perspective.

(1) *Indigenization: Protestantism and the Brazilian Culture and Temperament.* With the recent upsurge of nationalistic sentiment and the struggle of the Brazilian people to find their self-identity and to develop authentic forms of cultural life, we are now able to see to what extent Protestantism has been content with imported forms instead of trying to find more indigenous expressions of the Gospel. One of the leading Presbyterian pastors in Brazil today, the Rev. Boanerges Ribeiro, has shown a growing concern for this problem. In his excellent biography of José Manoel da Conceição, he expressed it this way: "With rare exceptions, the Protestant preaching has always found friends among the nationals who become converted; but the nascent congregations enter the mould of the churches from which the missionaries have come to us."[14]

This problem arose in the very first years of Presbyterian work in Brazil. There are two references in Simonton's *Journal* that may indicate that he was disturbed by it. Soon after his arrival in Rio de Janeiro, he records this conversation: "Having been often asked to take wine, I explained today to the Americans with whom I was dining my reasons for declining. Dr. L. thought, here where wine was not used to intoxicate, my reasons and example would not be understood."[15] The fact that Simonton took the trouble to record this conversation is a hint that he gave it serious consideration. More important, however, is his observation about the use of *Pilgrim's Progress*. On April 28, 1860, he tells of starting his first Sunday School class and remarks that the three textbooks he is using are "the Bible, a catechism of sacred history, and Bunyan's *Pilgrim's Progress*." After the second class, he makes this observation: "Amalia and Marroquinas think it hard to under-

[14] *Ibid.*, p. 124.
[15] *Journal*, Sept. 12, 1859.

stand John Bunyan. They have no substratum for his lessons, it is something different from all they have heard, seen or felt, so that they cannot get right hold of it."[16]

If he had lived a few years longer, it is quite probable that in dialogue with Conceição and in constant contact with his work Simonton's keen and open mind would have grasped the implications of the fact which he vaguely sensed. Boanerges Ribeiro has this to say about Conceição's vision of the Reformation in Brazil: "It seems that he did not desire the establishment of a Protestant Church transplanted from another race, another culture, different tradition or temperament, but a profound movement of Reformation in the sentiments and religious experience of the people, allied to Biblical instruction, which would make possible the creation of a pure and evangelical Brazilian Christianity, but which would be rooted in popular traditions and habits."[17] He then proceeds to quote a page from Conceição which, although referring directly to the Enlightenment, may have had a much wider application for him:

"If we unwisely wish to communicate to men, without any preparation, truths which are utterly incomprehensible to them, using these truths in this way falsely and harmfully, we will not thus promote enlightenment. To enlighten is to lead the thinking man to meditate, in order to make him courageous and capable of being able to discover for himself the truth which we communicate to him. . . . There are many uneducated men who are children in many respects, and who should be indoctrinated with great circumspection. For to destroy certain prejudices and useful customs, practices which are many times a substitute for the truth itself, is in no sense enlightenment; but rather inhuman levity and excessive cruelty. Respect then the customs and ancient practices of the people which, in the absence of more profound understanding, are capable of guiding them and keeping them on the right path. Oh my God! I will respect the religion of the ignorant—

[16] *Ibid.*, May 1, 1860.
[17] *O Padre Protestante*, p. 206.

the faith of those who have had few opportunities of knowing Thee and worshipping Thee in a worthy way. I will never allow myself to be dominated by vanity and presumption in such a way that I might shatter the pious faith of others by inconsiderate words and actions."[18]

This concern seems to have disappeared from the scene along with Simonton and Conceição, and another generation of missionaries took full direction of the orientation of the leadership of the Church. As a result, the national Church tended to accept these imported patterns without serious questioning. There was naturally much unconscious adaptation of the Protestant message and way of life to the Brazilian situation. Yet what was lacking for many decades was the acute awareness of this issue that we find in Conceição, which could have maintained a constant openness, among missionaries and national leaders, to the demands for indigenization. If this had happened, it might have been possible to avoid the development of such a rationalistic Calvinism among a strongly emotional people, or of a rigid Puritanism, which tended to stifle rather than liberate and transform the vitality of the Brazilian soul. It might have been possible to raise earlier the questions relating to a Brazilian theology, the use of the rich musical tradition in Brazil for Protestant hymns, and the adaptation of Church structures and patterns of congregational life to Brazilian reality, all of which would have made much less acute the situation in which we find ourselves today.

(2) *Ecclesiastical Structures.* The question of ecclesiastical structures is a serious one for Protestantism throughout the world today. In those Younger Churches where the alien patterns imported by the missionaries have not been transformed in creative encounter with the local situation, the problem has now become especially acute.

In the first years of Presbyterian work in Brazil, the foundations were laid for what might have become a creative struggle with this issue. In his encounter with Roman Catholicism,

[18] *Ibid.*, pp. 206-207.

Simonton was forced to make a serious theological study of the question and came to see very clearly the role of the Holy Spirit in giving form to the Church. In a pamphlet, "The Vicar of Christ," he affirmed that Christ indicated to his disciples "who was to take his place in the teaching and direction of the work of His visible church," namely, the Holy Spirit who not only accompanies the disciples and convicts them of sin but also "completes the revelation of the divine will and assists in the organization of the Christian Church and the propagation of the same until its final triumph throughout the world." The presence and work of the Spirit in the Church has tremendous consequences: " 'Where two or three are met together in my name, there am I in the midst of them.' The seat of Him who acts for the Savior on earth is established then in all the meetings of those who are true believers in his name. This seat is not established exclusively in any one particular place or city to which it is necessary to go in order to receive the benefits of his personal presence and work. Nor is it necessary to have a general council in order to guarantee the assistance of this Vicar in His Church and receive His teaching so that He may direct it in the doctrines of salvation and in the discipline of the house of God."[19]

Conceição, after years of experience within the rigid structures of the Roman Church, was especially sensitive at this point and was searching for a form of Christian community that would possess the depth and richness of life which the Spirit gives to the Body of Christ. When Simonton and his colleagues, however, went about setting up an ecclesiastical structure, they fell back, as was almost inevitable, on the patterns they knew at home. In the first decades, especially in the rich community life of the congregation in the rural areas, no serious problems arose. But as the ecclesiastical institution developed and as the theological insight of Simonton and the witness of Conceição were forgotten, a pattern developed in which a rather rigid and sterile organization came to the fore, and in which the absorption in administrative activities threat-

[19] "O Vigário de Cristo," Presbyterian Board of Publications, Philadelphia, n.d.

ened the development of the missionary community that represented, for Simonton, the supreme goal of his efforts.

The crucial problem arose in the definition of the role of the ministry in the Church. Here too Simonton's doctrine of the Spirit opened the way for a breakthrough. In his study of the sacraments is a paragraph which has a very modern ring about it: "All of the twelfth chapter of the First Epistle to the Corinthians treats of the structure of the Church and of the position which each one of its members should occupy, establishing this luminous principle, that the diversity of ministries was determined by the operation of the Holy Spirit. No one should aspire to any position without having received the precise spiritual gifts for the worthy exercise of it. The action of the Church was limited to the confirmation of these gifts."[20] The fact that this observation is followed by his conclusion that the one important ministry in the Church is that of the preacher of the Word should not detract from this insight and the possibilities it could have offered for the development of a new Church.

Likewise, Conceição dedicated himself to a most extraordinary expression of an indigenous ministry. With his rich educational training, culture, and sense of scholarship, he chose to begin an itinerant ministry that combined total identification with the people, communication of the Gospel in amazing depth, and a fantastic rapidity of evangelistic penetration in the interior of the country. Soon three or four young men received the call to the ministry and began to accompany him. If only this had been developed, it might have given form to a radically new type of ministry and to the spontaneous expansion of the Reformation in Brazil.

But Simonton and his colleagues took these men out of this situation of involvement and put them in a seminary organized on traditional lines. After a few years the seminary was closed, but by that time the traditional, imported pattern was firmly established. As a result, today both minister and

[20] *Os Sacramentos*, Presbyterian Board of Publications, Philadelphia, n.d., Chap. VII.

congregation often find themselves in a frustrating situation. The diverse gifts of the Spirit tend to be concentrated in one man who can easily understand his role, in a culture shaped by Roman Catholicism, as that of possessing and using authority to run the Church. The layman has restricted opportunities for using his gifts, while the majority of the Churches are unable to support a fulltime pastor. The ministry is considered very much like the liberal, middleclass professions, but without offering the advantages which these professions usually offer and tending to make the minister someone detached from the realities of a dynamic society rather than a militant participant in the center of its life.

(3) *Gospel, Church, and World.* Here we confront our most urgent question. The evangelical community knows modern man's interest in life in this world and the threats of disintegration that modern society brings into his personal life; it also feels the consequences of the breakdown of traditional culture and society under the impact of foreign forces and is caught up in the growing concern about social injustice. The result of all this is a deep sense of disorientation and anxiety, which can only be met to the degree that the Christian faith provides a foundation for the reintegration of human life in community and the redefinition of Christian responsibility through a new vision of God's redemptive activity in the world.

The early Presbyterian missionaries often revealed a strange mixture of Calvinistic concern for the world with pietistic ignoring of it, which we see demonstrated even in Simonton. His *Journal* reveals a keen interest in politics, the question of slavery, human need, and other major issues of his time. The Civil War distressed him greatly and led him not only to pray constantly for his country but also to see more clearly the relation of his faith to the struggles of his people: "I have seen and do see as I never did before, that God is the Savior of nations as well as of individuals and that he can bring the haughty low."[21]

[21] *Journal*, December 31, 1861.

His preaching did not develop this insight. Its message centers almost exclusively on individual piety. Even in his sermon on "Love" and a poem on the same theme, he never gets around to the implications of this for man's life in community.[22] His sensitivity to the American political scene was not matched by an equal awareness of what God was doing in Brazil nor of the relationship of the Gospel to social questions. As a result, one of the major dimensions of Calvin's Reformation in Geneva was absent from Simonton's plan for the Reformation in Brazil.[23]

Conceição conceived of the Gospel in a dynamic relationship to his country and its life and had great dreams of its influence on the total life of the nation.[24] He concluded his reply to the sentence of excommunication in these words: "The well being of my country, the moralization of society, whose felicity only the Gospel can guarantee, and the eternal salvation of men, are the objectives which I have in view. I am in the hands of God and at the service of all whom I may be able to serve in the Gospel of Jesus Christ."

Neither Conceição nor those who came after him had been provided with a theology capable of dealing with this. The result was almost complete separation between the Gospel and evangelical piety, on the one hand, and the major issues of life in the world, on the other. The Presbyterian Churches produced an unusual number of men who achieved positions of distinction in diverse areas of national life; but by and large they and their brethren in the faith did not succeed in presenting to their fellow Brazilians an understanding of the

[22] Published in *Sermões Escolhidos*.

[23] See the first part of André Biéler, *La Pensée économique et sociale de Calvin*, Georg & Cie., Geneva, 1959.

[24] See especially a paper which he presented before the presbytery, entitled: "Porque o Brasil Carece (da Pregação) do Evangelho?" Also the address which he made in Rio de Janeiro on the occasion of Lincoln's death in which he speaks of the power of free men in the building of a free society, and which would seem to indicate that Conceição and Simonton had discussed at length the influence of the Gospel in the development of a free society: "As Exequias de Abrahão Lincoln Presidente dos Estados-Unidos de América com um Esboço biographico do mesmo offerecido ao Povo Brasileiro por seu Patricio José Manoel da Conceição," Rio de Janeiro: Eduardo & Henrique Laemmert, 1956.

Gospel which was related creatively to the major intellectual and social issues before them. In the midst of the tremendous events now occurring in Brazil, the contributions our Calvinistic heritage might make remain largely unknown, while a growing number of laymen become convinced that what happens in the Church is quite irrelevant to the important issues of human existence and are oriented more by the ideologies which are dominant in the center of these struggles than by their Christian faith.

For Simonton the Gospel provided the basis for the total reconstruction of human life. In a sermon on "Eternal Life," he declared: "Eternal life consists in the greatest possible development of the virtues implanted and cultivated in the soul of the believer by the presence and operation of the Holy Spirit: to have the understanding illuminated and strengthened in order that it may contemplate God and know his perfections, to have the heart purified of its idols and consecrated to the worship of God, and to live in the constant practice and experience of the virtues enumerated by St. Paul; that is—to live in the enjoyment of God."[25] Because Calvinism in Brazil was not prepared to understand that this new man must take shape within the structures of the world, this pattern for the Christian life soon degenerated into legalism, and has now become for many a burden rather than an Evangel.

Underlying all of these issues is the question of what happened to the Calvinistic theology, for the failure to meet these problems is the failure of theology to be vital and relevant. We have already mentioned how Simonton makes practically no references to the decisive theological issues being debated in Princeton Seminary or in the Christian world; at the same time, he used the catechism as one of his first textbooks and urged the translation of A. A. Hodge's *Outlines of Theology* as the first book needed for the Brazilian seminary. This translation appeared in 1895, and since then very little basic theological literature has been written or translated in Brazil. At present there are many signs of a renewal of vitality as both laymen and ministers are revealing deep concern for theo-

[25] "A Vida Eterna," Presbyterian Board of Publications, Philadelphia, n.d.

logical studies. The issues we now face, however, possess the gravity they now have, in part at least, because this did not happen earlier.

VI

In this attempt to discover the historical origins and continuity of the problems now facing the Presbyterian Church in Brazil, we have no intention of diminishing the importance of Simonton's accomplishments. We have no right to judge his work from a perspective of historical development that he could not possibly have shared. His limitations are the limitations of the Calvinism that was dominant at the time. What is most disturbing in this whole picture is the fact that those who came after him did not become aware of these problems much sooner, that, in the decades immediately after Simonton, many of his successors went backward rather than forward in their awareness of these issues, and that our own generation has been so slow in discovering the frontiers of God's action in Church and world. We cannot sit in judgment on Simonton and his successors; we also dare not close our eyes to the serious questions God is raising for us at this time if we hope to be faithful to Simonton's objective.

The crucial question is the failure of Calvinism to be true to one of the fundamental principles of its own heritage: *ecclesia reformata semper reformanda*. For each generation, Christian obedience means keeping up with and responding creatively to what God is doing in the world and in the Church on those frontiers where renewal must take place. In terms of the mission of the Church, the question raised is that of the place of missiology in theological education as the study of what God demands of his people in their witness, at every moment and in every concrete situation, in a dynamic world. Especially in our day, the bringing to fruition of the work of the great missionary pioneers such as Simonton will depend largely upon the type of study and involvement in mission that will apply this Calvinistic principle and thus provide the foundation for the type of radical renewal which is now demanded in the Christian world mission.

VII. STEPHEN COLWELL (1800-1871)

Social Prophet before the Social Gospel*

BY BRUCE MORGAN

"A MAIN obstruction to the progress of truth lies in this, that most men have some little knowledge of these subjects. That little is magnified into much; infallibility becomes general. If we would make real attainments, we must abdicate these pretensions, admit our ignorance, and condescend to the position of learners."[1] So Stephen Colwell wrote in 1842 in an article discussing the will of James Smithson, from which of course finally issued the Smithsonian Institution in Washington. This, from one of Colwell's many contributions to the *Princeton Review*, sums up in a remarkable way the spirit of the man.

Born in western Virginia (now West Virginia) in 1800, educated in Jefferson College in Canonsburg, Pennsylvania, student of law, practicing attorney, and from the middle thirties a suc-

---

* Biographical material on Stephen Colwell is meager. Consult: Henry C. Carey, *A Memoir of Stephen Colwell*, Philadelphia: Collins, 1871, reprinted in *Proceedings of the American Philosophical Society*, xvii (1871-1872), pp. 195-209. Brief notices exist in the Philadelphia *Public Ledger*, Jan. 17, 1871, the *Index* volume (1825-1868) of the *Biblical Repertory*, pp. 139-140, *Dictionary of American Biography*, Volume 4, p. 827. The *Memoir* noted above contains a list of Colwell's published works, but there is no complete inventory of his many articles on economics, taxation, and social problems. For example, he prepared at least six major reports on trade and taxes for the United States Revenue Commission of which he was a member. He sometimes wrote under a pseudonym, "Mr. Penn," "Jonathan B. Wise," for the *Merchant's Magazine* and *Banker's Magazine*. Colwell's private library on political and social science subjects, amounting to 6,000 items, about one-half being bound pamphlets, was bequeathed to the University of Pennsylvania. The Stephen Colwell Chair of Applied Christianity was established at Princeton Theological Seminary in 1950, the first incumbent being Paul L. Lehmann. See his inaugural address with references to Colwell, "The Dynamics of Reformation Ethics," *Bulletin*, Princeton Theological Seminary, Volume XLIII, No. 4, pp. 17-22.

[1] Review of the Smithson bequest in the *Princeton Review*, July 1842, p. 393.

cessful iron manufacturer in southern New Jersey and around Philadelphia, Stephen Colwell was a notable churchman and lay Christian leader. He was a Trustee of Princeton Theological Seminary and also of the General Assembly of the Presbyterian Church. It was he who advocated a chair for the teaching of the social sciences at Princeton Theological Seminary and studies in applied Christianity in theological schools in general. The Princeton chair was inaugurated on September 27, 1871, shortly after Colwell's death. And it was Colwell who offered a prize of $500.00 for an essay "upon the law or doctrine of Christian charity as taught and exemplified by Christ and His disciples." He left his library to the University of Pennsylvania and coupled his bequest with his desire for the establishment of a chair of social science there. Colwell was an educational statesman, member of the Board of Trustees of the University of Pennsylvania, philanthropist and community leader, active member of the American Colonization Society and, after the war, of the Freedman's Aid Society. He presided over the first meeting of the Union League, organized at the outset of the Civil War to preserve the Union. (One can only reflect how many of his ideas would pass muster in that fortress of economic conservatism today.) He traveled to the hospitals of the Civil War and supplemented out of his own pocket provisions for the suffering.

Colwell was a man of affairs, member of the directorate of many corporations, and a most vigorous member of a Presidential Revenue Commission in 1865-1866, for which he wrote several of its reports and of parts of its draft legislation. He was in a most remarkable way a scholar in the wide area of what is now called social science. His major work in economics, *The Ways and Means of Payment*, 1860, is a monumental inquiry into the credit system leading him to far-reaching policy recommendations. Joseph Dorfman in *The Economic Mind in American Civilization* compares Colwell to Henry Carey, a much better-known figure in the history of American economic thought and the first really great American economist: "Colwell was far shrewder and more subtle than Carey" and "possessed the finest library in the country on economics and related subjects."² We are struck by his candid self-assessment when he wrote in 1852 "we have met with few who have explored a wider range of thought and fact on this subject than we have."³ As one reads his reviews, articles, and books on many subjects one is struck continually by his lucid and highly readable style and by the tremendous breadth and depth of factual knowledge with which he supports his analyses and arguments.

Through the middle decades of the nineteenth century we find Colwell "swimming against the stream," against what John Kenneth Galbraith has called "the conventional wisdom" of his time. As Henry Carey put it in his memoir of Stephen Colwell before the American Philosophical Society in November 1871, "to the commonly accepted authorities of Political Economy, Finance, and Policy of Public Affairs, he . . . gave no more than that amount of faith and acceptance which they should command from a mind well stored with the facts and philosophy of their subject."⁴ Colwell took to every task an original and well-disciplined mind and a devoted Christian commitment. Because he was in a very remarkable way open and receptive to the new possibilities of interpreting the Bible and Christian tradition on the one hand and to new social and political reality on the other, Colwell challenged uniquely the conventional wisdom of his generation.

I

In 1852 Colwell released over his own name the second edition of his *New Themes for the Protestant Clergy: Creeds Without Charity, Theology Without Humanity, Protestantism Without Christianity*. The first edition had been published anonymously in the preceding year. It had been both assailed

---

[2] Joseph Dorfman, *The Economic Mind in American Civilization, 1606-1865*, Vol. II, New York: Viking Press, 1946, pp. 809, 810.

[3] *New Themes for the Protestant Clergy*, 2nd edition, Philadelphia: Lippincott, Grambo and Co., 1852, p. vii.

[4] Henry C. Carey, *Stephen Colwell*, Philadelphia: Collins, 1871, p. 12. This "memoir" was reprinted with a bibliography of Colwell's works in the *Proceedings of the American Philosophical Society*, Volume XVII, 1871-1872, pp. 195-209.

and hailed in the interim and now Colwell came forth with his own signed preface to the second edition. There he declares, "The depths of divine wisdom in Revelation are not yet all sounded; divine truths have not received all their applications to the concerns of man of which they are capable. The teachings of Christ, in their bearings on social questions, require to be further studied, developed and applied. A vast domain of social, moral, and religious philosophy remains to be explored under the light of Christianity. To this investigation let Christians address themselves rather than to glorying in the past."

To his critics he replies, "It is not the least of our regret that these pages have given pain to some very worthy persons; but this we lament as much on their account as on our own; for while it was our part to present these views more free from defects and in a deserving form, it was theirs to receive them in a better spirit. Their reception, whether favorable or otherwise, has clearly shown it was time to bring the subject prominently into discussion."[5]

Thus the chair established at Princeton Seminary, the Stephen Colwell Chair in Applied Christianity, was singularly appropriate. It was Colwell's thesis that the Protestant Reformation had exhausted itself in the purification of doctrinal and ecclesiastical life and had in subsequent generations so divided and proliferated and hardened as to consume its energies in doctrinal and ecclesiological endeavor. As a result it had not been able to work out the social implications of the teaching and the action of Jesus, in the direction of compassion and love, or as Colwell put it in traditional terms, "charity." In *New Themes* he wrote, "If the scrutiny and time and talents which have thus been misapplied, had with equal industry and zeal, been turned to the science of human wellbeing, we should not now lament the little progress which has been made in that great and much abused department of knowledge."[6] He had earlier commented, "the responsibility

[5] Preface to second edition of *New Themes*, pp. xiii-xiv.
[6] *New Themes*, first edition, p. 244.

for the slow progress of Christianity lies at the door of those who profess to be the friends of Christ."[7]

As an evangelical Protestant of the nineteenth century Colwell is at times typically critical of Roman Catholicism. But he is often surprisingly appreciative of the way in which the Catholic Church in the Middle Ages retained at least the terminology and form and sometimes the reality of practicing Christian charity, compassion, and love.

He gathers together in his *New Themes* the teachings of Jesus and of the Apostolic witnesses on the subject of charity and the works of love, and he points out the slenderness or even absence of all concern or consideration for such matters in the creeds and standards of the various Protestant Reformation Churches. Protestantism's "framework of truth was of impregnable strength, yet it was cold, forbidding and uncomfortable; it was neither warmed nor lighted by charity. . . ." The Reformers "executed a task as great as any men ever achieved, but they should not continue to be our sole spiritual teachers."[8] Responding to his critics in the Preface to the second edition of *New Themes*, Colwell makes it very clear that he was in no way attempting to "wash out" or depreciate theology as such. He replies, "We did not attempt to present the whole of Christianity, but to indicate its bearing on humanity, its aspects on the side of humanity; we sought not to subvert sound doctrine, but asked to have the doctrine of charity or love to our fellow men incorporated with evangelical theology."[9]

II

Colwell engages in a scathing critique of the way in which the churches in the nineteenth century have linked themselves to a burgeoning free enterprise economy, have supported an industrial revolution in society, but have been little concerned about anything but the most palliative relief for the victims of social change. Colwell refused to look at eco-

[7] *Ibid.*, p. 9. [8] *Ibid.*, pp. 112-113.
[9] *New Themes*, 2nd Edition, p. ix.

nomic matters outside of the context of political reality, the welfare of the body politic. Writing in 1841 in a *Review* article on the British Poor Laws, Colwell commented, "The subject which should press with constant vigor upon the heart of every man that has power in the nation, is, what is to be done for the well-being of the people—not of the paupers, but *the people, all the people.* Abolish that legislation which legislates for the rich, as rich, and for the poor, as paupers."[10]

And in 1852 he wrote, "The Christian philosopher who surveys the masses of a nation with reference to their best temporal interests, knows, from his own observation, as well as from history and the testimony of Revelation, that men are by nature unequal in mind and body; in power of intellect and in physical endurance; he rejoices to see them united in communities or nations, that the weak may be protected against the strong, and the simple against the cunning; he knows that in the race of life many must fall behind, not only from mental and physical inability to cope with their superiors, but from accidental causes beyond their control; and that if these are not upheld and carried onward by their stronger associates, they must sink under the burdens of life: he knows these cases will be numerous, that Christianity forbids their being overlooked, and that they should also be an important subject of human legislation."[11]

Thus we see Colwell striving against the stream of his time, an anti-individualist, if individualism meant the energetic practice of the *laissez-faire* doctrine of every man for himself, which was becoming so popular in the economic life of the mid-nineteenth century. He comments on the anomaly in Protestantism, "There are not greater friends of political liberty than Protestants, but it is that liberty which lets every man take care of himself, and ruin seize the hindmost; it is that liberty which stimulates all to run, but permits the heat of competition to rise so high that none can stoop to pick up

[10] *The Princeton Review,* Jan. 1841, p. 127.
[11] *Politics for American Christians,* Philadelphia: Lippincott, Grambo and Co., 1852, pp. 22-23.

the multitudes who fall exhausted by the way."[12] Later on he adds, ". . . all this little comports with the stewardship of Christ's disciples, or with the command 'Go sell that thou hast and give to the poor.' "[13]

Unlike most of the Protestant leadership in his time, Colwell ran counter to the prevailing notions of the sanctity and inviolability of private property. He says, "The doctrine that property, real and personal, must, under all circumstances, remain inviolate, always under the ever watchful vigilance of the law, and its invaders subject to the severest penalties of dungeon or damages, may be very essential to the maintenance of our present social system, but totally disregards the consideration that labor, the poor man's capital, his only property, should, as his only means of securing a comfortable subsistence, be also under the special care and safeguard of the law."[14]

He also suggests that there is inequity in the rewards to the different participants in the industrial enterprise, ". . . the actual working of this mutual dependence has ever shown that a few men of superior mental power or attainments, or wealth or accidental advantages soon rise to positions of authority and control, which enable them to oppress those beneath them, and to draw to themselves, in various ways, and upon an infinity of pretexts, too large a proportion of the profits of labor."[15]

Although he was politically a Whig, later a Republican, an anti-Jacksonian, one is struck repeatedly by the non-doctrinaire quality of Colwell's thought. Again he displays the singular openness which is so much a mark of his life work. In a remarkable statement of his faith in the American experience, he comments in his Smithsonian article, "Our nation is the home of political truth: no possible discovery in that department of knowledge could give alarm here to the most timid, or threaten the peace of society."[16]

[12] *New Themes*, p. 190.
[13] *Ibid.*, p. 240.   [14] *Ibid.*, p. 242.
[15] *Politics for American Christians*, p. 23.
[16] *Princeton Review*, July 1842, pp. 368-369.

In this connection it is perhaps worthwhile to quote at some length his remarks concerning socialism, from the Notes on *New Themes*: "We belong not to that school which regards with a seemingly pious scorn all that passes under the name of socialism,—we are afraid to say even to the socialist, 'Stand by, for I am holier than thou.' We look upon the whole socialist movement as one of the greatest events of this age. We believe no man can understand the progress of humanity or its present tendencies who does not make himself, to some extent, acquainted with the teachings of socialism, and does not watch its movements. It is regarded by many, and especially by Protestant divines, as a war upon Christianity. This betrays ignorance, not only of socialism, but of human nature, and a sad misconception of Christianity itself. It is true, that a large mass of the socialists of France are not Christians, and that many of them openly express their disbelief; and it is just as true that many among us are not Christians who never scoff; and many more live in open and direct violation of Christ's injunctions of love and mercy, who make the loudest professions of Christianity. It is true enough that socialists are in error in many material or vital points, but they are earnestly seeking truth according to their opportunities and light."

He describes the socialists: ". . . they are a body of men who deem themselves injured; they point to the causes of their sufferings in the church and state, and demand a remedy; they insist that society is bound to amend their social position. They insist that no institutions can be wise or just which encourage or permit oppression—which fail of giving fair scope to industry and knowledge—which do not, as far as is practicable, secure to labor its proper reward, and to knowledge and enterprise an open field and due defence. It is true that those upon whom these doctrines have brought the epithet of socialists, have run into wild errors and mistaken theories, and many of them, perhaps, into absurd and crazy conceptions. But the mistakes of some, or all, by no means set aside or nullify the irrefutable truths they have announced. It is sheer nonsense to attempt to crush these truths by the cry of socialism; it is worse than nonsense not to know and appreciate truths which have already spread far and wide beyond the ranks of the socialists. . . .

"Although we totally dissent from the plans of reforming political institutions which the socialists have proposed, we cheerfully concede their having rendered a great service to social science by demonstrating the justice and necessity of reform. Their strong sympathy for human suffering throws an interest over many of their writings, very much in contrast with much of the theology, political economy, and politics of the present day. It would be a useful task to glance over pages thus in contrast, and entertain our readers with socialists pleading the cause of humanity, and Christians taking the part of wealth and power."

And finally, "Socialism can no longer be kept out of sight, and the subjects it involves can no longer be overlooked. That is the real triumph of socialism—it has raised the questions and forced on the discussion."[17]

Colwell sees an integral connection between Christianity and the revolution of the day—this is only three years after 1848—"All over Christendom, masses of men, long oppressed, are rising clamorous for relief, and a better condition. Light from Christianity has broken upon the night of their ignorance and helplessness, and they know that they are entitled to something better in the world's portion than has been alloted them. But the whole truth has not been told them, and their notions of remedy are wild and impracticable. This great movement should be met by Christians with rejoicing that light is at last penetrating such a dark mass of ignorance; and they should hasten to hold up to them the precepts of Christ, as meeting their entire case, and providing a complete remedy for all their grievances. But how is it that the outcries of these masses who have been hitherto strangers to the voice of Christian kindness, are now met by both Romanist and Protestant with a stern frown of rebuke and rejection? Christ is not preached to these poor, suffering millions as all-sufficient for them; much less do they anywhere behold any

[17] *New Themes*, pp. 359-365.

Christian movement in their behalf, which might at once explain to them their errors and show them their remedy. They are not sought for in the lanes and highways, and invited, nay, compelled to come into the feast of life; but they are rudely driven from the door as they present themselves, and are told that there is no room, no remedy, no alleviation; that the laws of property and the arrangements of society utterly forbid any amelioration of their sad condition."[18]

Colwell laments this tragedy of rejection by Christians. He says of the social reformers, "They find Christians arrayed against their plans, and they immediately array themselves against Christianity. The Christians may be right, and the reformers may be wrong, or there may be right and wrong on both sides, but what is chiefly to be lamented is that Christians suffer these controversies to assume a shape and aspect which have the appearance of infidelity being on the side of human well-being, while Christianity stands up in defence of ancient abuses, oppressive legislation, and social enormities."

What is the reason? Colwell asks the embarrassing question, "Is it that Christianity has so complicated her interests with those of governments, with the course of legislation, with the existing social evils, that Christians fear to have any of these touched lest the fabric of their respective churches may suffer?"[19]

III

As a man of wealth and power Colwell sometimes appears critical of mass democracy, of universal suffrage, and of the demagoguery, corruption, and incompetence that he felt were its consequences. His criticism, however, is not that of the typical Bourbon, who fears democracy because it may assail a vested interest of the privileged. It is rather that of one deeply committed to the well-being of the whole body politic, one who fears democracy's self-destruction. Interestingly enough, Colwell has no solution to propose except that somehow the politicians might be trained in a great university of

[18] *Ibid.*, pp. 194-195.   [19] *Ibid.*, pp. 267-268.

politics so that they might come to have the same kind of objectivity and independence of venal temptations which Colwell saw in the judiciary. He argues, ". . . the art of government and the whole mystery of legislation, are matters which require years of study and special opportunities to acquire, and it may be hoped that many will eventually be induced to qualify themselves suitably for public stations, as the only way to public favor. Let men with minds ripened by long study of these subjects, and stored with the lessons of history and experience, go forth yearly among their fellow citizens; and they will show the difference between the intuition of the demagogue and the actual attainments of the votary of truth."[20] This "university of politics" was what he proposed for the Smithsonian Institution.

Colwell had an understanding, unusual in his time, of the social, political, and economic causes of human distress, poverty, and suffering, which were more realistic than the theological and moral causes so frequently offered as explanations. He was concerned, of course, with the pauper on the dole, but even more with the working poor caught up in the grinding changes of the Industrial Revolution: "The beggar publishes his wants with busy clamor; the public has discovered the wretchedness of the inmates of its hospitals and almshouses; but who can find the abodes of modest want, of patient misery; who can number the poor whose food and raiment and shelter are far, far below the lowest standard of comfort; whose hopes for this world are cut off, and who have had no proper teaching for the world to come; who can tell their anguish who begin to feel their descent from a better condition into the abyss of helpless ruin, degradation and crime."[21]

Turning from England to America, he asks, "Have not we as a nation entered upon this career of over production? Are not our manufacturing establishments of the over-grown kind? Are not laborers crowded into them in multitudes? Are not single individuals and companies becoming the employers of thousands of their fellow men? Are not such laborers becom-

[20] *Princeton Review*, July 1842, p. 401.
[21] *Ibid.*, pp. 364-365.

ing more and more dependent upon their employers, as they become unfitted for other business, and as the present happy circumstances of the country, which now create a demand for labor are passing away? Human selfishness will display itself here as strongly as in England or France, as soon as it obtains an equal power over the bones and sinews of the working classes. Are not our cities already over-crowded with a redundant population, and is there not constantly exhibited in them a large mass of destitution and suffering? ... Now is the time that, availing ourselves of our positive advantages, we should adopt such measures as would secure our working population from the frightful destiny to which they are inevitably proceeding."[22]

Colwell did not see the solution in terms of an egalitarian division of human wealth. He was quite aware, probably too much so for today's egalitarian mood, of the inescapable differences among men; but he was committed to education and to economic development to the point where all could share in abundance. He exhibits a healthy caution about schemes of social betterment, "We freely admit there is a wide difference between pointing out an evil and finding a remedy. History abounds in cases where the remedy has proved worse than the disease."[23] But he displays a buoyant sense of Christian daring about the necessity for proposing and promoting change. He reminds us of Tillich's notions on intellectual justification when he says, "Happy are we indeed, that there is a way of salvation equally efficacious for errors of judgment as well as errors of life. No human scrutiny nor discrimination dare draw the line of doctrine or conduct which bounds the mercy of God in Christ."[24]

Colwell's analysis of the affinity between Protestantism and capitalism often prefigures that of Max Weber a half-century later. Speaking of the atmosphere commonly to be associated with Protestantism, he wrote, "... where Protestantism prevails, a free intellect but a hard and unrelenting selfishness,

[22] *Ibid.*, pp. 390, 391.
[23] *Princeton Review*, Jan. 1841, p. 129.
[24] *New Themes*, p. 43.

a devotion to mammon never before equaled, a grinding competition in all the pursuits of life, a race for wealth and power, in which the multitudes are distanced by a few, who become masters, and wield their power with unpitying severity; a scene of strife, of endless divisions, of hot discussions about trifles, of sectarian rivalry, in which every element of evil mingles, often without even a spice of human kindness, much less religious charity. Will the world adopt Christianity while this picture is before it? No ... the world sees much to admire in Christendom, but fearful evidence that neither the laws of brotherly kindness nor Christian charity control its institutions, social, political, or religious."[25]

"In the midst of all this turmoil, there arose a business morality exhibiting a punctuality, an adherence to contract, an honesty in the execution of trusts, a faithfulness to promises—far exceeding what the world had ever known. It was in fact, a necessity of business, without which by mutual consent, the immense transactions of which it was the bond, could never have been carried on. It borrowed some of its maxims from Christianity, and the whole of this vast movement had a tinge of Christian coloring thrown over it, yielding many of its deformities, but not sanctifying them."[26]

Assailing the clergy, Colwell goes on, "... we have too much reason to believe that a gradual compromise took place between the devotees of mammon and the ministers of Christ." In addition, "The whole expenditure of Protestant congregations of almost every denomination, for every purpose, religious and philanthropic, is derived, in a large degree, from those who are not acknowledged to be real disciples of Christ. ... We ask if there be not some danger in this co-mingling of the men of the world and the disciples of Christ in the business of the churches? Will not the former exercise an influence proportionate to their contributions?"

One of the results of this "hybrid system" "... is that the spirit of business which rules in the affairs of the world, has largely invaded the churches ... buildings are erected for the

[25] *Ibid.*, pp. 183-184.
[26] *Ibid.*, pp. 125-126.

worship of God where men are found to pay for them; ministers preach where men are found to pay them; congregations assemble in costly temples which they have contributed to build, or the services of which they contribute to maintain; ministers and missionaries are trained up and go forth where there is money provided to educate and maintain them; associations are created to promote every form of philanthropy where money can be had to sustain them. Every manner of good work is accomplished where money can be had to pay for it. A division of labor is established in religion and good works. Some furnish the head, some the heart, some the hands, and some the money. In these processes, the riches of this world become a ruling element, a foundation of all the system, and the cause of all the success . . . whence comes this money? It is not the voluntary offerings of crowds who come up cheerfully and pour their contributions into the treasury of the churches. It is levied, nay even exacted, by a system and under influences which do not permit denial; under such penalties as the givers are afraid to incur. It has become a great business to raise money for religious and benevolent purposes. A man may live in the house of another, if he pays the rent . . . he may occupy a respectable position in the church, and the society around it, if he contributes liberally, when called upon, to all the numerous demands which religious and charitable associations make upon him. It would be hard to conjecture how much of the money levied in this way would be got, if it were left to flow in solely by the spontaneous movements of the contributors. Certainly a very small portion. It is a regular system of business, this systematic benevolence; and, if this feature be taken away, the whole must fall to the ground, unless some other life be breathed into it."[27]

"Christianity," he says, "sits enthroned on high places, while poverty is struggling below. Christians find matters very well arranged for them; they are reaping the fruits of sobriety, economy, industry, and honesty, while the multitudes below are suffering the consequences of idleness, igno-

[27] *Ibid.*, pp. 126-131.

rance, vagrancy, intemperance, dishonesty, and crime. The complacency of the upper class is complete, but dangerous."

But, he says, "It is not Christianity to attend weekly in the stately church and well-cushioned pew, to hear expositions of difficult passages of scripture, while there is an utter failure to perform duties which are so plainly enjoined that the dullest intellect can comprehend."[28]

He is most critical, of course, of English Christianity, which confiscated the holdings of the Roman Catholic Church, at least one-fourth of which had been reserved for the relief of the poor, retained all of the holdings for the Church's own support, and left the poor to the tender, or not so tender, mercies of the state. "Thus arise the enormous revenues of the English bishops, which are a standing reproach to Christianity in a country where millions upon millions are groaning in poverty, with a clear right to all the relief these riches could afford."[29] He attacks the theories and proposals of the "Reverend Mr. Malthus" as a kind of predictable inhuman extension of the attitudes of English Christianity. He concludes his discussion of Malthusian population theory: "If this is not the doctrine of the Church of England in regard to the poor, it is the philosophy which has grown out of her neglect to teach and exemplify the great duty of Christian charity; if it is not her doctrine, it is the very essence and theory of her practice."[30]

IV

Although Colwell often lapses into the popular Protestant language of his time, the language of individual stewardship and generous philanthropy, he tends to think of the works of love in behalf of the socially distressed not as an optional act of generosity on the part of the fortunate, a common attitude in nineteenth-century Protestantism as well as today, but rather as a requirement of justice or a duty for Christians. In this he is reminiscent of the Roman Catholic Middle Ages

[28] *Ibid.*, pp. 199, 271.   [29] *Ibid.*, p. 141.
[30] *Ibid.*, p. 153.

and the Reformers, and prefigures one of the major thrusts of the Social Gospel. In his justification of the demands of the poor for redress of their grievances he approaches the Roman Catholic medieval notion that not only is charity owed as an obligation of justice to the poor but it is that which the poor themselves can demand and under certain circumstances take. He is thus very much out of step with the normative stewardship, "systematic benevolence," movement of his day.

Colwell tends to see Christian ethics as the religious ethic of Jesus rather than a religious ethic about Jesus.[31] But as all contemporary Christian ethicists are aware, even within a theological ethic about Jesus, the religious ethic of Jesus, though it may not be useful in terms of particular preceptive guidance, is still indicative of a posture of obedience, love, and suffering compassion. And this is true even when a Christian ethic is worked out in its most "contextual" form. Without this motif the Christian cannot move distinctively in this or any other ethical world. Superficially Colwell often sounds like a liberal proponent of "the teachings of Jesus" as a platform and program of Christian social ethic; actually, he is far more "contextual" than this.

But the most important thing about his concern with Jesus and the Bible is that he is deeply dedicated to going back to the Biblical resources in order to illuminate an area widely neglected by the Protestantism of his age and of the preceding generations.

And from this Biblical foundation Colwell moved repeatedly into the unchartered social reality of his time. Deeply committed to applying Christianity, he challenged and criticized the Church's failure to achieve social relevance. He was an exceptionally sophisticated economist, but he moved against the mainstream of the economic tradition that came to him. Most of the great economists who preceded him called themselves "political" economists. But, though Adam Smith had been deeply concerned about the welfare of the body politic, he had focused on the problem of the production of wealth, and many of his successors had been much more narrowly con-

[31] Paul Ramsey, *Basic Christian Ethics*, p. 23.

cerned with the technical "science" of economic development. Hence, few except for men like John Stuart Mill had given real attention to the word *political* in "political economy." Stephen Colwell speaks again and again of the general welfare, of the economic health of the whole society, of the well-being of the producers of wealth quite apart from the quantity and quality of production. In a much fuller sense than most of his predecessors and contemporaries, he was a *political* economist. Many of his schemes in the fields of tariffs, monetary policy, central banking, etc., were highly controversial in his time and some of them would find few supporters today. But those schemes were developed out of a concern for the general welfare. Speaking of trade, for example, Colwell argued, "All trade, both foreign and domestic, is but an instrument of industry; no theory of this instrument can be rightly formed, until the theory and laws of industry, and the rights of laborers, are known and established."[32] And again, "To shield its laborers is . . . the most important care of a nation; for labor is the most important item in the wealth of a nation, and the care of the laborer is the highest moral as well as political consideration which can claim the attention of a government."[33] Adam Smith had agreed that labor is the most important source of the wealth of the nation, but had not then felt it necessary to speak thus urgently of the care of the laborer.

Colwell's *New Themes* is in many ways a healthy anticleric attack. In a passage all too descriptive of our situation within the Church today, Colwell says, ". . . when the labors of the clergy are chiefly devoted to congregational management, the cause of Christ will suffer in proportion as the minister is successful."[34] He speaks of the tendency ". . . on the part of the people to flatter and pet their spiritual guides. Multitudes act as if they must be safe for the next world if they can secure the special favor or smiles of their pastors in this world. This has always been so obvious that even the most humble and modest among the clergy could not but see

[32] *Politics for American Christians*, p. 30.
[33] *Ibid.*, p. 34.
[34] *New Themes*, p. 207.

evidences of this servility; and none but the most firm and conscientious could help availing themselves of it."[35] And inevitably Colwell's protest is not only a challenge to the clergy to reform the ministry and the Church, but is also a call to a radical commitment to the lay apostolate on the part of all manner of Christians.

V

There are, of course, numerous points at which such a figure as Colwell must be subjected to criticism in any full length treatment of his work, especially when scrutinized from the vantage point of the mid-twentieth century. Such criticisms can simply be enumerated here. Like almost all Americans of his time, Colwell was a romantic optimist, though his optimism was tempered by his classical Christian background to a very significant degree. Presaging Reinhold Niebuhr's *Moral Man and Immoral Society*, Colwell sees the drag of public and group morality: "The morals of nations has always been far below the standard of the individuals composing them."[36] And his optimism is tempered also at the point of what Karl Mannheim has called the "sociology of knowledge," the Marxian "ideological taint," whereby everyone tends to think according to his own interest, to reflect in his intellectual formulations a deep-going and unconscious distortion in favor of his own interests and advantages in the body politic.

Like most of the leaders of the country at the time, Colwell was an American Messianist. He believed that God had somehow begun a new and radically discontinuous work on this continent, which was going to redound to the benefit of the whole race of mankind. But even this American Messianism was tempered by reality. "We know that our people of the Southern states hold men in slavery; we know that intemperate men in the North have, by indiscretion and wicked zeal, contributed to rivet more closely the chains of our poor Africans; [referring to the Abolitionists whom he opposed] we

[35] *Ibid.*, p. 209.
[36] *Princeton Review*, July 1842, pp. 375-376.

Stephen Colwell

acknowledge that we have as a nation sinned grievously against the poor Indians; we know that we have many other and great national sins, for which we must answer, one of the chief of which is a signal abuse of our civil and religious blessings. Every nation lies under heavy responsibilities. None have the right, however, to plead the oppressions of others in palliation of their own. We admit that many who are most loud in the condemnation of others, would, in the same circumstances, be guilty of the same acts themselves."[37]

Colwell believed unequivocally in the goal of a Christian America. His notions of the relation of Church and State, like most of those of the "theocrats" of his time, looked toward what Sydney Ahlstrom has called a quasi-Protestant establishment, in terms of the value patterns of legislation, introduction of Christianity into public education, etc. He was still intent on the *corpus Christianum*. But he was aware of the perils of too close an embrace between Church and State. Speaking of the decline of morals in Sweden, he pointed to the decline of evangelical Christianity as one of its causes: "The union of church and state is so close, and the embraces of government so strict, that it has produced a political religion, not a religious government. The form appears robust and imposing, but the *spirit* is departed."[38]

From his viewpoint, Christianity ". . . assumes that Christians will make Political Institutions ultimately effective in promoting human welfare; it regenerates the man, and leaves the man to regenerate the State; it works from the heart to the life. The grand result of Christian wisdom and love must, in the special respect in which we are regarding it, be developed upward from the individual to the masses, and be at last seen in the laws, manners, industry, and social institutions of a whole nation."[39]

His views on slavery were those of the conservatives of the northern Protestant Churches. He was anti-Abolitionist; he believed in the ultimate emancipation of the slaves but thought

[37] *Princeton Review*, January 1841, p. 124.
[38] *Princeton Review*, January 1843, p. 161.
[39] *Politics for American Christians*, p. 21.

their lot far better than that of millions of "free" working men in Europe and even America. At least in the view of the libertarian wing of both the Christian and political communities of that time—as witness the immediate absolutionists—the problem of technical, legal liberty did not loom large enough in Colwell's thinking.

Colwell's economic views are now dated and, of course, have been subjected to much criticism. His notions of charity and philanthropy and enhancement of the public good were sometimes colored by otherworldly considerations, i.e., that people could not hear the Gospel about eternal life until their temporal condition was improved; ergo, improve the temporal condition. But at other times he came close to an integral sense of the redemption of this world's life as an integral part of the Gospel in its own right. At one point he remarked that believers "have not realized that all the temporal, as well as the eternal interests of men, belong to their responsibilities."[40] His otherworldly inclinations are mild as compared to the views of his defender and fellow Presbyterian, the Reverend Dr. W. H. Ruffner, in whose argument the improvement of material well-being is seen far more as an evangelistic device.[41]

At times Colwell seems to be operating largely in the context of a notion of individual stewardship so characteristic of most of conservative Protestantism throughout the latter half of the century. To be sure, far more than most of his contemporaries, he saw problems of human distress as structural and social in origin, but he too tended to talk about their solution in terms of the voluntary goodness of good men and the re-creation of society in terms of the re-creation of individuals, good stewards of the resources which God had placed in their hands. At two points, however, he went well beyond this: (1) in his commitment to legislation embodying Christian understanding of social necessities—to be sure this legislation was to be sought by individual Christians; and (2) at the point where he appeals for the power of ecumenical Christian-

[40] *Ibid.*, p. 9.
[41] W. H. Ruffner, *Charity in the Clergy*, Philadelphia (Lippincott, Grambo and Co.), 1853.

ity which would be able to bring to bear social and political pressures of a kind not exhibited by the particular denominations in his own time.

"There should be a medium of communication, religious, political, and social, between the great Evangelical Denominations of this country, in which they might freely commune upon subjects of common interest to them all, to the whole country, and the whole family of man. Can men who hope to stand side by side in heaven refuse to stand side by side here, in the cause of their common Master, and especially in matters on which they could not differ in opinion? Such utter estrangement as forbids all coöperation for a common good, among those of different denominations, argues such a mutual enmity as is at utter variance with the injunction, '*to love thy neighbor as thyself.*' Can the indulgence of such a spirit be safe for any or for all?"[42]

VI

Both from what he said and what he did not say, Colwell leaves us a significant legacy. First of all, contemporary Protestantism finds itself, almost a century after the emergence of the Social Gospel, still riddled with individualistic notions of Christian obligation and discipleship and an inadequate theology of the "political" character of Christianity. This is paralleled by an inadequate notion of the political character of the operation of our society. On this subject Colwell has much to say to us. As a *political* economist he saw human problems in political terms. We must go well beyond Colwell because, in a society of mixed and diversified pressure groups, the very term *political* needs to be stretched far beyond a narrow application to the State. When Colwell used the term *politics*, he was thinking of the State. But he was already working in a context of voluntary associations that grew rapidly in his own lifetime and, since that time, have become a fixed part of the American system. They have in many ways evolved into agencies for pressure group activity across the whole body

[42] *Politics for American Christians*, p. 71.

politic. New political theory needs to be developed, and long overdue is a new understanding of the political pressure group character of the corporate Church and the churches which make up the Church. The development of such an understanding must be coupled with a rigorous examination of the possibilities and limitations imposed on the political pressure group activity of the Churches by the nature of the Gospel itself. As Protestants become enamored of the possibilities of pressure group power, it will be all too easy to succumb to the perilous temptations facing all wielders of such power and especially to those facing men and groups who exercise power in presumed obedience to a divine mandate.

As we have said, Colwell thought largely in terms of a Christian America, which for him meant Protestant America, a Protestant *corpus Christianum*. Appropriate as his attitudes may have been to the middle decades of the nineteenth century—and their appropriateness was even then rapidly being undermined—they must be seriously revised before they can become applicable to the latter decades of the twentieth. We have no adequate theory of the role of Christians and the role of the Churches and the ecumenical Church in a religiously and culturally pluralistic society. For a person working in his time, Colwell was in many ways sensitive to this problem. As he put it, "The relations of our national and state governments with the Christian religion, remain undefined and undetermined. Our country is deemed a part of Christendom. . . . No religion can be established among us by law; but we recognize Christianity by our officially proclaimed fasts, in the form of our oaths, in the enjoined abstinence from secular labors on the Sabbath, in the punishment of blasphemy, and in the appointment of chaplains in the Army, Navy, and legislative halls . . . in truth, nearly every form of worship except Judaism and Christianity are virtually excluded by our laws . . . how far we are bound to enforce the observance of the Christian Sabbath, and especially against those, who, like the Jews, do not believe in it as a divine institution, is yet unsettled. How far the rights of conscience are to be respected, is equally unknown: for men may profess to believe anything, and warp their faith and consciences at will. This great but delicate subject remains to be explored in its various aspects, and it demands a solemn regard for truth, and powers of discrimination of the highest order, and exercised under the most favorable circumstances."[43]

We have no adequate theory of the role of the Church in a world which has become thoroughly secularized, even in its religiosity. We must work out the meaning of Barth's injunction that Christians should take their Christianity anonymously into the world of public affairs. But one of the problems which now perplexes both the community-at-large and Christians in our country is the absence of an ethical and cultural ethos of sufficient homogeneity to provide direction to our pluralistic society.

Colwell, more than most of the Christians and other economic thinkers of the nineteenth century, was interested in economic justice in terms of the whole society sharing in plenty and abundance rather than in terms of an egalitarian distribution of the society's resources. This has proved to be the "wave of the future" for America. And since America now lives with an economy of widely, though far from universally, experienced abundance we find ourselves with a hopelessly inadequate theology of plenty. How can we define the good life in Christian terms in an era of comfort, a time of almost universal access to luxury and lushness, of physical and even cultural experience? This is a task which awaits creative Christian investigation and formulation.

Colwell's profound commitment to a political economy in which the whole of the nation would share in economic wellbeing is not adequate for our own time. Christians today are unable to escape the problems of planning for the development and integration and balance of a global economy. Just as Colwell was not willing to see groups or individuals sacrificed to a vigorous and unhampered flow of economic resources within the nation, so today we can no longer stand by and see groups or individuals or whole nations or areas sacrificed to a

[43] *Princeton Review*, July 1842, pp. 382-383.

vigorous and unhampered but humanly heedless flow of economic resources across the face of the world. We find ourselves faced with an inadequate theory of international economic integration and this is one of the major tasks of Christian ethics as of all other ethics in our time.

Though Colwell was not working out any articulate theology of the laity, he was playing out the role of a lay theologian and of a lay churchman with great sophistication. His anti-cleric sentiments displayed a sure feeling for the reality of full-blown Christianity. Contemporary Protestantism is run by multitudes of clerical executive-types who are supervising buildings and programs and administering enormously complex and financially successful structures of life within the Church, but again and again neglecting the possibilities for calling forth the lay apostolate in the world. That vocation is an urgent task of the Christian community for today and tomorrow.

Finally, Colwell, unlike many of his fellow Christian prophets in every age, was not so naïve as to think that good will and good intentions, a spirit of sweet if fuzzy-minded charity and compassion, were enough. Colwell knew that mastery and sophistication in the area of theory and fact, involving ceaseless dialogue with the world's wisdom, were necessary before any respectable Christian proposals could be put forth. Thus we have from him a heritage of devoted commitment, dedication, and concentration to technical and intellectual sophistication which we shall neglect to our hurt.

We shall not be faithful to our inheritance from Colwell if we take over his proposals and his analyses as if they were adequate for our time. He can help us most in two ways: first, in his singular openness and receptivity on the one hand to the Biblical and Church tradition and its possibilities of pouring out new treasures for a new day and, at the same time, to the actual structure, changes, and novelty within social reality. Secondly, he can help us as we examine the direction in which this sophisticated and sensitive Christian mind sought for solutions to the problems of his own time. It will be for us as for him a "political" direction. Obedience to the God who has been "political" with us, to the point of being with us in Jesus Christ to make community a possibility requires no less. We are heirs to that which Colwell so notably broke open and so modestly announced, "We propose to enter a little upon this examination, not with the hardihood of expecting to offer any solution of the difficulty, but merely to make a few suggestions—to mark out a line of thought, which, followed up by others more capable, may lead to profitable results."[44]

[44] *New Themes,* p. 9.

VIII. HENRY VAN DYKE (1852-1933)

*Many-sided Litterateur**

BY ROLAND MUSHAT FRYE

IN 1906, *The Illustrated Outdoor News* listed the ten greatest living sportsmen in America, and there, along with Theodore Roosevelt, was the Rev. Henry van Dyke. That fact indicates something of the diversity of van Dyke's career. He had already acquired national stature in several fields. Between 1884 and 1906, thirty-three books appeared over his name, some of them best-sellers; from 1883 to 1899 he served as minister of the Brick Presbyterian Church in New York City, and was regarded as one of the great preachers of his time; in 1902 he was elected Moderator of the General Assembly of the Presbyterian Church, and led both in the revision of doctrinal standards and in the provision of a book of common worship for Presbyterian use; since the fall of 1899 he had been Murray Professor of English Literature at Princeton. After Woodrow Wilson's election to the presidency of the United States, van Dyke was appointed chief of the diplomatic mission to the Netherlands, thus adding another dimension to his career; after the American entrance into the first World War he was commissioned a chaplain in the Navy at the age of sixty-five. Throughout his life he was an active outdoorsman, hunting and fishing all over North America and into much of the rest of the world.

* The major study of van Dyke's life and work is *Henry van Dyke: A Biography* (New York: Harper and Brothers, 1935), by his son Tertius van Dyke. This volume includes an extensive bibliography. Henry van Dyke's writings are available in the Avalon Edition of the *Works* (18 volumes; New York: Scribner's, 1920-1927). *The van Dyke Book* (New York: Scribner's, 1905, 1920) is an anthology prepared by Edwin Mims and revised by M. Struthers Burt. Henry van Dyke's most sustained effort in literary criticism was his *Studies in Tennyson* (New York: Scribner's, 1920); his *Essays in Application* (New York: Scribner's, 1905) contains typical pieces on both literary and cultural subjects.

HENRY VAN DYKE

A man of such varied talents is not easy to appraise, and his very versatility may make it more difficult to give him his due in any one of the fields of his interest, for we are after all a culture of specialists, devoted to specialism, and tend to be either uncomfortable or suspicious about the generalist. We are thus tempted to dismiss van Dyke as a gadfly, but we are prevented from doing so by the level of his achievements, which were quite substantial in each of these areas, though they were not preeminent in any.

Other problems arise, and these may be summarized in the famous remark attributed to Woodrow Wilson that Henry van Dyke was the only man he had ever known who could strut sitting down. Whether Wilson originated the remark I do not know, but it has been applied to van Dyke so frequently as to show that there was at least widespread suspicion of pride and pomposity in the man. But again, as with the suspicion of his versatility, we are drawn up short of an unequivocally adverse judgment by the presence of other evidence: frequent references by those who knew him to his lack of stuffiness; his wit; and the wide range of his friendships. Perhaps the "strutting" was only the physical posture of a small man—we remember that when a newsreel photographer said that he wanted to get a hundred feet of van Dyke, the latter replied that there were only five feet six inches to get—and we must be careful not to regard what may have been merely a physical compensation as though it were a basic psychological trait.

Again, there is the evidence of the man's style: his prose is highly mannered, moving through neat and geometrically arranged parallels and antitheses to conclusions that seem so inevitable within the context of the author's rhetoric that we are inclined at points to wonder whether the conclusions were not dictated more by the requirements of style than by the inner logic of the problem. We do not condemn him for writing clearly, which he always did, or for writing well, which he often did, but one begins to suspect that the highly mannered prose is almost an end in itself, and one even wonders whether van Dyke is not too often imitating his own best moments.

His prose style is like a uniform into which virtually every idea is fitted, regardless of size or shape. But again we cannot dismiss van Dyke as an empty rhetorician, for he had much of value to say, and he often said it quite well. Had the Church and the world paid more attention to him, both would have been spared much grief.

I think we may find the heart of this man's paradox in the remark of his son that "he had the soul of a poet and many qualities of the colonel of a cavalry regiment." That combination is not a common one, especially if we fill in the spectrum with a range of talents appropriate to the popular preacher, the Church statesman, the literary critic, the college professor, and the wartime diplomat—and when we have completed that list, we are back where we started, wondering how to appraise a man who was all these things as well as one of the ten great American sportsmen of his time! The combination was unique, and the man virtually so. The best I can hope to offer is a brief account of his life, and an evaluation of his place as a man of letters.

I

Henry van Dyke's long life began in 1852, in a Presbyterian manse in Germantown, Pennsylvania, and ended eighty years later in his handsome Princeton mansion, "Avalon." His connection with Princeton Seminary in any official way was restricted to his three-year B.D. work there, culminating in his graduation with the class of 1877, but as an undergraduate at Princeton College he had early established a kind of relationship with the Seminary, evidenced by the presence among his papers of a poster offering $50.00 reward for the persons who, as a prank, absconded with the Seminary gate in 1871, and in the margin of the reward poster is van Dyke's note: "They didn't catch us."

After his graduation from the Seminary, he spent several years abroad, studying and traveling in Europe. His first pastorate was in the Congregational Church of Newport, from which he was called to the pulpit of the Brick Presbyterian

Church, New York, in 1883. It was a remarkable testimony to his courage (and perhaps also to his cocksureness) that he at once established the principle that no important action be taken in the Church without the unanimous agreement of the elders in session, and in view of the fact that he accomplished much even under that rule, van Dyke must have been an exceptionally effective diplomat and strategist. His sermons at first appear to have been largely serious, but in 1886, he discovered almost as if by accident that he had a remarkable facility for using humor to serious effect, and from this time forward he made effective use of humor in his speaking.

His preaching interests and his concerns as a clergyman were consistently focused upon modern problems and the Church's relation to them. Being himself a convinced evolutionist, he tried to lead the Church into a confident cooperation with the expanding sciences. Churchmen, he said, should not regard science as a rival and a threat, so that they "tremble at every new theory and watch the progress of science with jealousy and mistrust." In one of his early sermons he sought to instill a proper understanding: "But why so restless, so fearful, so petulant, O Church of Christ bought with his blood? Stand firm and confident in thy faith. Enjoy the peace that Jesus has given thee. Say to every earnest seeker in every sphere of human thought, God speed, for all truth is God's truth and must be one. His revelation in Nature cannot contradict his revelation in Christ."

Like his father, he felt that doctrinal formulas should be subjected to fact, and not vice versa. "Let all ascertained and accepted facts," his father had preached at Princeton Seminary in 1882, "all demonstrated truth, be cast into the furnace: if our creed cannot walk into it without the smell of fire on its clothes, *let it be burned.*" If more clergymen had held to the position of the van Dykes, the Church today would have the reputation for honesty that it is still struggling to regain and that was denied to it by the bigotry of a vociferous minority of clergy and laity and the mute acquiescence of many others. As in the early years of his ministry, so too in the last decade of his life Henry van Dyke denounced "the declaration of war between science and religion," along with the fundamentalist efforts to enforce obscurantism upon the Church at large. In one of his original stories, he wrote that when it was known that a sinner had been accepted into heaven because he had clean hands and a pure heart, there began at once a contest between soap-makers as to which brand was "the only infallible soap" without which one could never hope to enter the Kingdom of God.

II

One of van Dyke's major aversions was the doctrine of infant damnation, to which, of course, there was linked the doctrine of reprobation in general, and it was in no small measure due to his efforts that these matters were reconsidered in the creedal revisions at the turn of the century. In the famous heresy trial involving Charles A. Briggs of Union Seminary in New York, van Dyke was one of Briggs' staunch defenders, though he did not claim to agree with his theology. In general he felt that the heresy-hunting of the literalists was doing the Church far more harm than good, and he viewed the literalists' crusades as offering men "the stone of controversy" instead of the bread of life. He was unwilling to make any such affirmations about the original Biblical manuscripts as the fundamentalists wished all to make, and he wrote that for the Church to accept the fundamentalist position would "result in the condemnation of a very large number of our ministers, including myself and others, who accept the Bible as it is as the word of God and our only infallible rule of faith and practice, but know nothing about the 'original autographs' and are not willing to make any affirmation concerning them." As for the labels "fundamentalist" and "modernist," he wrote that "they only becloud the issue and confuse the minds of plain folks. The real difference (which I pray may not become a division) is between the *Literalists*, who interpret the Scripture according to the letter, and the *Liberals*, who interpret according to the spirit."

In all events, van Dyke opposed the imposition of an abso-

HENRY VAN DYKE

lute uniformity which, he said, "in any association of men means the absence of thought or the presence of hypocrisy." In that phrase he demonstrated his ability to pose issues in words so clear that few could escape the significance involved. He clearly saw that the heresy-hunters would drive many of the best minds and most honest spirits out of the Church and would in the long run damage traditional Christianity rather than reinforce it. "Heresy trials," he wrote, "are the delight of the ungodly and the despair of religion."

In his attitude toward the literalists van Dyke has been amply supported by history, but there must be some suspicion as to the depth of theological acumen in a man who could say of President Eliot of Harvard, who was at most a Unitarian, that " 'faith in the eternal' on Eliot's lips signifies just what 'come to Jesus' does," and there must also be some suspicion of the kind of preaching van Dyke did at Harvard when we learn that President Eliot remarked after hearing him that "that sermon could do no harm." The point is that van Dyke was at times theologically naïve, not that he was a Unitarian, for his essential adherence to the central Christian doctrines seems to have been above suspicion.

Van Dyke regarded himself as an "adventurous conservative," and though he did not hold what our generation regards as a sophisticated social gospel, he was active in so many social and political causes while in his Brick Church pulpit that the *New York Sun* proposed that he run for mayor of the city and so settle once and for all whether he would be in or out of politics. He preached against the existence of slums on top of which "we build our houses of comfort as it were on the thin crust of hell," he fought for the institution of Civil Service as a corrective of the spoils system, sought an international copyright law to prohibit unscrupulous though respectable American publishers from pirating the works of foreign authors, actively campaigned for conservation of natural resources, courageously opposed United States imperialism in the Philippines in the face of charges of un-Americanism, and in later years opposed Prohibition. As United States minister to Holland, he displayed a willingness for political and social involvement, which he thought of as but another aspect of his ministry, as he actively sought international arbitration of disputes, while after war came to Europe he tirelessly cared for refugees from all nations. When the United States entered the war, van Dyke, though thirty years over the age limit, obtained a naval chaplain's commission and even sought, though without success, to be given combat duty. Then, during the presidential campaign of 1928, van Dyke vigorously attacked the position of those who would deny the presidency to a Roman Catholic. Such a man can scarcely be dismissed as socially neutral and politically unconcerned, but when asked whether he belonged to any reform societies he replied that the only such societies to which he belonged were the Christian Church and the United States of America.

III

His major influence throughout his career was exerted through his mastery of words, whether the words were spoken or written, and he addressed himself to virtually every issue upon which his interests touched. In a very real sense, he squandered his talents, for by writing too much he failed to realize the promise held out by his abilities. Though he undoubtedly had literary gifts, he seems to have found methods for mass-producing his own talents, so as to pour out books and articles for a wide audience that found him both easy and pleasant to read. Literarily, he simply spread himself too thin, and as a result we find it difficult to take him very seriously today. *The Other Wise Man* is skillfully executed, but of no more lasting literary worth than most best sellers. Many of the outdoor tales have signal vitality—and Brander Mathews, the critic, said that van Dyke interested him in nature for the first time—but they are again only very commendable works of the second or third rank. Some of the poetry is good, and though it is radically different from most twentieth-century verse, it is a delight to read such poems as "The Maryland Yellow-Throat" and "The Whip-Poor-Will," to name only two.

HENRY VAN DYKE

Van Dyke himself regarded *The Book of Common Worship of the Presbyterian Church* as his most important contribution, and in this judgment he was, I think, quite correct. He served as chairman of the committee of 1903, which produced the work, and of the committee of 1928, which revised it. In both committees, his influence was the decisive factor in the production of a volume of varied forms for public worship that has proved of great benefit throughout the major forms of American Presbyterianism. *The Book of Common Worship* is a masterly achievement, blending traditional and modern prayers into a rich texture whose value to the Church can scarcely be overestimated. The marriage service, the five litanies, and many of the prayers are van Dyke's own contribution, but his fine literary discrimination marks the entire volume just as Thomas Cranmer's marks the Episcopal *Book of Common Prayer.* Both volumes are literary masterpieces.

It was here, rather than in his own original and critical writings, that van Dyke's lasting influence may be found. In his own writing he was too often mannered and even affected, but in the editing of the Presbyterian service book his wide reading of the great English writers and his undeniable literary taste made him the ideal editor and arbiter. On this subject there is surely need for study, and an excellent book could be produced as a result. "Truth and goodness," van Dyke declared, "are not complete until beauty is added to the trinity of excellence," and it is principally due to his efforts that American Presbyterianism has available a service book containing varied and beautiful orders of worship for all occasions in the life of the Church.

IV

For twenty-three years, counting his leave-of-absence as diplomat and naval chaplain, van Dyke occupied the Murray Professorship of English Literature at Princeton University, and it was his persistent contention that the task of an English professor was the teaching of reading. He had no developed philosophy of aesthetics, and he wrote no scholarly magnum opus in his field: he concentrated upon teaching his students to read and appreciate great literature, and in that effort he would appear to have been considerably more successful than most. It is doubtful that van Dyke could, in 1963, attain the status of a major chair at Princeton or any other university of comparable stature, for the new standards of academic advancement put a premium on scholarly and critical production in a way that would exclude van Dyke. It is true that he produced a great deal: the bibliography of his books numbers over seventy items, not counting articles and reviews. Indeed, he produced too much, for no man can write that much and write it well, and with the exception of certain isolated pieces he may best be seen as a popularizer.

To say this is not to damn the man. The ideas he sought to popularize were generally sound. In his moral teaching, he was consistently virile in his Christianity, shunning both sentimental tripe and Pharasaic prudishness. When a dear old lady wrote to rebuke him because she heard that he sometimes smoked, he replied: "Dear Madam: It is not true that I sometimes smoke: I *always* smoke."

Though he was scarcely a profound critic, van Dyke's view of literature was essentially sound. In the haste of composition he sometimes blurred the distinction, but he knew well enough the difference between telling a story and preaching a sermon. "After all, what profit is there in a sermon after a great story," he asked. Quite correctly, he criticized the proletarian fiction of the first third of the twentieth century because it unduly imposed a kind of preachiness in its writing: "I do not believe in 'proletarian literature' any more than I believe in 'capitalistic literature.'" His criticism at this point was based in literary criteria, not in political prejudice, though he has sometimes been misinterpreted on this issue.

Misinterpreted, too, was his criticism of Sinclair Lewis, and Lewis himself seems to have been willing to capitalize on a somewhat warped version of the remarks by this "most amiable old gentleman." Actually, van Dyke's criticism of Lewis concerned his literary narrowness, not his literary morality, for he clearly stated that his objections to Lewis' work "were not

Henry van Dyke

based on moral grounds, but on literary and philosophic grounds. An out and out pessimist cannot be a really great writer any more than an out and out optimist can be." To criticize Lewis on these grounds showed courage, at a time when the entire literary climate was becoming increasingly pessimistic and proletarian. Similarly in poetry, van Dyke attacked the growing reliance upon free verse and the abandonment of metrical discipline, though he defended metrical innovations, for "metre and rhyme have a deep relation to the rhythm of human emotion, of which I grow more sure the less I can explain it. Some call them a bondage, but the natural harmony of such laws makes for true freedom." Again, his judgment was sound.

In all his writing, van Dyke represented the genteel tradition, but he was far more democratic than many of those who represented the new creative and critical movements in literature by which the genteel tradition was overwhelmed. In van Dyke's view, the common reader was to be elevated to the level of appreciating good writing, and the good writer was to make himself intelligible to the common reader. The elevation of taste as well as conduct was the aim of the genteel tradition, but since the turn of the century other forces have been at work. These forces have come to dominate literature, though their influence seems now to be at least beginning to wane. Van Dyke opposed the new tendency to make culture a coterie province, and he described certain emerging twentieth-century characteristics in a lively and polemic fashion:

"Their mark is eccentricity. Their aim is the visible separation of the cultured person from the common herd. His favorite poet must be one who is caviar to the vulgar. His chosen philosopher must be able to express himself with such obscurity that few, if any, can comprehend him. He must know more than anyone else about the things that are not worth knowing, and care very passionately for the things that are not usually considered worth caring about. He must believe that Homer and Dante and Milton and the Bible have been very much overrated, and carefully guard himself, as Oscar Wilde did in the presence of the ocean, from giving away to sentiments of vulgar admiration. His views of history must be based upon the principle of depreciating familiar heroes and whitewashing extraordinary villains. He must measure the worth of literature by its unpopularity, and find his chief joy in the consciousness that his tastes, his opinions, and his aspirations are unlike those of common people."

No polemic statement is ever altogether fair, but in this passage van Dyke has struck home on many targets. The genteel tradition was essentially democratic, but what followed it was often the height of snobbism, even when it was the snobbery that regards vulgarity as sophistication.

V

It is here, perhaps, that we today stand at the farthest remove from van Dyke. The literature of our age avidly exploits the new, the different, the sensational, the exotic, even the aberrant and the perverse, and even where it does not follow the well-beaten path of novelty, it still hesitates to say the obvious. Not so van Dyke, who was not afraid of saying something obvious if he could put it in a finely wrought phrase. "It is by forgetting platitudes," he wrote, "that men and nations are ruined"; and he was doubtless correct, but he makes himself look rather silly when he blares his verbal trumpets and parades his platitudes as though they were great and original ideas.

We can only regard as pompous such expressions as these: "Individualism is a fatal poison. But individuality is the salt of common life," and "What we call society is very narrow. But life is very broad." There is value in both expressions, but van Dyke's mannerisms as a writer often call attention away from the validity of what he is trying to say. Recalling Wilson's remark, we may say that van Dyke's prose also struts, and that, when that prose would introduce us to the common wisdom of the race, it often does so in a manner so pretentious as to seem a parody of itself.

In the following passage we see a perfect example of the

manner in which rhetorical style and structure become ends in themselves, with the result that the first three sentences are false, and while the climactic fourth sentence contains some basic truth, the very style focuses attention upon its pretentiousness rather than its truth:

"A great general like Napoleon may be produced in a military school. A great diplomatist like Metternich may be developed in a court. A great philosopher like Hegel may be evolved in a university. But a great man like Washington can come only from a pure and noble home."

Time after time van Dyke undercuts himself as he does in this passage, but, at his best, his high moral seriousness and wide learning combine in fluent expression to say things to which we can still listen with profit and pleasure. But if we listen very long, we become tired.

But perhaps we are too harsh on van Dyke. Few writers can stand the scrutiny of later generations, and if a man has served his own time well, that in itself is a great deal. There can be no doubt of van Dyke's contributions to his contemporaries in the course of a long and useful life, and many of those contributions (most notably the assaults upon literalism and the production of *The Book of Common Worship*) still benefit us in a direct way. His basic ideas were sound, if not original, and he managed to present these ideas in a form that was not only palatable but even attractive to large numbers of people. He served his Church, his nation, and his University with integrity and distinction in the most varied capacities over the course of eighty years, during which time he played an honorable part in almost every major event.

What is the present significance of Henry van Dyke? It is, I think, in his vision, and in his attempt to hold together the triad of truth, goodness, and beauty, though we must be careful to note that truth for him contained both scientific and religious aspects. He sought a viable openness to new scientific understanding on the part of traditional Christianity, a flexibility of relationship, a means of riding the waves of new knowledge. He openly faced these problems, and though the solutions he proposed were generally accepted, they did not gain sufficient support to save the Church from much controversy and bitterness. In regard to beauty, he insisted (and would to God that more clergymen would follow him here) that beauty in art and worship should be merged—indeed, must be merged—in the modern Church, and here he contributed much in a liturgical way. His own writings are less successful, and though some of his verse and of his prose on nature may well be regarded as minor classics, he was neither a great creative writer nor a great critic.

Van Dyke's largest significance for us is not to be found in what he wrote or accomplished, but rather in the fact that he saw so clearly that the modern world challenges the modern Church with the necessity of achieving a viable and Christian sophistication. The frontier was dead, and a new urban society was emerging with which the Christian could deal only in terms of a Christian urbanity, which van Dyke attempted to achieve, not always with success. He attempted, like Robert Louis Stevenson, to be an "adventurer in a velvet jacket," and words which he wrote of Stevenson may well serve as the fittest summary of his own aims in life:

"On one side are the puritans who frown at a preacher in a velvet jacket; on the other side the pagans who scoff at an artist who cares for morals. Yet surely there is a way between the two extremes where an artist-man may follow his conscience with joy to deal justly, to love mercy, and to walk humbly with his God. And having caught sight of that path, though he may trace it but dimly and follow it stumblingly, surely such a man may say to his fellows, 'This is the good way; let us walk in it.'"

IX. FRANCIS JAMES GRIMKÉ
(1850-1937)

Christian Moralist and Civil Rights*

BY CLIFTON E. OLMSTEAD

IT was Sunday, October 26, 1913. In Washington, D.C., the congregation of the Fifteenth Street Presbyterian Church sat in silence as the words of a beloved pastor, now, at a venerable sixty-three, in the thirty-fifth year of his ministry, came winging their way into mind and heart. Dr. Francis James Grimké stood erect in the pulpit, his serene countenance testified to his senior citizenship. His pince-nez spectacles, tilted at the appropriate angle, gave added distinction to a firm but compassionate face marked by the personal sorrows and victories of more than half a century. The sermon, bright but never florid, was intensely moving in its pathos and sincerity; it bespoke the bitter experience of a downtrodden race striving to greet the dawn of its social redemption. There had been heartbreak and defeat, but there had also been progress. The future seemed auspicious.

"The struggle before us is a long and hard one," prophesied the pastor, "but with faith in God, and faith in ourselves, and indomitable perseverance, and the purpose to do right, in spite of the forces that are arrayed against us, we need have no fears as to the ultimate result. Success is sure to crown our efforts. We are not always going to be behind; we are not always going to be discriminated against; we are not always

---

* See *The Works of Francis James Grimké* (Washington: The Associated Publishers, 1942, 4 volumes); *Anniversary Address on the Occasion of the Seventy-Fifth Anniversary of the Fifteenth Street Presbyterian Church, Washington, D.C.* (Washington: R. L. Pendleton, 1916), by Francis James Grimké; *The Journal of Charlotte L. Forten* [Mrs. Francis James Grimké] (New York: Collier Books, 1961), edited by Ray Allen Billington; *Theodore Weld, Crusader for Freedom* (New Brunswick: Rutgers University Press, 1950), by Benjamin P. Thomas; *Records* of the Presbytery of the District of Columbia i (1823-1849); *Records* of the Presbytery of Washington City i (1870-1878); x (1916-1920); xv (1936-1946).

going to be denied our rights. For, as Sojourner Truth said, 'God is not dead.' And some day, in His own good time, the right will triumph."[1]

I

No smug complacency prompted Pastor Grimké's sanguine hope. His conviction that the lot of the Negro must and would be improved had been baptized in the fire of civil conflict and the smoldering antipathies that lived on in the aftermath of war. He was the scion of two traditions, master and slave, and he bore in his body all the qualities of that passion that characterized intersocial relationships in the antebellum South. His sire, Henry Grimké, member of a prominent South Carolinian family, had compelled Nancy Weston, a slave, to serve him as wife. Three children, Archibald Henry, Francis James, and John, were born of the union.[2]

Francis Grimké was born on November 4, 1850. He was reared in Charleston, South Carolina, first by his father and then, after the father's death, by his half-brother, E. Montague Grimké. At the outset of the Civil War, Montague attempted to enslave Francis, though his father had provided in his will that Francis should be free. The young Negro lad escaped, however, and for a time served an officer in the Confederate Army. Two years later, when Francis was on a visit to Charleston, his half-brother had him thrown into the "workhouse," where he became seriously ill and might have died had it not been for the ministrations of his mother. No sooner had Francis regained his health than his half-brother sold him to a Confederate officer who held him in bondage until the close of the war.[3]

Through the good offices of two benefactors, the years immediately following Appomattox found Francis and his brother Archibald in the North in pursuit of an education. Arrangements were made for them to attend Lincoln University in Oxford, Pennsylvania; they graduated in 1870, Francis

[1] *The Works of Francis James Grimké*, I, 513.
[2] *Ibid.*, p. vii.   [3] *Ibid.*, p. viii.

at the head of his class. Archibald went on to Harvard Law School and to a distinguished career as lawyer, editor, author, diplomat, and public servant.[4]

During the year before their graduation, the two brothers made a providential encounter with two famous aunts on their father's side who had long since removed from Charleston to become Quaker abolitionists in Philadelphia and who, therefore, had no knowledge of the boys' existence. Angelina Grimké, now married to the eminent abolitionist Theodore Dwight Weld, and her older sister, Sarah, had chanced to read in a Boston newspaper of the enviable record maintained at Lincoln University by a Negro youth named Grimké. Knowing that the surname Grimké was unique to Charleston, Mrs. Weld wrote to Francis for an explanation. Later she visited the university and publicly declared her relationship to the two brothers. Thereafter she and her husband treated them as members of the family and gave them much-needed financial assistance.[5]

For a time Francis pursued the study of law at Lincoln University and later at Howard University in Washington, D.C. Failing to find satisfaction in this calling, he determined at length to prepare himself for the Christian ministry. In the fall of 1875 he matriculated in Princeton Theological Seminary.

II

At Princeton he roomed in the dormitories and encountered little if any racial prejudice.[6] Here he came under the tutelage of such illustrious scholars as Charles Hodge, Archibald Alexander Hodge, Caspar Wistar Hodge, and William Henry Green.[7] He never departed from the thorough methods of study that he learned at their feet. A year after his graduation in 1878, James McCosh, President of Princeton College, wrote

[4] Charlotte L. Forten, *The Journal of Charlotte L. Forten*, pp. 38-39.
[5] Benjamin P. Thomas, *Theodore Weld, Crusader for Freedom*, pp. 256-258.
[6] Grimké, *op.cit.*, I, 526.
[7] Orion C. Hopper, compiler, *Biographical Catalogue of Princeton Theological Seminary, 1815-1954*, pp. xxiii-xxiv.

that "the late Dr. Hodge reckoned him equal to the ablest of his students."[8] In another letter, written in 1881, Dr. McCosh testified: "While here he convinced all the professors under whom he studied as a young man of a very high order of talent and of excellent character."[9]

Despite the demands of his ministerial studies, the young seminarian found time for an affair of the heart. The lady was Charlotte Forten, member of a wealthy and influential Negro family of Philadelphia. Her grandfather, James Forten, had amassed a fortune through his sailmaking business and was widely respected as a man of high moral principles whose life was dedicated to public service, especially to the elevation of the Negro.[10] Charlotte carried on the family tradition in her early career as a teacher and author of considerable repute. Both before and after her marriage to Mr. Grimké, on December 19, 1878, she labored tirelessly for the people of her race. Her husband found her a constant strength in his own crusade for social reform. Theirs was an idyllic marriage, nurtured by tender and loving devotion, and saddened only by the loss of their child in 1880.[11] When Mrs. Grimké passed away in 1914 after a long and painful illness, her husband could write with perfect candor: "She was a most devoted companion and a woman in whom there was no guile. And yet with all her sweetness, gentleness and rare delicacy of nature, she was a woman of great strength of character. She could take a stand and hold it against the world."[12]

III

Francis Grimké's public ministry began with a call to the nation's capital. There, in 1841, the Fifteenth Street Presbyterian Church had been organized under the leadership of the Reverend John F. Cook in order that there might be an adequate ministry to the colored people of Washington.[13] By the

---

[8] Grimké, *op.cit.*, I, x. [9] *Ibid.*
[10] Forten, *op.cit.*, pp. 17-19. [11] *Ibid.*, pp. 37-38.
[12] Grimké, *op.cit.*, III, 5.
[13] Presbytery of the District of Columbia, *Records*, I (October 6, 1841, and May 4, 1842), 305-306, 313.

1870's the congregation, which occupied a handsome edifice on Fifteenth Street between I and K Streets, Northwest, numbered one hundred and fifty communicants.[14] Francis Grimké, even as a young licentiate, seemed to this well-educated, relatively affluent Negro congregation an ideal choice for the pastorate. Having received a unanimous call, he was ordained and installed on July 7, 1878.[15] The work prospered under his leadership, but in 1885 his health failed him and he accepted a call to the Laura Street Church, Jacksonville, Florida. There he ministered effectively until 1889 and, in the salubrious climate, gradually regained his health. By that time the pulpit of the Fifteenth Street Church was again vacant; and when a second call was issued to Pastor Grimké, he accepted it. He returned to Washington and assumed the pastoral obligations of what proved to be his first and last parish.[16]

It was not long before Francis Grimké came to be recognized as the most outstanding Negro clergyman in the capital city. As a craftsman of the homiletic art, he had few peers. His messages were consistently the product of careful and mature reflection, and they were delivered with power and conviction. As his reputation spread, he found himself ever more in demand as a preacher and lecturer. He became a regular lecturer at the Tuskegee Institute and for several years preached during the summer at the Hampton Negro Conference. Always conscious of his civic responsibility, he served with distinction as a Trustee of Howard University and as a Trustee of the Public Schools of the District of Columbia. In recognition of his meritorious service, Lincoln University, in 1888, conferred upon him the degree of Doctor of Divinity.[17]

Physically the Fifteenth Street Church enjoyed a healthy growth during Dr. Grimké's pastorate: the record shows that the congregation expanded from one hundred and fifty communicants to more than five hundred.[18] In 1918 the congre-

[14] Presbytery of Washington City, *Records*, I (April 5, 1871), 60.
[15] Presbytery of Washington City, *Records*, I (July 7, 1878), 476.
[16] Grimké, *op.cit.*, I, xii.
[17] *Ibid.*, pp. xii-xiii.
[18] Presbyterian Church in the U.S.A., *Minutes of the General Assembly* (1930), p. 588.

gation moved to a handsome brick building at Fifteenth and R Streets, Northwest.[19] Dr. Grimké remained in its active service until 1925, when he felt the necessity to relinquish his pastoral responsibilities. Out of gratitude, however, the congregation refused to accept his resignation, and, though most of his duties were taken by another minister, he held the title of pastor until his death on October 11, 1937.[20]

Early in his career, Dr. Grimké endeavored to establish a warm and friendly relationship with the white ministers and churches of the Presbytery of Washington City. Unfortunately racial prejudice significantly limited the contacts he could make, and as the years passed he entered into increasingly fewer associations with his ministerial brethren. As a protest to unfair discrimination against the Negro, he even refused to attend the meetings of his presbytery; the white churches within its bounds, he maintained, were largely apathetic or hostile to his people's advancement. In 1908 he wrote to the presbytery: "if there is any one thing that Jesus himself desired to accomplish, more than others it was to break down these artificial and anti-christian walls of separation. When will the church of Jesus Christ cease its hypocritical cant about religion, and begin to live it, in spirit and in truth?"[21]

Never a man to compromise with principle, Dr. Grimké habitually endeavored to proclaim the truth as he saw it. Tactfulness was hardly one of his virtues, a circumstance that cost him many friends and brought him excoriation from his critics. Some of his associates agreed with him in principle but felt that he was attempting to accomplish his purposes in a deleterious manner. Perhaps his most loyal friend in the presbytery was the distinguished pastor of the New York Avenue Church, Dr. Wallace Radcliffe. Writing to Grimké in 1919, he reflected on the question of race. "The only philosophy that will settle this question is the philosophy of Jesus Christ. The only solution is as you say to treat the Negro everywhere as a

[19] Presbytery of Washington City, *Records*, x (April 5, 1918), 208.
[20] Presbytery of Washington City, *Records*, xv (November 8, 1937), 48.
[21] Grimké, *op.cit.*, IV, 115.

man and brother. And it will certainly come or the Republic will go down. Its life is in its righteousness."[22]

IV

The central purpose of Dr. Grimké's life was the application of the Gospel to the social order, particularly in regard to the elevation of his people. He labored in a time of great social ferment, one by-product of which was an increasing predilection, in both the North and South, to relegate the Negro to inferior status. At the close of the Civil War, most southern whites, though reconciled to the abolition of slavery, were determined that the Negro should remain in a servile capacity.[23] In the North, Negro workers encountered stern opposition from white artisans and factory workers, who regarded the freedmen as a threat to their economic security.[24]

Republican politicians regularly sought civil rights legislation, but their primary motivation was the strengthening of their party in the South. With the application of Radical Reconstruction, however, secret societies such as the Ku Klux Klan were founded to maintain white supremacy, through violence whenever it seemed necessary.[25] After the eventual passing of Reconstruction, southern Democrats returned to power; wherever possible legislatures disfranchised Negroes and enacted laws for the segregation of the races. By the end of the century it was apparent that the Negro had lost the peace. Any attempt to gain his civil rights was met with threats, beatings, and finally lynchings.[26]

If the last half of the nineteenth century brought few gains in the economic and social position of the Negro, at least it witnessed significant advances in the area of education. Thousands of Negroes enjoyed the benefits of secondary and higher education as a result of enlightened giving by philanthropic

[22] *Ibid.*, p. 252.
[23] John Hope Franklin, *From Slavery to Freedom, A History of American Negroes*, p. 299.
[24] *Ibid.*, p. 308. [25] *Ibid.*, pp. 321-323.
[26] *Ibid.*, pp. 328, 338.

and ecclesiastical agencies. Though most professions were scarcely open to Negroes, by 1900 there were 28,560 persons of that race in the teaching profession.[27] A new era in Negro education began in 1881 with the coming of the indomitable Booker T. Washington to Tuskegee Institute in Alabama. Washington believed in Negro advancement through a combination of hard work and respect for the white authorities. He favored a program of industrial education that would enable the Negro to serve where he was and not antagonize southern leaders. A man of conciliatory nature, he became, paradoxically, to his own people the colored version of an Horatio Alger hero, while to the white man he was invariably a symbol of placid conformity to a fixed social and economic system.[28]

It might be said of Francis Grimké that during the early years of his ministry his solution to the Negro problem was not unlike that of his friend Booker T. Washington. In 1892, for example, he told the Ministers' Union of Washington: "The future of the Negro, his ability to hold his own as a permanent factor in the world's civilization, and against the aggressions of his enemies, in this country, depends more upon character than upon anything else, and therefore upon that the chief emphasis should be laid. Every Negro, in every part of the country, by some means should be made to feel, and to feel at once, the transcendent importance of character."[29]

The sobering evidences of racial prejudice during the next few years, however, caused Dr. Grimké to view the social conditions of his time with considerably more realism. In a sermon delivered on November 20, 1900, he declared with considerable justification: "After thirty-three years of freedom, our civil and political rights are still denied us; the Fourteenth and Fifteenth Amendments to the Constitution are still a dead letter. The spirit of opposition, of oppression, of injustice is not diminishing but increasing. The determination to keep us in a state of civil and political inferiority and to surround us with such conditions as will tend to crush out of us a manly and

[27] *Ibid.*, p. 383.   [28] *Ibid.*, pp. 384-386.
[29] Grimké, *op.cit.*, I, 224.

self-respecting spirit is stronger now than it was at the close of the war."[30]

Still, Dr. Grimké was convinced that the doors of opportunity would yet open to the Negro of high character and training who was devoted to his work. He told a conference at Hampton Institute, Virginia, in July 1897: "This is the lesson which you need, and which I need, and which we all need to learn if this poor race of ours is to survive in the struggle. Here is the key to the future, and that key will respond to no touch but our own. White men cannot help us except in an indirect way. We have got to work out our own salvation. The power that is to level the mountains of prejudice and opposition, and make clear our path in this country, lies within ourselves—in our own intelligence and pluck and fidelity and conscientiousness and high resolve to make the most of ourselves,—to put our best into whatever we do. If we use this power we will succeed; if we do not we will fail, and ought to fail."[31]

If Pastor Grimké believed that self-help was the major clue to progress, he was not unmindful of the value inherent in well-placed connections. He had his favorite champions among the nation's white leadership, and he never ceased to extol them for their benefactions. Theodore Roosevelt's record in matters Negritic was not impeccable; but it was good, and Dr. Grimké held him in highest esteem. When the President invited Booker T. Washington to dinner at the White House in 1901, Grimké was ecstatic in his praise. "We have at last in the White House one who is every inch a man; one who has convictions, and convictions in the right direction, and who has the courage of his convictions."[32] Although the incident evoked a rash of excited and vitriolic comment from prejudiced observers, the colored minister saw in it an omen of a brighter future.

V

Meanwhile, a virile and vociferous segment of the Negro community had determined to reject the moderation of Booker

[30] *Ibid.*, p. 237. [31] *Ibid.*, II, 565-566. [32] *Ibid.*, I, 340.

T. Washington and to press immediately for full civil rights. They met at Niagara Falls, Canada, in June 1905 under the leadership of W. E. B. DuBois and drafted a manifesto that called for Negro suffrage and the abolition of all distinctions founded upon race. Thus was initiated the Niagara Movement with its militant program for the achievement of Negro rights.[33]

At this juncture the brothers Grimké sided with the anti-Washington faction; thereafter Francis Grimké was publicly critical of Washington's work.[34] When Washington passed away in 1915, the minister wrote of him: "His attitude on the rights of the Negro, as an American citizen, was also anything but satisfactory. He either dodged the issue when he came face to face with it, or dealt with it in such a way as not to offend those who were not in favor of according to him full citizenship rights. He never squarely faced the issue, and, in a straightforward, manly spirit declared his belief in the Negro as a man and a citizen, and as entitled to the same treatment as other men."[35] Whether this judgment was just, only history can determine. It should be noted, however, that many responsible and dedicated white friends of the Negro regarded Washington as the greatest man of his race and were convinced that the polemical Niagara Movement would serve only to impede the Negro's advancement. Lyman Abbott's editorial in the *Outlook* of July 29, 1905, was perhaps representative: "The real leaders of the American negroes are not complaining; they are too busy inculcating habits of thrift, energy, and self-control among the people to whom they are proud to belong."[36]

Within a few years the leaders of the Niagara Movement joined forces with a group of distinguished white reformers, among whom were numbered Jane Addams, William Dean Howells, and John Dewey. Together they made plans for a permanent organization pledged to fight segregation and to

[33] Franklin, *op.cit.*, p. 437.
[34] Grimké, *op.cit.*, IV, 89-90.
[35] *Ibid.*, III, 16.
[36] Quoted in Ira V. Brown, *Lyman Abbott, Christian Evolutionist*, Harvard Univ. Press: Cambridge, Mass., 1953, p. 207.

campaign for the full civil rights of Negro citizens. In May 1910, the National Association for the Advancement of Colored People was born. Immediately it inaugurated a crusade to gain better legal protection for Negroes and to win for them greater opportunities in industry.[37]

From the outset the N.A.A.C.P. had the loyal support of Pastor Grimké. In 1914 he urged his congregation to give thanks for the Association, which he believed was inspired of God.[38] Seven years later he was no less enthusiastic: "I do not hesitate to say that, of the great, live forces today at work helping to make this race manly, self-respecting; helping to batter down the walls that race prejudice is ever setting up in the way of our progress, there is not one of them that is doing more than this National Association for the Advancement of Colored People. Its very existence is a constant protest against the vile treatment to which we are subjected in this country; is a notification to the enemies of the race that we are not going to be put down...."[39] By the 1930's Dr. Grimké noted with some concern that the Association was becoming more secular in its outlook and inclined toward a routine professionalism, but he continued his support of the organization in the faith that it would recapture something of its pristine idealism.[40]

The second decade of the twentieth century found Dr. Grimké becoming steadily more vehement in his denunciation of those who were not avid supporters of Negro advancement. He was sharply critical of President Woodrow Wilson for "the disposition, under your Administration, to segregate colored people in the various departments of the Government."[41] On the occasion of William A. (Billy) Sunday's Washington, D.C., campaign in 1918, the colored minister became highly censorious. "This man, Rev. Billy Sunday, at times, seems to be a little courageous, judged by his vigorous denunciation of many sins; but when it comes to this big devil of race prejudice, the craven in him comes out; he cowers before it; he is afraid to

[37] Franklin, *op.cit.*, p. 439. [38] Grimké, *op.cit.*, I, 518-519.
[39] *Ibid.*, p. 626. [40] *Ibid.*, III, 612-613.
[41] *Ibid.*, I, 518.

speak out; at heart, he is seen to be a moral coward in spite of his bluster and pretense of being brave. What are you afraid of Mr. Sunday, and, what are your ministerial brethren afraid of?"[42] Many clergymen in high places felt the bite of Grimké's words when they did not stand militantly in favor of integration. Even the citizens of Washington were censured in 1917 for the ovation they gave a troop of Confederate veterans marching in parade. It was unthinkable, cried Grimké, that these "unreconstructed, unrepentant rebĕls" should be "treated as if they had been fighting in the most holy cause!"[43]

Then came 1917 and America's entrance into World War I. Most American Negroes responded to the crisis in a fine patriotic manner and supported the government in every way possible. There are records of exceptional heroism on the part of Negro troops in battle. Much discrimination was evident in the military services, and most Negroes reacted to it with nobility.[44] Dr. Grimké's attitude toward the political order was rabidly critical and would have been rejected by most of his fellow Negroes. In 1918 he wrote these acrid lines: "As a government, we pretend that we are fighting to safeguard democracy in the world, are fighting in the interest of justice, of equal rights for all. It is a lie. What we are really fighting for, and what the Allies are fighting for is to insure white supremacy throughout the world, and the only difference between Germany and this country and the Allies is that Germany wants not only white supremacy, but German supremacy, which the rest of the white nations are not willing for her to have."[45] Later that year he refused to make some short addresses for the government in the interest of the Fourth Liberty Loan, arguing that "the money is not to be used in defense of liberty, but only in defense of the liberty of white men, with no thought or desire of safeguarding the liberty of colored people."[46] Thus wrote the man who regarded Booker T. Washington as a detriment to Negro advancement.

[42] *Ibid.*, p. 559.
[43] *Ibid.*, III, 31.
[44] Franklin, *op.cit.*, pp. 447-453.
[45] Grimké, *op.cit.*, III, 45.
[46] *Ibid.*, p. 73.

Francis James Grimké

FRANCIS JAMES GRIMKÉ

VI

In 1919 Pastor Grimké addressed himself more positively to the Negro problem. He found the Negro's responsibility to be small in relation to that of the white man. "The problem with the Negro is largely that of self-development; with the white man, that of getting rid of his prejudice, his race-hating spirit."[47] No solution could be found that did not involve a change of attitude on the part of white citizens. Above all, the white churches would have to become centers in which the Christian doctrine of the brotherhood of man is both taught and lived. "There is but one solution to the race problem, and, it is to treat the Negro as a man and brother. It will be solved on principles laid down by Jesus Christ, or it never will be solved.... Let us hope there will be an awakening; that common sense and the principle of love, of righteousness, will somehow get the ascendency, and so shall begin the ushering in of a better day."[48]

Francis Grimké did not live to see the death of racial prejudice. He did witness the virtual annihilation of lynching, the establishment of greater benefits for the Negro worker through unionization, the election of Negroes to public office, and the beginning of a large-scale effort to end segregation. If there had been retrogression during his lifetime, there had also been progress. With the support of the churches or without it, legal discrimination would continue to decline and the Negro would come finally to enjoy the full rights of citizenship.

Since Dr. Grimké understood Christianity to be essentially a way of life rather than a system of thought, he would not have aspired to the title of theologian. Theologian he was, nevertheless, and, in the grand tradition of Protestant orthodoxy, modified somewhat by the idealistic temper of the age. He believed in a God who was at once transcendent and immanent, a God who stood at the center of a civilization, "directing, controlling, influencing it in all of its movements."[49] He believed that this God was incarnate in Christ and that,

[47] *Ibid.*, I, 595.   [48] *Ibid.*, pp. 596-599.
[49] *Ibid.*, II, 429.

through Christ's life and sacrificial death on the cross, salvation for sinful men had been made possible. With all his being he trusted that Christ had been victorious over the power of death and that in his name men might inherit eternal life. Men are called to Christ in the proclamation of the Gospel, and, though they are saved by grace, "there must be the most earnest cooperation on our part with the Spirit of God."[50] The doctrine of God's irresistible decree held no place in his thinking. "The direction in which we go is determined by ourselves, we go the way that we want to go, that we will to go. We are free and responsible moral agents, and are not in the midst of forces that destroy our freedom."[51]

In his view of the Christian life, Pastor Grimké reflected the ethos of middle-class pietistic evangelicalism. He stood firm in the conviction that Christianity was best exemplified in personal character, especially in the virtues of diligence, trustworthiness, thrift, punctuality, and forthrightness. He shared in the repudiation, common among Protestant moralists, of liquor, tobacco, dancing, and the theater.

Liquor was the chief devil to be conquered. In many a sermon he expatiated on this evil, never more eloquently than in a discourse delivered in 1906: "Strong drink has done more to unman men, to degrade them to the level of the brute than any other single influence. It makes no difference what our gifts may be, if this appetite is awakened within us, if we yield ourselves to the seductive influence of the wine cup, it is only a matter of time when we shall be brought low. The intoxicating bowl has never, in all its history, been a stepping stone to anything worthy or honorable. Its trend has always been downward."[52]

As a Puritan reformer of public morals, Dr. Grimké gave his full support to the movement that culminated in the passage of the Eighteenth Amendment on National Prohibition in 1919. During the 1920's, when the law came under attack by persons who insisted that it bred crime, the Negro pastor

[50] *Ibid.*, III, 625-626.
[51] *Ibid.*, pp. 627-628.
[52] *Ibid.*, II, 473.

was adamant in its defense. The repeal of the Eighteenth Amendment at the advent of President Franklin Roosevelt's administration was for him a crushing blow. In 1934 he wrote with great feeling: "As to what conditions were, you know, I know, we all know. Bad as they were under prohibition . . . they were nothing like as bad as before the 18th Amendment was enacted and the Volstead Act passed. Already the evil effects are being seen and felt, and things are growing steadily worse. Our streets are already witnessing a steady increase of drunken men and women on them, and the number of arrests for drunkenness is steadily on the increase."[53] And yet Dr. Grimké's pious though justified fulminations could not dispel the indisputable fact: the lights of an old order were going out, and they would not be lit again in his time.

What manner of man was Dr. Francis James Grimké? Perhaps no one dares speak with finality on the subject. There are at best impressions, and these are highly subjective. To the present writer, Dr. Grimké was a Negro Puritan, a man of exceptional character who possessed a strong sense of right and wrong and the unfailing courage to defend his cause against overwhelming opposition. He had all the aggressiveness common to minority groups that experience the dynamics of social prejudice, and occasionally he displayed an attitude of vindictiveness wholly inconsistent with the Christian love that he regularly preached and often practiced. His vision carried him into the ideal world that was not yet and that would not be in his generation; it was largely because he lived so much in this utopian realm that the present world of stark reality seemed so unbearable. He was a prophet, and so he attempted to bring the ideal world into the dreams of men. If he failed, then all men are the losers, for life without dreams is empty and vain. If he succeeded, then all men are the better for his having lived. For into a broken, fragmented world he came bearing the Gospel of the Christ he loved and the assurance that with God all things are possible.

[53] *Ibid.*, pp. 529-530.

X. WALTER LOWRIE (1868-1959)

Man and Churchman Extraordinary*

BY HOWARD A. JOHNSON

WALTER LOWRIE, ardent advocate of Episcopacy, knew what it was, on occasion, to tangle with bishops. When once he was embroiled in controversy with a particular bishop, he flung at his episcopal opponent this stinging remark: "Until two years ago I lived in completest harmony with my bishops, being treated rather as a pet. And it might be considered in my favor that I have written two books to prove the necessity of having bishops for the Church. If I once in a while betray the suspicion that they are a necessary evil, some extenuation may be found in the fact that I was brought up a Presbyterian."

I

This same Walter Lowrie, one of the chief intellectual ornaments of the Protestant Episcopal Church, was indeed brought up a Presbyterian. He came from a long lineage of Presbyterian divines and was graduated from Princeton Theological Seminary in 1893. He won not only a degree from the Seminary but also several of its prizes, one of which was to take him to Germany for graduate study. Before going abroad, he successfully stood his examinations before Presbytery and was licensed to preach. He decided to defer ordination, however, on the ground that two or three years of graduate study

---

* An annotated bibliography prepared by Walter Lowrie himself appears (pp. 233-241) in the volume of essays, *Dr. Lowrie of Princeton and Rome* (Greenwich: The Seabury Press, 1957), edited by Alexander C. Zabriskie and Howard A. Johnson. Since then, some of the Kierkegaard translations have been reissued, several of them in paperback editions, and Lowrie's *Ministers of Christ* (first published in 1946) is in a new edition with accompanying critical essays (Greenwich: The Seabury Press, 1963), edited by Theodore O. Wedel.

stood between him and the exercise of the pastoral ministry. There was also a deeper ground for hesitation. Lowrie had begun to have scruples about his fitness for ministering under the terms that at that time the Presbyterian Church would have required of him.

I, an Episcopalian myself, am too uninstructed in the in's and out's of American Presbyterian history to know with what justice the young Walter Lowrie assessed the situation in the Gay Nineties, but I do know—from letters I have read since his death—that there were three chief things about the Church in which he had been reared that finally drove him away from its fold.

He was repelled by its fundamentalism. (I here report his own words. I do not presume to evaluate them or endorse their historical justification.) His professor of Old Testament seemed to him "hell bent on maintaining positions already antiquated in the 1890's and which absolutely nobody today [in the 1950's] is minded to maintain." Lowrie's deeper complaint, as registered in letters to his parents at the time, is that the New Testament Department at Princeton failed him abysmally. It seems that he hit the Seminary at a period when New Testament studies were at a low ebb. The principal teacher in that subject had died, and his two successive replacements seemed to the youthful and hotheaded Walter Lowrie "unequal to their task." He complains that one of the men could hold forth on nothing but the Epistle to the Hebrews—about which Walter Lowrie felt that his father, a Trustee of the Seminary, had already said enough in a gigantic commentary of his own composition. He complains of the second teacher that he was "tongue-tied except for the Acts of the Apostles." "Thus it came about," Lowrie lamented in later years, "that during my three years in the Princeton Theological Seminary I had no instruction whatever in the Gospels, which was my most ardent interest. About the New Testament we had nothing but the exegesis of several passages in Romans and Galatians which deal with the doctrine of predestination." Lowrie felt—with what justice I do not presume to say—that the Scriptures were exploited in the interest of underwriting one or another preconceived dogmatic notion. He objected in particular to the doctrine of the literal inerrancy of Scripture. As the time approached for graduation from the Seminary and for ordination, Walter Lowrie held back. In conscience he could not affirm, as the Westminster Confession seemed to require of him, the literal inerrancy of the Holy Scriptures. Yet Professor B. B. Warfield, if Lowrie gives a correct report, told him that he should not seek ordination unless he could ascribe to the Confession *ex animo*. To this stand Lowrie took no exception, but he knew that for integrity's sake he must therefore rule himself out.

Yet this fundamentalism was only one of three things that unsettled Walter Lowrie in the early nineties. He was troubled early in the game about problems of ecclesiastical polity. There are letters to show that already as a youth he had very mature doubts about the efforts of the Reformed Churches, whether stemming from Calvin or from Zwingli, to prove that some particular form of Church government is "*jure divino* and by the will and appointment of Jesus Christ." To this fiery young seminarian it seemed preposterous that a system of ecclesiastical organization should be elevated to the status of "an article of faith—hardly inferior in importance to belief in God."

A chief Lowrie indictment against the Seminary, which nevertheless he loved, was that it gave him no guidance in the field of liturgics. His skill in Greek, aided no doubt by a certain esthetic bent, propelled him into a study of liturgics, the ancient Greek liturgies in particular. From a study of these liturgies he was to be led eventually into a fascination for Christian archaeology and for the art of the early Church. If our forebears in the faith worshipped in such and such a manner, in what surroundings did they carry on their devotions? How was the "house of the Church" arranged, how decorated? To Lowrie's mind these were not trivial questions, and the pursuit of their answers was to have revolutionary consequences.

For awhile it was touch and go whether or not Walter Lowrie would even get his degree from Princeton Seminary. Having been at one time a seminary professor myself, I can see that it requires no inspired guesswork to understand how difficult a student this Lowrie boy must have been. In multiple ways he was disobedient. Ale and tobacco, for example. He did not come regularly to lectures. He was at no pains to conceal his scorn of certain "unprofitable lecturers" on the faculty. He more than once incited students to sign petitions when he thought that an injustice had been done to a student ... or to a dismissed professor. Always quick with the tongue and the pen, he talked a lot (sometimes out of turn) and circulated to every Presbyterian magazine in the country inflammatory articles (some of which got published) exposing one or another flaw in the Princeton gem. I marvel that Princeton Seminary was able to put up with him at all. In an Episcopal seminary I think he would have been booted.

With the utmost forebearance, however, Princeton Seminary tolerated him despite a triumvirate of professors who worked for his ouster. The stormy young petrel had swept the board, winning every prize offered. One prize was designed to carry its winner to Europe for graduate study. Student Lowrie was called to task by the three professors. Did he feel that he could accept the prize when there was a question about whether or not he would get his degree in theology? And did he even want a degree when there was a question about his willingness and suitability to be ordained? Other members of the faculty, however, remarked on how embarrassing it would be to refuse a degree to the student who had distinguished himself above all others. Recognizing quality when they saw it, even when they could not agree with all of the conclusions to which Lowrie's studies had carried him, they voted that the prize was well earned and must be bestowed.

How exceedingly well earned can be judged by reading the first book Lowrie published, *The Doctrine of S. John: An Essay in Biblical Theology*. Although it did not appear until 1899, it was but a revision of his prize-winning essay of 1893; there were virtually no changes in substance. The book is as fresh today as when it was written nearly seven decades ago. It anticipated many of the assured results of present-day Johannine scholarship. It is not yet as widely recognized as it ought to be that Walter Lowrie (in the words of Holt Graham) belongs "in the front rank of New Testament critics." Not only *The Doctrine of S. John* but also Lowrie's *Jesus according to St. Mark* (1929) and *The Short Story of Jesus* (1943) are there to prove it.

In the end, Lowrie got the degree and the prize, together with the kindly admonition not to be hasty about deciding against the ministry and to take his time before deciding on withdrawal from the Presbyterian Church. Germany, the Seminary authorities hoped, would work wonders, effect a cure, and solve everything. It did. But not quite in the direction they had expected.

Armed with his $600 fellowship from the Seminary, Lowrie went to Greifswald, having chosen that place because there he would be the only foreigner. Because of the reach of the Lowrie mind and the length of the Lowrie stride, Greifswald's Professor Victor Schultze welcomed the young American as a companion on many long hikes. From the friendship thus formed were to come lengthy sessions together for the purpose of investigating the earliest forms of Christian worship. This was Schultze's specialty, along with Church History and Christian Archaeology. For him as for Lowrie, preoccupation with liturgics led on, by a logical progression, to an intensified interest in the arts and architecture of the early Church. In this way the Presbyterian-sponsored Walter Lowrie, unaware of what was happening to him in Germany, was being prepared, as he said later, "to accept the fellowship in archeology which took me to Rome two years later and thereby determined the course of my life."

II

Before going to Rome, however, he "went to Canterbury" —i.e., he returned to America and became an Episcopalian. "The period of quarantine prescribed to disabuse me of my sectarian errors seemed to me unduly long," Lowrie remarked drily in one of his reminiscences, but after being "fumigated" for eight months he was made deacon in 1895 and priest the follow-

Walter Lowrie

ing year. Shortly after becoming a deacon a chance to dig in Latium was then presented to him in the form of a fellowship in the new School of Classical Studies. To Rome he went in 1895 for an academic year, and when the fellowship was renewed he went again for a second year in 1899. The spade work done there bore fruit in 1901, when Lowrie published his great work called *Monuments of the Early Church,* in the American edition, and *Christian Art and Archaeology,* in the English edition. Its author was thirty-three years old. Of the book Dr. A. W. Van Buren, a professor at the American Academy in Rome, has recently said, "Only a scholar at the height of his youthful powers could have produced it. That volume has served its purpose, being admitted by common consent into the inner circle of essential theological literature. It perfectly filled a gap—it put into effective form the material widely scattered throughout publications great and small, and it set forth judiciously and serviceably the results which had been reached by generations of scholars." The book had a long run. There were reprintings innumerable, and perhaps there would have been even more of them had it not been necessary, during World War II, to melt down the metal plates for the making of bullets.

The suppression of the book occasioned Lowrie no discontentment, for he felt he had learned a thing or two in the forty years that had elapsed since he wrote it. He had second thoughts about a number of things and, at the age of seventy-nine, felt spry enough for a new excursion in the field of Christian archaeology. The result was the publication in 1947 of *Art in the Early Church.* The critics gave it a mixed reception, yet I know of none who would quarrel with Dr. Van Buren's verdict: "Its five hundred illustrations are the most adequate pageant of their artistic material ever presented in printed form. For this alone, gratitude will be unbounded; for what a pageant is here presented! And how the treasures thus displayed follow one another in orderly sequence, one theme leading on to the next, one illustration preparing for another!" An elegantly printed book with so many illustrations was necessarily a costly thing, and this kept it too much out of the hands of penurious students and underpaid parsons. One therefore hails with joy the recent decision of Harper & Brothers to bring it out as a paperback book.

But to return to the young Walter Lowrie in Rome. There he made the friendships that were probably the cause of his being summoned back to Rome in 1907 to be installed as Rector of St. Paul's-within-the-Walls. For twenty-three years he ministered in this place. And, although many of his finest books were written there, he could later say, justly enough, that he always looked upon his writing as "incidental to my work as a parochial pastor." While in Rome he became fast friends with both Roman Catholics and Waldensians—and often acted as go-between when the two groups had matters at issue. There too he won for himself a distinction uncommon for a commoner: the Gold Medal of the King of Italy for Valor. This was in recognition of his having helped to raise and then having ably spent nearly one million dollars to rebuild two Italian towns which had collapsed in the great earthquake of 1915. Moreover, he showed heroism doing Red Cross work at the front during the first World War.

But to tell all he did, in Italy or anywhere else, is clearly impossible. After all, this son of Princeton lived a very long time! I must make place, however, for the preservation of one glimpse of the Lowrie wit. When this archaeologist was in the United States to solicit money for the American Academy in Rome, he concluded his fund-raising speech with the words, "I *can* dig, and I am *not* ashamed to beg!"

The word "dig" reminds me that I am ahead of my story. We must go back once more to the young Princetonian who had become enamored of the study of the liturgical practices of the early Church. The deeper he dug into liturgics, the more deeply he became involved in Christian art and archaeology; and there precisely he found the clue he had been seeking, the answer to tormenting questions about ecclesiastical polity. From a study of how the early Christians *worshipped* and of how they adorned that worship architecturally and artistically, Lowrie—with a copy of Rudolph Sohm's *Kirchenrecht* in his pocket and a shovel in his hand—succeeded in hitting upon a simple, startling, and liberating solution to problems of ecclesiastical government that have vexed the Church and divided it for centuries.

He lost little time before sharing his discovery with the world. In 1904 he published a big book entitled *The Church and Its Organization*. Modestly, he gave it a subtitle: *An Interpretation of Rudolph Sohm's Kirchenrecht*. The German professor promptly dispatched to Lowrie this courteous letter: "Your work is by no means merely an 'interpretation' of my book: it is an original creation. Your agreement with me in the main thesis has all the greater worth on account of the independent way in which you handle both the historical and the theoretical questions. The precision of your conceptions and the lucidity of your exposition will surely avail to carry the truth to wider circles."

In this expectation Sohm was too sanguine. Lowrie's book went virtually unnoticed. One seeks reviews of it in vain, and in the whole literature on problems of Church unity it is hardly ever alluded to. It was a book which came too early—came, that is, before the birth of the Ecumenical Movement; and when that movement got underway, Lowrie's pioneer effort was already forgotten. Yet not exactly forgotten, for how might it be possible to forget something that was never remembered or even noticed? But for my part I am in entire agreement with Theodore O. Wedel, who maintains that Sohm and Lowrie have achieved a "masterly unravelling of the mystery of 'bishop or elder' in the early Church" and that the Sohm-Lowrie insights provide "the only way of breaking the present ecumenical log-jam."

III

In 1924 Lowrie again raised his voice—more succinctly, more urgently than before—in a book called *Problems of Church Unity*. This book fared no better than its predecessor, even though it also appeared in Italian translation. Reader response was nil. It is almost as if these books had never been written. Yet I know of no books on the subject more illuminating, more liberating, more likely to promote unity.

Not easily discouraged when so much was at stake, Walter Lowrie tried a third time. This was in 1946, a year in which American Presbyterians and American Episcopalians were trying to woo each other. Temerity and tenaciousness were marks of the Lowrie character. An ecclesiastical matchmaker by divine constraint, Lowrie had his heart set on getting Presbyterians and Episcopalians together. To this end he brought out a little book (little only in size) called *Ministers of Christ*. It represented the crystallization of fifty years of agonized thinking about the disunity of the Church—an agony all the greater because he knew how fairly simple the solution was. What in 1904 it had taken him 402 pages to say, and what in 1924 he said in 328 pages, he was now able to say—but without so many evident signs of erudition—in 113 pages, pages so pungent, so cogent, that they sizzle. It was Lowrie's intention to send a complimentary copy of this book to every presbyter in both of the negotiating Churches. But a sad fatality that rested over much of Lowrie's authorship visited him also here. A printers' strike delayed publication. By the time the book was out, it was too late. It could no longer hope to influence decisions, for the brief romance between Episcopalians and Presbyterians was already over. The engagement had been broken—blame for which (as I see it) must be laid squarely to the charge of the Episcopalians. One wonders if things might not have gone differently had Walter Lowrie's *Ministers of Christ* appeared in time.

But now that Presbyterians and Episcopalians in America have once again resumed their flirtation—this time with more earnestness, more theological depth (and with Methodists and Congregationalists taken into the picture too)—Walter Lowrie may *yet* have a chance to be heard. He shows persuasively why bishops there must be, yet in such a way that no Episcopalian could retain the hauteur and the theological delusion which now separate him from his Brothers in Christ; while non-Episcopalians, subjected to no humiliating loss of face, would to their good gain bishops, and the whole Church thus be mutually corrected, mutually enriched.

Simple as the Sohm-Lowrie insights are, they are nonetheless too complicated to be set forth here within the compass of a brief essay that must necessarily touch upon many other matters as well. Unfortunately, Lowrie's three books on the subject of the Church and its organization are now out of print. Nevertheless, many copies must be lurking, unread still, in manses and rectories and on the shelves of seminary libraries. And if Lowrie's own books cannot be had, there is a place where the kernel of his thought is easily accessible: Chapter IV of a book called *Dr. Lowrie of Princeton and Rome*. This is a *Festschrift* that nine Episcopalians presented to Walter Lowrie on the occasion of his eighty-ninth birthday "in acknowledgment of a debt."

If I had any power to command, the Lowrie trilogy on Church unity would be required reading for everybody having anything to do whatsoever with the present explorations, both here in America and also in the United Kingdom, where conversations are in progress between the Church of Scotland and the Church of England. Were these books to be read, marked, learned, and inwardly digested by all parties concerned, we would be well on our way to "godly union and concord." I do not believe I exaggerate in claiming so much for Walter Lowrie. And if I am mistaken in this, then I must abdicate: my judgment counts for nothing.

From liturgics to archaeology to polity. This was the progress of Lowrie's development. "In a way," he writes, "my whole life was shaped by the fact that as a student in Princeton Seminary I had been unreasonable enough to devote myself to the study of the Liturgy." There is, in this utterance, the characteristic light play of his good humored irony. The New Testament and liturgical interests he cultivated in Princeton led him to Germany, where he acquired the taste for art and archaeology that carried him on to Rome; and there, instructed by what he read in the testimony of ancient Christian monuments, he found a key to the problems of Church unity. Thereafter forever he could not hold his peace. He anticipated the Ecumenical Movement as a pioneer and even now must be summoned to help if that movement is to find its way with godly celerity.

SONS OF THE PROPHETS

Recently, in the course of a two-year trip around the world to survey the work of the Anglican Communion, I visited Pakistan, India, and Ceylon. To leaders in the already existing Church of South India and to those who are laboring to bring into being a Church of Lanka and a united Church for North India and Pakistan I showed the results of Lowrie's studies. "But great heavens!" these men exclaimed. "Your Dr. Lowrie had already done all of our work for us! How much brain-racking and heart-searching we might have been spared, if only we had known of him!" It is a comfort to find in the independent researches of these Singhalese, Indian, and Pakistani Christians a corroboration of most of the positions that Lowrie had taken up a half-century before.

In the long run and in the large view of things it matters very little that a Presbyterian became an Episcopalian. Unless by a mean trick of history Lowrie is again ignored, he will be remembered chiefly for the fact that he helped to show the way for the coming together of Presbyterians and Episcopalians in such a way that neither side loses anything essential and in such a way that both sides gain much in discovering each other as participants together in the same Eucharist.

It is greatly to the credit of Princeton Theological Seminary—a gauge of the charitableness of its spirit—that in a volume of this sort, where it singles out for honorable mention a mere dozen of its most notable sons, it should elect to include a man who ordinarily would have been written off as a turncoat. For the record it should also be noted that there was charity on Walter Lowrie's side as well. It was not his practice as a grown man to go around voicing disappointment with the theological education he had received. He was fully aware that things are different now. It is only from letters he anciently wrote to his parents (letters I have been permitted to read now that he is gone) and from typewritten reminiscences (never intended for publication and hammered out by an octogenarian) that I have learned of his dissatisfaction. Recurrent and emphatic is his latter day affirmation: "I have been happily associated with this seminary during the thirty years I have lived in Princeton [since retirement from the active ministry]. The admiration I feel for teachers I know there now, especially for President John Mackay, suggests some regret that in my youth the place offered far less advantages than it does for the youth of today."

IV

Lowrie was a man of many talents, with many irons in the fire simultaneously. If I have dealt at disproportionate length with his relationship to Princeton Seminary and with his significance as an ecumenical prophet it is only because this side of his story is less well known.

Well known is his role in making Kierkegaard available to the English-speaking world. So well is it known, in fact, that it threatens by its brilliance to eclipse his claims to fame in his own right. I have therefore preferred to stress his importance as an ecumenical prophet, a New Testament critic, and an expert in archaeology and liturgics.

Yet Kierkegaard cannot be kept out of the picture if we are to focus on Lowrie. I somewhere wrote that the plain fact is: *Ubi* Walter Lowrie *ibi* Sören Kierkegaard. Kierkegaard would have been "discovered," even by theologically sluggish British and Americans, sooner or later. We have Walter Lowrie to thank that it came sooner rather than later.

In passing we should note that Lowrie was an experienced hand at introducing European authors to the Anglo-American public. The first translation of Albert Schweitzer into English was the doing of Walter Lowrie. In 1914 he gave to Schweitzer's *Skizze des Lebens Jesu* the title *The Mystery of the Kingdom of God*. "Thereby hangs a story strange and sad," Lowrie tells us. "This book, the first translation of a work by Schweitzer, was ready for publication just when World War I broke out. Dodd, Mead & Company were horrified at having a *German* author on their list, and, without telling me, without stopping to reflect that the name Schweitzer indicates a Swiss and that Albert Schweitzer was actually a

Frenchman, got rid of the whole edition by selling it to a jobber, who sold it to department stores at 10 cents a copy, which in their turn got rid of it at 25 cents a copy."

This defeat found parallels in two others. Lowrie wanted the Russian Orthodox Soloviev to be known. Though he took the appropriate steps, he got nowhere. Then, undeterred by the great William James' lack of success, he brought out a large book called *Religion of a Scientist* so that we might benefit from the teachings of Gustav Theodor Fechner. This availed but little. Two other "introductions" should also be mentioned: a longish essay *Johann Georg Hamann—An Existentialist* was published in 1950 as Number 6 in the *Princeton Pamphlet Series*, and in 1955 Princeton University Press published "The Book on Adler" under the title *On Authority and Revelation*. Only in the case of Kierkegaard, however, did Lowrie's exertions receive general acceptance.

In 1930, feeling himself "a superannuated clergyman," he quit Rome for Princeton. On coming home he was struck by the fact that hardly anybody in America seemed to know even the names of Kierkegaard, Barth, Brunner, Unamuno, Tillich, Bultmann, let alone betraying any awareness of the gauntlet which these giants, each in his own way, had thrown down. As capable of indignation in 1930 as he had been in 1893, Lowrie launched out on two projects. First, although he was already sixty-two years old, he began teaching himself Danish in order that he might read Kierkegaard in the original. Second, he prepared a series of lectures which he gave in many places, including China and Japan, and which were to result in a book named *Our Concern with the Theology of Crisis* (1932). In that book—in an inconspicuous place and in the smallest possible type—he permitted himself a venting of his spleen. "For what reason," he demanded with angry rhetoric, "have we so many universities? Is it to insure that studious youth shall be shielded from all contacts with contemporary thought?" With this salvo a campaign was begun. By lectures, by translations, by interpretations it was carried through.

Providentially a superannuated and unemployed Walter Lowrie had money. When nobody else believed in the enterprise, he did. Devoid of support from his environment, he went ahead, though family and friends deemed him mad. To his convictions he added cash. At one point he was more than $18,000 out of pocket because he had to pay publishers in order that they might have the privilege and one day enjoy the prestige of having produced in English translation the works of Kierkegaard.

I am not good at arithmetic, but if you are willing to overlook such niceties of precision as the fact that some pages are bigger, some smaller, it will give a generally accurate notion of the ground he covered when I compute that Lowrie's translations of Kierkegaard amount to 3790 printed pages. Add to that the 979 pages he wrote in his own name to interpret Kierkegaard and you have a sum so tidy that you no longer marvel that this enterprise took him the better part of twenty-seven years. If your knowledge of Danish permits you to be a judge, you marvel rather that the task could have been accomplished with such excellence in so short a time, especially when you consider the workman's age and the fact that in the same period he was writing articles left and right for a variety of learned journals on a variety of learned topics, not to mention the books he wrote reflecting the incredible scope of his far-ranging interests.

There is no need for me to tell the story of "How Kierkegaard got into English." It has already been told by the man best qualified to tell it, by Walter Lowrie himself, in a supplement to Kierkegaard's *Repetition*. Nor is there any need for me to say here what Lowrie's modesty inhibited him from saying there about his expertness as a translator and expositor, for I have recorded it elsewhere (in the *Festschrift* entitled *Dr. Lowrie of Princeton and Rome*). It is sufficient here to make the following points. Erudite Danes will tell you that "Kierkegaard cannot be translated." Then immediately they add, with astonished admiration, "But when you read Walter Lowrie you are reading Sören Kierkegaard!"

Lowrie's massive biography, which is called simply *Kierkegaard*, was acclaimed by Denmark's leading Kierkegaard scholar as "the greatest one-volume work on Kierkegaard in any language." Although this was said many years ago, I think there is still no chance of its being successfully challenged. I am glad to note that the big *Kierkegaard* is being translated into Italian as I write, and that a paperback edition in English will be out before my present essay comes into print. Meanwhile, Lowrie's *Short Life of Kierkegaard* enjoys a lively sale as a paperback. Its popularity on the American market has its exact counterpart in Germany, Holland, and Japan, for these are the languages into which it has already been translated—with more yet to come. For all of this a well-advised King of Denmark knighted Walter Lowrie. *Ridder af Dannebrog*—Knight of the Order of Dannebrog—is in Scandinavia a proud title. It well becomes the universally recognized mentor of Kierkegaard studies.

V

In this brief account I have had to leave entirely out of the reckoning many of Lowrie's writings. Even to list his books and weightier essays requires nine pages in print. When once he was compelled to draw up a bibliography of his works he made this comment: "I have enumerated nearly 100 items: 38 books and 59 substantial articles in reviews. It would be tedious to write, or even to read, a bare list of the more trivial items I have contributed in the course of a long life to daily or weekly papers. Most of them I have kept, but I haven't the heart to count them. Suppose they amount to one thousand and one—that would be a sorry record for eighty-eight years, as compared with many a columnist who turns out a column a day! My output comes to barely 12 items a year, or one a month, in the course of a long and misspent life."

Alexander Zabriskie, editor of the Lowrie *Festschrift*, did not account it a misspent life. He computed, rather, that this life, like all Gaul, was divided into three parts: 27 years of active preparation, 35 years of active ministry, and 28 years of active retirement. So in 1959 Lowrie died in his ninety-first year, lucid and active to the end, able even in the last week of his mortal life to look at television, grumble over newscasts, express concern about several promising young students he had befriended and was abetting, enjoy a bit of wine for his stomach's sake, and heartily make all the responses in a Communion Service celebrated at his bedside—a sacrament which then, as in all his writings, he understood as designed by Christ to be to us poor sinners a sure and certain pledge of eternal life.

As I gazed upon the countenance of this venerable man who had known for years what it is to live eschatologically—who stood, as he preferred to think of himself and of all Christians, not on the brink of death but the brink of eternity—I had occasion to remember above all else the decision he made when it was up to him to choose a text to be emblazoned on the exterior west wall of the Church of St. Paul-within-the-Walls in the City of Rome. The text he selected and ordered carved in Latin letters so large that even he who runs along the Via Nazionale may read is: "Whether it were I or they, so we preach, and so ye believed." At once irenic and unflinching. In one stroke he makes it plain to us all that, although various mergers of Protestant bodies may have to come first, he has no ultimate interest in a mighty pan-Protestantism designed to overawe Rome and force concessions from it. By the same stroke he makes it clear to a sometimes arrogant Rome that they without us cannot be made perfect. Indeed, until we all can find each other in common worship, none of us is perfect.

"I was born a Presbyterian but was predestinated to become an Episcopalian" is the playful way in which an indefatigable nonagenarian described himself. Yes, but more than that: predestinated, because of his knowledge and appreciation of Protestantism, Anglicanism, and Roman Catholicism, to see how pointless, wasteful, ruinous are our unhappy divisions—and how needless.

XI. TOYOHIKO KAGAWA (1888-1960)

Blessed Are the Poor*

BY YASUO CARL FURUYA

In order to explain what "instrumental good" would be, an American philosopher once gave this illustration: "A railroad train carrying a saint like Kagawa from San Francisco to New York is an instrumental good, for Kagawa may be able to achieve worthy ends in New York which would never be achieved if he did not go there."[1] It was September of 1914 when Toyohiko Kagawa for the first time crossed the continent by train. At that time, however, he was not yet considered a "saint" nor did he go to New York. He was a student and got off at a town between New York and Philadelphia instead. Nevertheless, the train that carried him was an "instrumental good."

During the two years that he stayed at Princeton, in addition to theology, which he studied at the Seminary, he also took courses in psychology, mathematics, and biology at the University. While attending classes, Kagawa found interesting scribbling on desks at both institutions and made a study of it. "On one of the desks in the Seminary," wrote the serious student from Japan, "I counted forty-two faces of girls!" Although he made this study public later as a part of his study of the psychology of American students, Kagawa was already a self-taught psychologist before going to Princeton. A few

---

* There is no critical biography of Kagawa, and curiously there is very little of any importance written about him in Japanese. A number of popular and inspirational accounts give the main facts of his career and something of his Christian message. See, for example: *Kagawa*, by W. Axling (New York: Harper and Brothers, 1932; revised edition, 1946); *Kagawa, An Apostle of Japan*, by Margaret Baumann (New York: Macmillan, 1936); *Unconquerable Kagawa*, by E. O. Bradshaw (St. Paul: Macalester Park Publishing Co., 1952); *Kagawa of Japan*, by C. J. Davey (London: Epworth Press, 1960).

[1] E. S. Brightman, *A Philosophy of Religion*, Prentice-Hall, Inc.: 1940, p. 242.

months after he arrived, in his room at the Seminary dormitory, he was writing a preface for his coming book. It was *A Study of the Psychology of the Poor*, published in 1915. This book of 654 pages was unique and the first study of this kind ever made in Japan, if not in the world. Kagawa was, however, more than a psychologist. He went to Princeton directly from the Shinkawa slums of Kobe, one of the worst slums conceivable, where he had lived nearly five years. Probably no faculty member nor fellow-student at Princeton at that time could think of him as a "saint." He was a rather quiet student, and he spent most of his time reading non-theological books. He was, however, already a "saint" in the full sense of the title given to him in later years by the people of America. Upon his return from the States, he went back to the same slums to preach the Gospel and to serve the poor, as he had done before.

The name and life of Kagawa may not be so well known to the postwar generation as it was to the prewar generation in America. There is, nevertheless, no Japanese like Kagawa whose name is still widely known and remembered outside of Japan, particularly in the United States. There are several biographies of Kagawa available in English, admirably written by men like William Axling in the early thirties and Cyril J. Davey more recently.[2] Instead of giving a biographical sketch of the man, therefore, I would like to point out some strange facts about Kagawa and ponder the problems which these facts imply.

I

On April 23, 1960, Kagawa died. He would have been seventy-two on July 10. Strange as it may sound, it was not the Japanese but the foreign press that first dispatched the news to Japan. At the public funeral which was held a week later, foreign correspondents were more in evidence than Japanese citizens. These instances are not accidents but indications of the strange position Kagawa had long held in his own country.

[2] W. Axling, *Kagawa*, New York, 1932, revised edition, 1946; C. J. Davey, *Kagawa of Japan*, London, 1960.

He was better known and more appreciated outside Japan than within.

To tell of my own experience, I learned how great a Christian Kagawa was after I went to America and Europe, where I was often asked about him. When I first read the illustration quoted in the beginning of this essay, I was amazed. No Japanese, not even a Christian philosopher, would use Kagawa as an illustration of a saint, though he might so think of Albert Schweitzer. Indeed, as Jesus said: "a prophet is not without honor except in his own country." It is quite a recent and new phenomenon that serious and positive attempts to evaluate Kagawa have begun to be undertaken among academic circles in Japan. One of the first attempts of this kind is an article, "An Essay on Kagawa Toyohiko—The Place of Man in his Social Theory," written by Professor Kiyoko Takeda Cho.[3] In this article, having shown Kagawa as one deeply involved in the labor movement in its early stage, she said "However, many other images of Kagawa can be painted: He was the evangelist who worked self-sacrificingly in the Kobe slums of Shinkawa in Fukiai; a famous social worker; the author of innumerable books including a best seller of that time, *Across the Line of Death*; and the preacher who converted one or two hundred farmers to Christianity at one time. He is the man whom the world called the Saint of Japan; the representative of Christians; and a man nominated several times for the Nobel Prize. Within Japan, however, he was not considered to be as great a man as Westerners are led to believe. Even within Japanese Christian circles he was treated with an air of indifference."[4] This is a pretty accurate impression of the image of Kagawa in Japan, though it may sound strange to westerners. I would like, however, to add two things which may sound more strange in order to clarify the problems I see.

First is the fact that there are many, if not a great majority of people *outside* Christian circles who know Kagawa and ap-

---

[3] This article first appeared in a secular journal *Shiso no Kagaku* (Science of Thought), Jan./Feb. 1960. The English translation is in *Asian Cultural Studies*, Sept. 1960.

[4] *Ibid.*, pp. 48f.

preciate him very much. Ten years ago, *Yomiuri Shimbun,* one of the nation-wide newspapers, had a popularity competition. Kagawa was the top and only Christian among the highest six in the religious world of Japan. Soichi Oya, the leading journalist and one very popular in mass media, is one of those who regard Kagawa highly. He said about Kagawa:

"If one chooses the best-ten who had a great influence upon the Japanese people during the modern age, Toyohiko Kagawa would be certainly included in them, perhaps even in the best-three.

"The influence of Toyohiko Kagawa is seen not only in religion, which was both starting-point and goal for him, but in all fields of modern culture. It would not be too much to say that most of what we call movements of people such as political, social, labor-union, farmers-union, cooperative movements, etc., were derived from Toyohiko Kagawa as their source.

"If I were asked to name one who is the representative of modern Japan and who can be recommended to the world with confidence and pride, I would without any hesitation name Toyohiko Kagawa. The personality which had never been in Japan before and which seems to be impossible to reproduce in the future—that is Toyohiko Kagawa."[5]

Even if one takes into consideration the fact that Mr. Oya was baptized by Kagawa in his youth, these are unusual compliments to hear from a man who has had nothing to do with the Church for many years.

Another of those who appreciated Kagawa was the present Emperor of Japan. He conferred a posthumous honor, the Order of the Sacred Treasure, first class, on Kagawa. Though the secular press failed, again, to mention the honor, this is an extraordinary prize, which only the nation's most eminent persons are given. Apart from the question on what basis the Emperor gave Kagawa such an honor, no one can deny that there are some people like the Emperor outside of Christian circles who acknowledged Kagawa's work as first class.

[5] "Alas Kagawa Toyohiko," in *God Is My Shepherd* (a collection of Japanese essays in memory of the life and work of Kagawa), 1960, pp. 1f.

Second is the fact that there are a great many people *within* Japanese Christian circles who respected and appreciated Kagawa as a "saint" or "prophet." Kagawa had many friends, many supporters and many devoted followers in Japanese Churches. Even before he died, several biographies of him were written by his friends. There are very few Christians in Japan whose biographies have been written while they were still alive, though there have been not a few autobiographies. After Kagawa died, two volumes entitled *Biography of Kagawa by 103 People* were published.[6] It was more than one year before Kagawa's death that those 103 essays in honor of him were collected from Christians all over Japan. The contributors were: ministers, professors, kindergarten and school teachers, social workers, doctors, patients in sanatoriums, businessmen, farmers, factory workers, writers, company presidents, shop employees, housewives, a former minister of finance, and others. But there is one thing in common: all of them remember Kagawa with great respect and deep gratitude.

At present, another publication is being undertaken. Kagawa was a voluminous writer; there are about 200 books written by him. Recently a large project was started by Christians from different denominations. They organized a committee to publish *Kagawa's Complete Works* in 24 volumes. More than three hundred names are listed as promoters of the project. Many of them are leading clergy and laymen: bishops, moderators, local ministers, university presidents, professors, congressmen, businessmen. This will make it appear that the entire Japanese Christian community pays honor and tribute to Kagawa.

After Kagawa died, a tribute in English translation appeared in *The Japan Christian Quarterly*, a journal of foreign missionaries. As a sort of comment, the following explanation was attached to it: "In view of the fact that it has often been said Dr. Kagawa was not without honor save in his own country, your editor felt that it would be wise to listen to the voices of his fellow-countrymen as they gave their estimate of his contribution. This tribute appeared in the *Kirisuto*

[6] Edited by Tomio Muto, 1960.

Toyohiko Kagawa

Shimbun for April 30th, and is here translated by your editor and reprinted with the permission of the publishers."[7] The editor is trying to show that there are some people who respect Kagawa *even among Japanese*. The two publications I mentioned above confirm the fact and support his intention.

One may wonder which is the truer picture of Kagawa in Japan. Was he with or without honor in his own country? Generally speaking, within Japan Kagawa was not considered to be as great a man as westerners are led to believe. But, at the same time, I must say that within Japan Kagawa was not without honor. Then, one would like to raise a question: why has it often been said and why does one usually get the impression that "even within Japanese Christian circles he was treated with an air of indifference?" The truth seems to be this: within *certain, not all*, Japanese Christian circles he was treated with contempt. And because of the great influence of those certain circles, it gave people the impression that Kagawa was treated by all the Churches with an air of indifference.

What kind of people were in those certain circles? And why was Kagawa treated with contempt by those people? In order to give a comprehensive answer to these questions, perhaps I shall have to wait some time until the results of research and study, which have just been started from different points of view, become available. They are highly complex problems. Certainly, problems exist on both sides. Moreover, some are peculiarly local, namely Japanese Church problems, and others are personal, namely Kagawa's own problems. What I would like to deal with here is not those specific problems in detail, but some general and yet basic problems that underlie those specific questions, namely those problems which all of the Churches in the world today are facing. To put it in other words, I would like to consider those problems of the Church that Kagawa himself raised and challenged.

As far as I can see, there are three basic problems about

[7] "The Final Prayer of a Saint," *The Japan Christian Quarterly*, July 1960, p. 193. *Kirisuto Shimbun* is an interdenominational Christian weekly paper founded by Kagawa.

which Kagawa has much to say for us today. They are symbolically shown in a story of the twenty-one-year-old Kagawa. It was Christmas Eve of 1909 when he carried his few belongings from a Presbyterian Seminary to the slums, while the Churches were busy celebrating Christmas. Although they are closely related to each other, let us see three problems in turn. They are, first the *Seminary* he moved from, second, the *Church* he passed by, and third, the *slums* he went into.

II

The problem of the Seminary. By "Seminary" I mean a certain group of people who are very theologically-minded and among the intelligentsia. Kagawa was famous for his omnivorous reading and erudition, covering an amazing range of subjects. Not only had he studied theology but also he had the experience of teaching at several theological schools. Before he went to Princeton, he had translated Albert Schweitzer's *The Quest of the Historical Jesus* into Japanese. Theology as such, however, did not attract him. Not even theology at Princeton! "There was," he said, "nothing particular to learn." He was rather anti-theological. One of his fellow-ministers remembers that Kagawa often said: "We must emancipate the Japanese Church from theology." His anti-theologism was one of the main reasons why Kagawa was treated with a sneer by Japanese theological circles and by the Christian intelligentsia. Of these people, he said:

"There are theologians, preachers, and religious leaders, not a few, who think that the essential thing about Christianity is to clothe Christ with forms and formulas. They look with disdain upon those who actually follow Christ and toil and moil, motivated by brotherly love and passion to serve.

"To them formulating definitions about the truth is a higher thing and of more value than to emancipate the under-privileged masses. They conceive pulpit religion to be much more refined than movements for the actual realization of brotherly love among men. Hence, religion becomes calloused and an empty cast-off shell. The religion which Jesus taught was diametrically the opposite of this. He set up no definitions about God, but taught the actual practical practice of love."[8]

Kagawa simply could not get along with those theologians who were more interested in the doctrine of God than in God himself, more in Christology than in Christ, and more in the teaching of love than in the practicing of love. He was impatient with those Christian intelligentsia who called Jesus "Lord, Lord," and did not what he told them. He could not go along with his fellow-ministers who preached the word of God but did not try to make the word of God incarnate among the people's actual life. For him to be a good Samaritan was more essential than to teach the story of a good Samaritan. Moreover, Kagawa challenged those intellectually-minded Christians not with mere words but with action and life itself, namely by his personal example.

After Kagawa gave a lecture at a university in the States, a student asked a professor: "Because his English was not clear, I could not understand what he was talking about. Could you?" The professor answered: "Yes, it was hard to understand. But the greatness of that man is not in his words. There are many who can explain the word of God with words. There are, however, very few who can speak living words with the living body." Kagawa was one of those very few.

Kagawa was not only an evangelist and preacher but a social worker; yet he was never a theologian in the strict sense of the word. That was the reason why he was almost completely neglected by theological circles. In the index of *Japanese Contributions to Christian Theology*, the name of Kagawa is mentioned only once. There we read:

"The Japanese name most familiar to the West, which has yet to appear in this volume, is Toyohiko Kagawa. Kagawa's essential contribution to the Christian life of Japan is not theological but evangelistic and social. He will be remembered as one who understood the importance of expressing the Christian faith through the structure of society. That emphasis was the strength of the liberal Christianity of which Kagawa has

[8] Quoted from Axling, *op.cit.*, 1932, pp. 132f.

been a leading representative. The weakness of the liberals was their tendency to identify Christianity with morals, thus weakening the significance of the doctrinal dimension."[9]

It is true that Kagawa did not contribute to theology by writing systematic theology. But is not his whole life itself a great challenge to the tendency of theology to identify Christianity with doctrine or knowledge, thus weakening the significance of the life dimension, regardless of whether it be orthodox or liberal?[10] Can we not, then, call his challenge a contribution, an important contribution to theology today?

III

The problem of the Church. By "Church" I mean a group of people who are very church-minded but indifferent to the rest of the world. It is widely recognized that the early labor and social movements in Japan were initiated mainly by Christians who were liberal in theology and critical of the institutional Churches. Most of them, however, in later years either lost their Christian faith or left the Church completely.

Kagawa was one of the very few who not only remained in the movement as a Christian but also remained within the Church as a minister of a local church and as an evangelist for all Churches. It was, strange to say, within his own denomination that he was treated the coldest. For Kagawa was critical of the tendency of Churches to isolate themselves from the rest of the world. He could not enjoy the *service* in the Church that did not also carry *service* to the world. He was angry at the Churches which remained indifferent toward the actual problems of society. He could not, therefore, win support from his fellow-ministers who were concerned about forming institutional Churches. Very sharply he said: "The religion of imposing edifices is a heart-breaking affair. It is the soul's cast-

[9] Carl Michalson, *Japanese Contributions to Christian Theology*, Philadelphia, 1959, p. 149.

[10] Not a few Japanese ministers insist that at the basis of Kagawa's life and thought lay the profound orthodox faith which he learned from Presbyterian missionaries and seminaries. Cf. R. H. Drummond, "Kagawa: Christian Evangelist," in *The Christian Century*, July 6, 1960.

off shell. A religion which builds men rather than temples is much to be preferred. For this reason I reject everything connected with the religion of imposing architecture.

"Under the eaves of the cathedral nestle the slums. Before the Vatican Palace, mercenary troops stand guard. Nothing is so pitiful as the religion of cathedrals, temples, and stately edifices.

"Well would it be if the world's Churches and temples were razed to the ground. Then possibly we would understand genuine religion. True religion must invade the bedroom, the study, the street, the factory, invention, our outings, our toil, our recreation, our meals, yes, even our sleep."[11]

The Church does not exist for itself but for the world. Kagawa could not tolerate, accordingly, Churches that were busy in Church affairs alone. Especially he did not like narrow and closed denominationalism. Because of his accent, when he said "denomination," some people thought he was saying "damnation." Having been told so, he said: "I am not surprised. To me, they are very much the same thing."[12] Such anti-denominationalism naturally irritated some of his fellow-ministers. This was one of the main reasons why he was not much supported by his own Presbyterian denomination but more often by inter-denominational bodies. It was natural, therefore, that he himself supported the formation of the Kyodan (the United Church of Christ in Japan) and remained loyal to it even when other Churches left it after the war.

Furthermore, his inter-denominationalism was not limited to Japan. He was a truly ecumenical Christian. No Japanese Christian, like Kagawa, so often went abroad and preached in different Churches of various nations. Between his first evangelistic trip to America in 1924 and his last trip to Malaya in 1958, he made extensive evangelistic visits in countries such as Great Britain, Canada, China, India, Australia, New Zealand, Norway, Sweden, Denmark, Germany, Brazil, Thailand, and others.

[11] Quoted from Axling, *op.cit.*, p. 84.
[12] Davey, *op.cit.*, p. 84.

However, even ecumenism as such was for him not the end itself, but rather, as his final prayer put it, "for the salvation of Japan and the peace of the world." In other words, the Church exists for the world. For Jesus Christ is not only the Lord of the Church but of the world. To use Richard Niebuhr's phrase, for Kagawa Christ was "the transformer of culture."[13] And he challenged the Church, as an instrument of Christ, to go into the world in order to transform it.

IV

The problem of the slums. By "slums" I mean the poor who are neglected by the bourgeois-minded Church. Although it was for about twelve years that Kagawa lived in the midst of the slums, he worked throughout his life for the poor. Probably there are very few like Kagawa, who lived like the poor, with the poor, and for the poor, while all the time he could have lived otherwise. He simply could not think of being Christian or religious without being concerned about the poor. For him it was one of the most essential things of religion, particularly of Christianity, to take care of the poor. Once he spoke at a National Religious Conference, and in front of the leaders of the then three major religions in Japan, he warned them as follows:

"The time has come when the priests of the shrines and temples and the pastors of Churches should come out of their somnolence and face realities.

"You Buddhists! Read again your scriptures and find in them the spirit which animated your pioneers. If you cannot rediscover and reincarnate their spirit, roll up your scrolls and carry them back to India whence they came.

"You Shintoists! If you cannot grasp the vision which impels to service for the weakest and the most unfortunate, of what avail are your numerous and elaborate rituals?

"And you Christians! Shame on you for erecting huge and

[13] R. Niebuhr, *Christ and Culture*, Harper and Bros., 1951. I wonder why the author did not mention Kagawa in the fifth type?

costly Churches and failing to follow the Man born in a manger and buried in another's tomb."[14]

Is this the voice of a Christian or a socialist? Kagawa was a Christian Socialist, influenced by men such as Charles Kingsley, Frederick D. Maurice, Arnold Toynbee, and Canon Barnett. "I am not," he said, "a Christian because I am a Socialist. I am a Socialist because I am a Christian." Throughout his life he fought against the evil of exploiting capitalism and warned Churches of consciously or unconsciously being its tools. In this respect, he may be called "Rauschenbusch in Japan." As in the case of Rauschenbusch, present-day readers of Kagawa may have difficulty with some of his specific socio-economical remedies. We should not, however, be deaf to his essential message, being misled by such words as "capitalism" and "socialism," however various and vague the meanings of these words have become today.

The problem that Kagawa challenged was not basically the matter of this or that social structure but the matter of the life and death of the Christian Church. He said:

"God dwells among the lowliest of men. He sits on the dust-heap among the prison convicts. With the juvenile delinquents he stands at the door, begging bread. He throngs with the beggars at the place of alms. He is among the sick. He stands in line with the unemployed in front of the free employment bureaus.

"Therefore, let him who would meet God visit the prison cell before going to the temple. Before he goes to Church let him visit the hospital. Before he reads his Bible let him help the beggar standing at his door.

"If he visits the prison after going to the temple, does he not, by so much, delay his meeting with God? If he goes first to the Church and then to the hospital, does he not, by so much, postpone beholding God? If he fails to help the beggar at his door and indulges himself in Bible-reading, there is a danger lest God, who lives among the mean, will go elsewhere. In truth he who forgets the unemployed forgets God."[15]

[14] Quoted from Axling, *op.cit.*, pp. 93f.   [15] *Ibid.*, p. 28.

Are there any Churches in the world today that do not need to be reminded of the poor? In the age of the welfare state, does not the Church need to be concerned about the problem of the poor any more? Half of God's children on this earth still go to bed hungry every night. Two-thirds of them have an annual per capita income of less than a hundred dollars. Is it possible that a Church is truly concerned about social injustice or international problems, while not being concerned about the poor? Is it possible that a Christian can have true faith without love for the poor? Kagawa's work among the poor, from slum work to labor movements, was nothing but his response to the redemptive love of God revealed in the cross of Jesus Christ. The problem of the poor is not the problem of "rich" Churches in the West only, but of "poor" Churches in the East as well. For this is, in essence, the question as to whether a Church truly understands and responds to the essence of the Gospel.

It was the priests, scribes, and Pharisees, according to the Gospels, that did not honor Jesus, the friend of the poor. Is it too much to say that Kagawa was not honored by modern "priests, scribes, and Pharisees" while he was loved by the "poor"? At least, one can say that Kagawa challenged and warned the Churches of the danger of becoming Churches of "priests, scribes, and Pharisees." Sometimes I wonder whether Kagawa would have been honored if he had been born and had worked in the West. On his part, Kagawa tried to be faithful throughout his life to the first prayer he ever made before a missionary, when he was sixteen years old: "Oh God, make me like Christ!"

XII. JOSEF LUKL HROMADKA
(1889-   )

Theology and Ideology*

BY CHARLES C. WEST

JOSEF LUKL HROMADKA has lived for eight of his seventy-two years in the United States. Between 1939 and 1947, during which he made his home in Princeton and taught at Princeton Theological Seminary, he won a place in the hearts and minds of thousands of students and others who came to know him. As a Christian, as a friend, and as a teacher of the Church he became one of us. But it is just this unity that has become for American Christians today a provocation and a challenge. For Josef Hromadka was and remains a European and a Czech. His sense of the total crisis of western Christendom, his acceptance of the Communist revolution as God's judgment upon it, and his decision to serve Christ and the Church in his own country on the other side of that revolution, can only be understood against the background of a personal and cultural history which for most of us is strange. Yet when Professor

---

* In addition to items mentioned in the footnotes, the following deserve attention: *Sprung über die Mauer* (Berlin 1961) is a German translation of *Doom and Resurrection* (Richmond: Madrus House, 1945) with a new section in which Hromadka reflects on developments in the interim; *Von der Reformation zum Morgen* (Leipzig 1956) is an East German translation of a Czech work by several authors, the final chapter being by Hromadka; *Communio Viatorum*, a theological quarterly edited by Hromadka and printed in German and English, devoted Volume II, No. 2-3, Summer 1959, to Hromadka and selections from some of his untranslated works; *Church News from Czechoslovakia* is a news service in English which often carries brief items from Hromadka; *Church in Communist Society: A Study of J. L. Hromadka's Theological Politics*, by Matthew Spinka (Hartford: Hartford Seminary Foundation Bulletin, No. 17, June 1954) is written by a fellow Czech and former intimate friend of Hromadka's; Hromadka wrote several major articles during his Princeton sojourn for *Theology Today* (Cumulative Index, Volume X, No. 4, January 1954); most of Hromadka's works in Czech are in Speer Library, Princeton Seminary.

Hromadka speaks from Prague we cannot be indifferent to him because of his foreignness, any more than we were in those days when he shared and misunderstood (or did he?) our common life in this country. His words still echo as if they came from the classroom in Stuart Hall; they come from the midst of the congregation of which we also are members. They call for understanding, and response.

I

Hromadka was born on June 8, 1889, in the Moravian village of Hodslavice. His father was a small farmer and an active Lutheran layman; later he was a member of the Synod of the Czech Brethren Church after the union. The son absorbed from his days in secondary school the intellectual ferment that was breaking down the old Europe of the Congress of Vienna. His decision to study theology, at the University of Vienna, was born out of the conflict between the faith of his family and the critical, skeptical attitude toward all religion that this ferment carried with it. From the beginning Hromadka had little use for half-way solutions. His continued studies in Basel and in Heidelberg made of him a radical defender of freedom and a methodological critic in Biblical studies, doctrine, and history. These lessons he learned well from Ernst Troeltsch, Johannes Weiss, and others. At the same time, however, he could not make his own the relativism, the basically humanist religion which much of this criticism implied. Probably inspired by Bernhard Duhm, and later in Aberdeen by D. S. Cairns, his own pilgrimage led him to rediscover the objective message of the prophets.

In his own words, quoted in a biographical article by his friend and colleague, J. B. Soucek, it was around 1918 that "it became clear that the central problem of theology is the problem of God; that what matters are not religious experiences but the absolute truth; that God is no mere principle of life, but the first starting point of any theological thinking; that it is not important what men experience, but what they are to experience; that the problem of faith is no problem of the human mind and of internal spiritual process, but the question who is God, what He wants us to do, and what are his plans with the world."[1] Hromadka, in other words, came to his basic conviction—that the starting point of theology lies in God and his revelation rather than in man and his experience—at about the same time as Karl Barth but independently of him.

After completing his education at the University of Aberdeen, Hromadka returned to his native country, to serve Lutheran congregations first in Vsetin, in Moravia, and then in Prague. For a time, in the last year of the First World War he served as a chaplain in the Austro-Hungarian Army, an experience that intensified his feelings for the disintegration of the great "cathedral of common norms and ideas" in which he had grown up. In 1920 he was called to the chair of systematic theology at the John Hus (since 1950 the Comenius) faculty of Protestant theology at the University of Prague, which post he has occupied (as full professor since 1927), except for his Princeton interlude, until this day.

This occupancy has not been a peaceful one. Hromadka the theologian is inconceivable apart from his engagement in the controversies of the day. Already in 1918 he was a member of the Lutheran delegation which helped prepare the union with the Reformed Church which resulted in the Evangelical Church of the Czech Brethren. This meant a shift of emphasis for the uniting Churches from Luther and Calvin to the central principles of the Bohemian Reformation of John Hus and John Amos Comenius. Yet as a leading theologian of the new Church, which he quickly became, Hromadka was involved in debates on several fronts. He opposed the liberal religious tradition with all the force of his faith and conviction. At the same time he fought his Church's tendency to interpret its Bohemian tradition too narrowly and emphasized its dependence on the whole of the Reformation of which Luther and Calvin also were fathers.

In the mid-twenties he stirred up a tempest by pleading for

[1] J. B. Soucek, "Theology in Action," in *Communio Viatorum*, Summer, 1959, pp. 278-279.

a new appreciation of the Roman Catholic Church as a judgment on Protestantism and as a representative of some of the essential features of Christianity, thus questioning the spirit of the movement away from the Roman Church then in progress. His contacts with the Eastern Orthodox Church, with the revivalist, and ultra-conservative Protestant Churches and groups were similarly self-questioning and provocative at times for the comfortable members of his own Church. At the same time he identified himself closely with the work of the Czechoslovak Student Christian Movement and through it with the World Student Christian Federation, that free, radical pioneer of ecumenism unfettered by ecclesiastical institutions or confessional bondage.

II

This Churchly-theological struggle has been matched by a political involvement even more controversial. Hromadka's opponents in both have been the same: the contented religious bourgeois, narrowly nationalistic in loyalty, class-limited in outlook, lacking the faith to move out from traditional securities, to perceive the judgment of God in the forces of our times, and to accept the grace that comes from continually dying and rising with Christ. This opposition has made him a sympathizer with the socialist movement from his earliest years and a sharp critic of the social status quo. As early as 1920 he warned the Czech people that the Bolshevik Revolution in Russia, however much one must criticize it, is a call to the Church to repent for its class selfishness and narrow nationalism. In the 1930's he was one of the most vigorous anti-fascists in his country, denouncing Hitler before it was at all popular in his land to do so and working for the defense of the Spanish government against Franco's rebels. This activity brought him into cooperation with Communists who were working for the same ends, which he accepted as an opportunity for Christian witness, though the Moscow purge trials drew strong denunciation from him.

There followed the shock of the Munich Pact, which a man in Hromadka's position could only interpret as a betrayal by the western democracies not only of Czechoslovakia but of the whole spiritual and cultural heritage on which the democracies were based. He escaped with his family, first to Switzerland, then to the United States, where he lived eight years teaching theology at the invitation of John A. Mackay at Princeton Seminary, and working with the Czechoslovak government in exile, nourishing and testing the hope that the wartime cooperation of the western allies with the Soviet Union would herald a new era of cooperation in which the best of western bourgeois Christendom would be purged and invigorated by Communist faith, while Communism would be healed of its extremism.

This is the man who in 1947 returned to his country and his native post to face with his people the consequences of the complete disillusionment of his political hopes. His recent political and theological history—his acceptance of the Communist *coup d'état*, his churchmanship in Communist society, his continued efforts to combine theological independence with a positive attitude toward the political power under which his nation lives, his uneasy position as chief spokesman for this point of view among Christians in ecumenical circles— is too well known to need recapitulation.[2] It needs, rather, interpretation against the background of the basic themes in Hromadka's whole life and ministry, of which it is the most recent expression. To these we now turn. They are basically two.

III

Western civilization, according to Hromadka, is enveloped in a total crisis, a revolution, in which all of the norms and ideals, all the political and spiritual realities on which it was based are crumbling. Hromadka's most sweeping and eloquent statement of this theme is in *Doom and Resurrection*, the book that reflects his teaching during his Princeton years: "The crisis of our civilization is deep, deeper than many of us are

[2] For an analysis, cf. C. West, *Communism and the Theologians*, Westminster Press, Philadelphia, 1958, Chapter 2.

prepared to admit. The civilization as it existed prior to 1914 and, in a way, until 1930 is gone. The cathedral of common norms and ideas, standards and hopes disintegrated from within."[3]

But this is not only a reflection of the trauma of the war; it is a perennial emphasis in Hromadka's thinking and the deepest experience of his life, if we are to believe his writings and his biographer.[4] It is at once the conclusion he draws from and the premise he brings to the analysis of every major reality of politics, culture, and religion: the end of the Austro-Hungarian Empire, the Bolshevik Revolution in Russia, the rise of Hitler, the Munich Pact, the spirit of the people in Britain and America during the war and the policies of these countries after it, the rise of Russian power and the rapid changes in Asia, Africa, and Latin America, existentialism and secularism in postwar Europe, and the bourgeois liberal spirit with its comfortable complacent ways of life and belief, in the whole western world. In all of this, Hromadka believed himself to be continuing the prophetic tradition of Fyodor Dostoievski, and later of Thomas Masaryk.

Dostoievski, in Hromadka's eyes, was the great Christian prophet who foresaw at once the personal and social catastrophe that threatened western man from within, and the hope for all mankind which lay beyond. It was he who read in the rationalist individualism and the positivist naturalism of which western Europe was so proud, the disintegration of all that is truly human. "This is the point at which modern man has arrived," Hromadka paraphrases him: "First he declares himself to be the sovereign lord and his reason to be the supreme authority; in the name of his reason he launches out into rebellion against the eternal sovereign authority of God—and in the end by his reason he denies his reason itself and declares himself to be a powerless expression of the processes of nature or of the social milieu. This confusion of modern thought is gradually disintegrating everything that holds so-

[3] Madrus House, Richmond, Va., 1945, p. 118.
[4] Soucek, *op.cit.*

ciety together and opens the way to chaos and confusion."[5]

At the same time Dostoievski extended this crisis to the innermost consciousness of man, expressed over and over again in the main characters of his novels. Human beings, victims of their own vital forces, the passions of their bodies and souls, "cut loose from the discipline of standards, and without awe before what is unconditionally sacred, are doomed to perish in incurable disease and self-destruction. Modern civilization is a macabre dance of men without bones, without sense of rhythm and melody, without order and discipline, without beauty and joy. A macabre dance at the edge of an abyss."[6] For this condition man himself is responsible. "The wall protecting us from the horror of passions and impulses, from the powers of moral chaos, lust, debauchery, licentiousness, and death, has been torn down by a deliberate, conscious, and responsible act of the human mind."

Salvation then, for the nineteenth-century prophet, as for Hromadka today, lies through suffering and death. It comes through sharing the "grief, sorrow, corruption, and misery" of the world and taking upon ourselves responsibility for the human tragedy, as Sonia did for Raskolnikov in *Crime and Punishment*. It is in the moment of our deepest abandonment, when all other help is gone, that we suddenly become aware of the companionship and the power of Christ. He is there in our depths, with his forgiveness on which new life can be built. He "challenges the power of death and sin by his real presence —without moralizing, and patronizing, without sanctimonious poise, without orthodox self-complacency."[7] He is there with the weakness of love to raise up all the victims of society. "Only through him can we build a new cathedral both on the debris of impotent, dumb, and dull reaction and on the ruins of destructive revolution."[8]

This is Dostoievski through Hromadka's eyes. There are, of course, differences between the two. Dostoievski's piety was

[5] "Russia and the West," in *The Fortnightly*, London, January, 1944, p. 35.
[6] *Doom and Resurrection*, p. 36.
[7] *Ibid.*, pp. 40-41.   [8] *Ibid.*, p. 50.

Russian Orthodox and his hope was rooted in a sense of the holiness of Russia as a sacred community. Hromadka remains a theologian of the Reformation for whom the sovereignty of Christ over the world in the Word determines the relation of man with God. But the sense of total crisis through which all human life is seen and interpreted, the longing, both past and future, for the "cathedral of common norms and ideas," is common to them both. For Dostoievski in his Russian Orthodox context, this was natural. For Hromadka it has led to continual contradiction between his diagnosis and hope for our time and his theology and faith, a contradiction already evident in his attitude toward the other great prophet whom he honored and followed, Thomas Garrigue Masaryk.

IV

Masaryk was in almost every way a sharp contrast to Dostoievski. He was a philosopher and a statesman. He was a disciplined rational thinker, though not a rationalist. He was a liberal and an optimist, though not an individualist or utopian. Above all he was a man of action. "There was nothing academic, abstract, or impersonal about Masaryk. He saw the old world crumbling and asked what to do about it."[9] Their kinship of spiritual insight, however, Hromadka believes, was deeper than their differences. Masaryk too was convinced that the old world, where authority values and loyalties were maintained by the tacit consent of the whole community, had crumbled. Its priests and princes could not cope with modern man's needs and aspirations in the framework of old dogmas and privileges. Yet he, like Dostoievski, believed that there was nothing in modern philosophy or politics to fill the vacuum. "Unbelief, skepticism, and revolt are sufficient for destruction, but not equal to building new cathedrals, institutions, and moral discipline."[10] The moralism of Kant is impersonal and inhuman. Comte's positivism is at least an attempt to help real human beings, but in the long run it destroys man by reducing him to nature. "Positivism, monistic Hegelianism, and

[9] *Ibid.*, p. 66. [10] *Ibid.*, p. 59.

Josef Lukl Hromadka

Marxian socialism deprived the human moral and spiritual freedom of all ontological, metaphysical, and religious safeguards, and subjected the human personality to history, to the state, to the masses, to the absorbing, devouring Leviathan of the all-powerful society."[11]

In their analysis of the total crisis of mankind then, Hromadka finds Dostoievski and Masaryk to be at one. In their prescription for the cure they were, however, significantly different. Dostoievski's evangelical extremism, and the lingering doubt in his writings as to whether the witness of Christ is really a victory in this world, did not appeal to the philosopher-statesman. If the choice for man is between Jesus and Caesar, it must be Jesus as the truth, the eternal truth about man and society. Masaryk set himself the task of bringing out the true insights in the whole intellectual and religious heritage of the West, from Plato through the medieval philosophers to Kant and Dostoievski. He strove as a statesman to make these the foundation for a workable social order which would conquer the destructive extremes of every ideology and reverse the disintegration of society. "His slogan, 'Jesus, not Caesar,' indicated his genuine hope that the morally and spiritually vigorous democratic mind would do its upbuilding, constructive work in the post-war world."[12]

This was the hope which Hromadka held up to the world at the end of the Second World War. He found in Masaryk a statesman who had plumbed the depths of the disintegration of our times and was not defending the past in fear against it. He saw him and his Czechoslovakia as agents of reconciliation between the truths of a pre-revolutionary and a post-revolutionary world, between Communist Russia and the West. Masaryk was no Communist. "The revolutionary practice of the Bolsheviks shocked him by its cruelty and ruthlessness."[13] But Hromadka read in him the attitude that he himself adopted, which saw underneath the violence and destruction of the old way, a nation's awakened sense of mission, the disci-

[11] *Ibid.*, p. 73.
[12] *Ibid.*, p. 80.
[13] "Russia and the West," p. 39.

plined, self-sacrificing passion of masses of people for a new society of universal brotherhood and love. This he believed to be the continuing theme of Russian history behind its Communist façade, the vitality that put to shame the "moral and spiritual weariness, disintegrating skepticism, and anarchical individualism" of the West.

Masaryk, a believer in the humanitarian democratic tradition of the West, set himself to build a left-of-center, social democratic society that would bring Communist Russia and the western democracies into dialogue and cooperation with one another. In his own land, despite sharp attacks from left and right, he largely succeeded, Hromadka reports. His hope for Europe was betrayed at Munich, but the wartime collaboration of Russia with the Allies opened new possibilities, and such statesmen as Franklin D. Roosevelt and Henry Wallace seemed to have caught his vision. Russia herself, Hromadka believed, had changed. She had rediscovered the wealth of her tradition, including its Christian themes. New questions were being asked in the wake of the terrible experience of the war. His great plea to the western world at the end of his Princeton sojourn was that it recover the revolutionary dynamic of its own traditions, shake off defensiveness, and meet the vital forces of the East in cooperative endeavor. His great hope was that this vision of Masaryk's might yet be realized.

V

This hope was disappointed, and with the disillusionment came a change in Hromadka's judgment of Masaryk. Since this comment has not appeared in English, it is worth quoting at some length:

"The second world war revealed the greatness and worth of his personality and of his political and spiritual activity. He stood like a monument to a great epoch of humanistic ideals. But soon after the war it became clear that he had in fact become a monument, and that his epoch had passed. I myself have had to wrestle with his heritage in order to realize that he belongs to the past, and that our future cannot be formed according to his pattern. Despite his fabulous knowledge of Russian history and Russian thinkers, he misunderstood and underestimated the historical meaning of the Soviet Revolution of 1917 . . . My own attitude toward this Revolution was from the beginning more open and affirmative; but I hoped nevertheless that men like Masaryk—and in America Franklin D. Roosevelt—would be able to work creatively on the synthesis of which I have already spoken, between East and West. History has decided otherwise. Soon after the war it became clear that the preconditions were lacking on the Western side for carrying out Masaryk's program, and that Eastern Communism, disillusioned by the west European politics of 1936-39, was not prepared to reckon with a bridge-builder like Masaryk. Both west European socialism and Russian Communism pushed men like Masaryk aside. The historical situation has demonstrated that even the heritage of Masaryk, however, can be preserved and rendered fruitful on another level. Even my own country will be able to preserve the great values of classical and Western civilization, Masaryk included, on the level of a radical socialist structure. The reactionary elements and groups who fight Communism under the flag of Masaryk at home, and even more abroad, destroy thereby all the fruits of his life which are useful and irreplaceable for the future.

"Furthermore it is clear today that Masaryk was a child of the nineteenth century, of the Enlightenment, and of a positivist understanding of man. His philosophy, noble and sublime as it was, is out of date and unusable today in coming to grips with the upheaval of peoples and the needs of the contemporary world. Masaryk did not penetrate the last depths of human existence. He did not correctly judge the hard reality of a disintegrating humanity. Even in his understanding of Christian faith he was not able to see beyond the limits of rational and moral values, the religion of Jesus . . . He has become a classic, but he is no longer a valid lodestar for our action and our decisions of faith."[14]

[14] *Sprung über die Mauer*, Käthe Vogt Verlag, Berlin, 1959, pp. 132-134.

This is Hromadka's final settlement with one side of his social-political analysis and hope. There will be no synthesis between East and West. We will live for the foreseeable future as citizens and as Christians *in* East or *in* West, in Communist and bourgeois worlds each of which is blind to essential truths that the other embodies, each threatening destruction to the other. We are left with Dostoievski's analysis and hope alone. For this condition Hromadka does not hesitate to blame primarily the western world and to excuse the policy of the Communists. But nowhere does he extol the Communist order as being in itself the promised synthesis.

In one recent writing he throws the whole competition between the Communist and the western worlds into the perspective of Asian and African development. The breakdown of "Christian civilization" takes on a new meaning in the light of the vitality of non-Christian peoples there. "We must not only be prepared for the political expression of the extra-Christian peoples, but for their participation in the scientific, cultural, and spiritual construction of the international community as well."[15] Here is the new field of historical action, and although Hromadka suggests that the Soviet-Chinese social order may prove more attractive there, he leaves the future open. For the true hope of mankind, for the effective answer to the total crisis of western civilization, Hromadka turns more and more to the second great theme of his life and ministry: the sovereignty of a gracious God and the freedom of the Christian's witness to the hope he has in Christ.

VI

To call theology Hromadka's second major theme is perhaps unfair. Certainly he himself would want to be called first of all a theologian, and only secondarily a philosopher of culture or politics. It is the reality of his faith and the force of his theology that places him, despite all the social judgments and actions which are alien to us, in the intimate relation of Christian brotherhood. It is because he speaks in

[15] *Von der Reformation zum Morgen,* Koehler und Amelang, Leipzig, 1959, p. 816.

the authentic tones of a fellow Christian that we cannot ignore him. When we call theology his second theme, therefore, we do not mean to doubt the primacy of his faith, but rather to assert that, for him, as for many, perhaps most, other Christians, theology gives the answers to questions posed by pretheological experience in the world. World crisis was Hromadka's first experience. The sovereignty of God was the answer he found. His career, as we have seen, has been informed by a continuing theme of worldly hope for a Communist-western synthesis. The hope of the kingdom of God and the victory of Christ has been the deepening, the translation of that earthly longing into its proper sphere.

In all of this Hromadka has differed from Karl Barth, despite the kinship of their theological outlook. Hromadka, like Barth, turned from a vigorous critical liberalism to a central preoccupation with God and his Word in the aftermath of the First World War, and he struggled in the following years to overcome and re-evaluate all the categories of his liberal theological training in the light of this new insight. When he discovered Barth, he was especially delighted with the latter's confrontation of man with the total crisis of his existence when faced by the living God.[16] But Hromadka remained more preoccupied with the crisis of culture throughout his career than Barth ever was. Where Barth was overwhelmed directly by his confrontation with the Biblical message itself, Hromadka received that message as a deepening of the crisis already defined for him in Dostoievski and his own experience. Where Barth rejected all natural theology, even that implied in the experience of the existentialists from Kierkegaard and Dostoievski to his own time, Hromadka maintained staunchly that "Christian theology is unthinkable without a positive doctrine of the natural knowledge of God." This conviction he based on the very premise that Barth rejected: that a creator God can be known in his works apart from or before his revelation of himself as the electing and gracious God in Jesus Christ:

"Belief in Creation means that the world possesses full on-

[16] *Doom and Resurrection*, Chapter V.

tological reality, that the world as a work of God is an objective reality . . . The observation and investigation of this world has meaning for the perception of the creative work of God. The laws of natural and historical events, the mathematical, physical, and sociological laws are an indication of the wisdom and power of God. Still more are the norms of human legal and moral thought and of artistic creativity a pointer in the direction of the essence and goal of God's creative act. The knowledge of nature, of society, and of the human soul has a positive meaning for the thinking of a Christian . . . The theologian believes that in the God-created human spirit the presupposition is present by which man can perceive the traces of the work of God in the world and his duty before God."[17]

To be sure Hromadka hedged this about with a number of qualifications. We do not thus recognize God, but only his work. Reason and conscience are sinful. They "remain stuck in religious immanentism." The natural knowledge of God is only the porch or narthex of the temple of theology. But Hromadka's concern here reflects the fundamental fear, which was never Barth's, lest theology become irrelevant to the previously defined concerns of human society, lest there be a double standard of truth in these different areas. In all of this his spirit is closer to Reinhold Niebuhr than to Karl Barth. This is perhaps why, in the period of Hitler's ascendancy and the Second World War, his theological work was somewhat overshadowed by his political thought and action and his cultural analysis.

Nevertheless, Hromadka has become more deeply theological, and he has moved closer to Barth's independence of worldly hopes, crises, and anxieties as the postwar world has hardened in its divisions and as the sobering realities of everyday life in a Communist society have impressed themselves on his mind and commended themselves to his responsible churchmanship for attention. This will not be encouraging for those who test his ministry by that time when he will at last say No. But for most who are concerned that the Gospel be preached

[17] "Aus den Schriften von J. L. Hromadka," *Communio Viatorum,* op.cit., p. 116.

and lived even in present-day Czechoslovakia and points east, it may be a source of profound hope and gratitude.

VII

The evidence for this interpretation can be gleaned in many places in Hromadka's German and English writings. Let the following serve as examples. There has been no more questionable strand in Hromadka's thinking than his use of the idea of history. To confront "naked history" has too often been his euphemism for accepting that interpretation of Communist power that grows out of his peculiar understanding of crisis. His greatest historical hope, as we have seen, ended in a confession of its failure. But in 1956, in his most recent book in English, *Theology Between Yesterday and Tomorrow*, we find in the midst of sober theological analysis a new type of confession on the subject: "My own theology is strongly molded by what we call the eschatological motif of the Biblical message ... No matter how deeply we may be interested in the affairs of this world, we nevertheless look beyond history and any human ideology. Our perspective is the perspective of faith, of the Biblical message, not a perspective of history."[18]

Such words as these Hromadka has been saying not only to Americans but to the Communists themselves, reminding them that the classless society, when they achieve it, with all its social justice will not be utopia but still a society of sinners in need of control, forgiveness, and redemption. But in 1959 in a German volume, he goes a step further. After discussing the burden of history with special reference to the relations of Czechoslovakia and Germany with their legacy of guilt and sin he adds: "But the Gospel frees also from the burden and the fetters of history. The past loses in the light of the Gospel its binding power. Peoples live in history and are formed by their past. They are divided from each other by historical events and prejudices. But when the word of the Gospel sounds, those who have heard its voice come to the crucified

[18] *Theology Between Yesterday and Tomorrow*, Westminster Press, Philadelphia, 1956, p. 58.

and risen Christ as sinners. They are freed from that which has historically divided them and can truly begin to write a new chapter."[19]

Significantly there is no mention in this whole section of Communist power, or of accepting any reality save that of the Gospel itself, through which history is made and remade. The ghost of naked history has vanished and hope has found its proper context.

Our argument so far has left Hromadka with a Christ more akin to Dostoievski's than to either Barth's or the Bible's. In a sense this criticism still applies, even to his most recent writings. So deeply concerned is he with the failure of the Christian Churches and their culture, so eager to emphasize the urgency of going with Christ into the depths of human despair and need, so cautious lest we express ourselves to Communists or others in ways which would raise misunderstanding, or justify ourselves against them, that one cannot help but wonder whether it is faith that is speaking in some writings, or only longing. This question is not so much related to words as to their contexts. Of ringing declarations of the sovereign power of Christ there is no lack in the Hromadka corpus, from the earliest years. They become more convincing sometimes when they ring less but are surrounded by a description of churchly and worldly reality which does not stand by itself but is truly captive to Him. Such is the case for example in the eloquently simple exposition of missionary Christology in *Theology Between Yesterday and Tomorrow*: "We are living in a time of witness: to go back to the central theme and reality of the Biblical message, to go there where Jesus Christ himself stands, walks, and acts. What have we that the world does not possess?"

There follows an analysis of the sins of all the Churches and the examples of dedication and service among non-Christians. "And yet, in repentance and longing for the integrity of faith we may, I repeat we may, answer: What we have that the world does not possess is Jesus Christ. Have we him, or

[19] *Von der Reformation zum Morgen*, p. 342.

better to say, has he prevailed in his struggle for us? Have we opened the door and let him come in?"[20]

Hromadka has severely criticized the Church from the beginning of his career in the prophetic attempt to awaken and renew it. Like Barth and Marx he finds much of human religion to be the expression of human attempts to make God in their own image. But in recent years his positive doctrine of the Church has come more into focus:

"As the Word will ever sound and work anew, so will the Church ever be formed anew by the prophetic word and the preaching of the Gospel. It is not possible to press the Word of God into finished theological formulas. But it is also not possible to bundle up the Church in finished ecclesiastical orders and laws. The Church is a gathering around the Word and the present Christ according to the Scriptures each day anew. The Church is a continually fresh bestowal of the Holy Spirit."[21]

The Word creates new realities in the world, and these realities are expressed in the Church. The Word shocks and upsets people, brings them through death to new life, and the Church is the fellowship in which this takes place. The Word reconciles enemies and conquers hate and fear so that the Church is the first place in the world where sinners love and forgive one another. It makes men free from guilt, from the past, from fear, and from self, for serving the neighbor, and the Church is first of all, therefore, a community of free men. All this can be said about the Church not by virtue of what it is at any moment, but because of what God is doing to shake and reform it, and through it the whole world. In this context must be placed the ministry of the Church to the Communist part of the world: "From the beginning of this new period it has been clear to me that we are carrying on and will carry on, in the part of the world which stretches from the Elbe to the Pacific Ocean and in which hundreds of millions of people live, one of the most responsible struggles of the Church of Jesus Christ. It must be a struggle in the full affirmation of

[20] *Theology Between Yesterday and Tomorrow*, pp. 89, 91.
[21] *Von der Reformation zum Morgen*, p. 302.

our faith, with a mighty Yes and Amen which sounds forth from the Gospel of Jesus Christ for the whole world; for the Church and also for those who are outside its borders."[22]

To the Communists it must be a witness that refuses to take their atheism at face value, for "their resistance to the god they have thought up cannot reach the God whom we confess in Jesus Christ, and in whose light we recognize other men, from whose grace we receive joy and peace and out of whose mercy we draw new strength each day for true service to our fellow men."[23] The witness of the Christian here relativizes ideology and points all men toward practical purposeful social action for justice and freedom. Here, in the fellowship of common work, is where Christian witness takes place whether by way of cooperation or at other times protest, whether in its Yes, or in its No.

VIII

So run some of the themes of Hromadka's ministry. We have dealt with themes rather than with specific acts, although our subject's thought was formed in action and reaction, because it is the basic character and mind of the man that concern us. The essential question is not our reaction to his peace propaganda activities or to his statement on the Hungarian revolution, but whether we have heard his challenging questions to us and considered them in the light of our own understanding of the culture in which we live.

Few of us will accept the total crisis in which he has placed us, and there is some evidence that he himself is moving away from this analysis. But how then do we understand the social implications of the crisis in which we are placed when we confront the judgment of God? What does it mean to know that we live each day in security and prosperity by grace and not by the nature of our social order? Few of us would allow that the Bolshevik Revolution is the wave of the future, the expression of masses longing for a fuller life. But there is a revolution abroad in the world today. How do we understand it in

[22] *Ibid.*, p. 384.   [23] *Ibid.*, p. 369.

the providence of God? What is our part in ministering to it, through which we might bear witness to Hromadka?

Most of us believe that our Christian responsibility calls for defense and support of the plans and hopes of the western world for the freedom and prosperity of all peoples. How can we explain this so that our colleague across the Iron Curtain will understand it as a ministry of the Church in which he shares? There is evidence that such questions as these are worth our thoughtful answer, for, says our subject's biographer: "Hromadka's criticism of Western nations and their leadership . . . is by no means an expression of aversion against them as nations, of blindness to the values of their great historic heritage nor of lack of solidarity with Christians in their midst who feel responsible for that heritage. Quite the contrary, it is an expression of the anxiety that this heritage may be deprived of any fruition for the future of the world by the blindness of its present guardians and by the lack of spiritual insight and of faith courageously looking towards the uncharted future on the part of church and theological leaders."[24]

[24] Soucek, *op.cit.*, p. 285.

THE CONTRIBUTORS

ERNEST THEODORE BACHMANN, a graduate of Haverford, Harvard, Lutheran Theological Seminary, University of Chicago, Tübingen, and Erlangen, has served Lutheran Churches in Pottsville, Pennsylvania, and Wilmington, Delaware. He was Professor of Church History at Chicago Lutheran Seminary and for two years was Deputy Chief of Religious Affairs Branch, Office of U.S. High Commissioner for Germany. He was Professor of Church History and Missions, Pacific Lutheran Theological Seminary, and is now Secretary of Theological Education of the United Lutheran Church of America, residing in Princeton and commuting to New York. He is the author of: *They Called Him Father: The Life Story of Christian Frederick Heyer* (1942); *Epic of Faith* (1952); *The Emerging Perspective* (1956); *Word and Sacrament* (1960).

ROLAND MUSHAT FRYE, a graduate of Princeton University, 1943, received his doctorate in English Literature from Princeton, 1952. He taught English at Howard College and Emory University. He is now Research Professor of the Folger Shakespeare Library in Washington, D.C. He is the author of: *God, Man, and Satan* (1960); *Perspective on Man* (1961), which comprises the Stone Lectures delivered at Princeton Theological Seminary.

YASUO CARL FURUYA is a graduate of Tokyo Union Theological Seminary and San Francisco Theological Seminary. He received his doctorate at Princeton Seminary in 1959. He is Director of the Religious Center and Instructor in the Division of Humanities, International Christian University, Tokyo, Japan.

HOWARD ALBERT JOHNSON, a graduate of the University of California at Los Angeles and the Protestant Episcopal Theological Seminary at Alexandria, Virginia, did graduate work at Princeton University in 1942. He has held parishes in California and Washington and taught theology at the Uni-

THE CONTRIBUTORS

versity of the South. He is now Canon Theologian at the Cathedral Church of St. John the Divine in New York. He is the author of: *Kierkegaard Rikaino Kagi* (1953); *Man in the Middle* (with James A. Pike, 1956); *A Kierkegaard Critique* (with Niels Thulstrup, 1962).

HUGH THOMSON KERR, a graduate of Princeton University, 1931, and Western Theological Seminary, Pittsburgh, Pennsylvania, did graduate work at the University of Pittsburgh and received his Ph.D. from the Universities of Edinburgh, Scotland, and Tübingen, Germany. He taught theology at Louisville Theological Seminary and is now Professor of Theology at Princeton Theological Seminary and Editor of *Theology Today*. He is the author of: *A Compend of Calvin's Institutes* (1938); *A Compend of Luther's Theology* (1943); *Positive Protestantism* (1950); *Mystery and Meaning in the Christian Faith* (1958); *What Divides Protestants Today* (1958); *By John Calvin* (1960).

JOHN ALEXANDER MACKAY, a graduate of the University of Aberdeen and Princeton Theological Seminary, 1915, did graduate work at the University of Madrid, taught philosophy at the National University of Peru, and received the Doctor of Divinity degree, Princeton University, 1937. He is President Emeritus of Princeton Theological Seminary and founder of *Theology Today*. He has been Secretary of the International Missionary Council, Moderator of the General Assembly of the Presbyterian Church, and a member of the Central Committee of the World Council of Churches. He is now serving as Professor of Hispanic Thought at the American University in Washington, D.C. He is the author of: *The Other Spanish Christ* (1932); *That Other America* (1935); *A Preface to Christian Theology* (1941); *Heritage and Destiny* (1943); *Christianity on the Frontier* (1950); *God's Order: The Ephesian Letter and This Present Time* (1952); *The Presbyterian Way of Life* (1960).

FRED BRUCE MORGAN, a graduate of Maryville College and Princeton Theological Seminary, 1942, has been minister of rural churches in West Virginia and Pennsylvania. He took graduate work in Chinese Language and Culture at Yale and served as a missionary in China and Thailand. He was in the Religion Department at Wilson College and Director of the Westminster Foundation of Princeton University. He received his doctorate at Princeton Seminary in 1958. He has taught at Syracuse University and is now Professor of Religion at Amherst College. He is the author of: *Called in Revolution* (1956); *Christians, the Church, and Property* (1963).

HERMANN NELSON MORSE, a graduate of Alma College and Union Theological Seminary, N.Y., is the former Executive Vice President of the Presbyterian Board of National Missions. He has been Moderator of the General Assembly of the Presbyterian Church and a Vice President of the National Council of Churches. He has recently been serving as Visiting Professor in Field Education at Princeton Theological Seminary. He is the author of: *The Country Church in Industrial Zones* (1922); *Toward a Christian America* (1935); *These Moving Times* (1945); *From Frontier to Frontier* (1952).

JAMES HASTINGS NICHOLS, a graduate of Yale, where he received both his A.B. and Ph.D. degrees, has taught at Macalester College and the Divinity School of the University of Chicago. He is now Professor of Church History at Princeton Theological Seminary. He is the author of: *Primer for Protestants* (1947); *Democracy and the Churches* (1951); *Evanston: An Interpretation* (1954); *A History of Christianity, 1650-1950* (1956); *Romanticism in American Theology* (1961).

CLIFTON EARL OLMSTEAD, a graduate of American University, Washington, D.C., received the B.D. degree from Princeton Theological Seminary in 1949 and the Th.D. degree in 1951. He has been an associate pastor in Maryland, a Professor of Religion and Philosophy at American University, and most recently the Executive Officer of the Department of Re-

THE CONTRIBUTORS

ligion at George Washington University, Washington, D.C. He is the author of: *History of Religion in the United States* (1960). Professor Olmstead died, Dec. 1, 1962.

MILLARD RICHARD SHAULL, a graduate of Elizabeth College and Princeton Theological Seminary, B.D., 1941, and Th.D., 1959, has been a minister in Texas and a missionary in Colombia and Brazil. He has been Dean and Professor of Theology at the Campinas Theological Seminary and more recently Professor of Religion and Philosophy at the Instituto Mackenzie, Sao Paulo, Brazil. He is now Professor of Ecumenics at Princeton Theological Seminary. He is the author of: *Encounter with Revolution* (1955).

LEONARD JOHN TRINTERUD, a graduate of the University of Washington and Princeton Theological Seminary, 1938, took his doctorate at the University of Lund, Sweden. He was Religious Book Editor of the Westminster Press, Philadelphia, and is now Professor of Church History at McCormick Theological Seminary, Chicago. He is the author of: *The Forming of An American Tradition* (1949); *The Gospel of God*, by Anders Nygren (translation, 1951); *The Architectural Setting for Reformed Worship* (with J. H. Nichols, 1961).

CHARLES CONVERSE WEST, a graduate of Columbia University, Union Theological Seminary, New York, and Yale, where he received the doctorate, has been a missionary and a teacher in China and Hong Kong. He served as Associate Director of the Ecumenical Institute, Chateau de Bossey, Geneva, Switzerland. He is now Associate Professor of Christian Ethics at Princeton Theological Seminary. He is the author of: *Communism and the Theologians* (1958); *The Missionary Church in East and West* (edited with D. M. Paton, 1959); *Outside the Camp* (1959).

GPSR Authorized Representative: Easy Access System Europe - Mustamäe tee 50, 10621 Tallinn, Estonia, gpsr.requests@easproject.com

www.ingramcontent.com/pod-product-compliance
Lightning Source LLC
Chambersburg PA
CBHW061438300426
44114CB00014B/1738